WITHDRAWN

AFRICAN
REVOLUTIONARY

AFRICAN REVOLUTIONARY

THE LIFE AND TIMES OF NIGERIA'S AMINU KANO

Alan Feinstein

Quadrangle / The New York Times Book Co.

72234

ACKNOWLEDGMENTS

So much of the writing of this book was dependent upon the cooperation of others that, at best, it is a difficult task to single out the individuals involved. I must say first that, in the process of hunting down pertinent information, I gained the unexpected bonus of a number of warm and wonderful friends who, I hope, will remain so, far into the future. Among the scholars in this category are Dr. John Paden of Northwestern University, and Professor C. S. Whitaker of Princeton University. Both went far out of their way to give unstinting access to their sources, time, and, not least, their friendship and guidance.

To the many, many people in Nigeria, England, and the United States who willingly submitted to the extensive interviews I put them through, and especially to Bello Ahmed Yakasai, my interpreter in northern Nigeria, thank you. Here too, I feel that I now number many of them among my good friends.

There was one person whose advice and personal concern guided me through the writing process: David Winsor, currently with Macmillan Publishers and resident in England. And, most certainly, my editor Emanuel Geltman was key to the process. Fred Feinstein, my son, was responsible for the photographs.

But on a more personal level, if I had to single out one person who made the whole project possible, it was my wife, Mary Kotick Feinstein. Not only did she fend off all distractions from a very tight schedule, but in a traveling household such as ours, with a "together" family (including my two children, and severest critics, Fred and Nancy), it meant a whole new life style for Mary, and she participated wholeheartedly for the two-year period it took to complete the job.

CONTENTS

FOREWORD

by BASIL DAVIDSON

Alhajji Aminu Kano is a radical and modernizing reformer in the great tradition of Sudanese Islam, and, as such, already holds a distinguished place in the history of Africa today. As an active and courageous leader of modern Nigeria he has played, and he is playing now, a key part in carrying his country, but more especially his own people of Hausaland, across the bridge that has lain between their traditional or colonial past, and their liberation in the present and the future.

Aminu Kano is happily a strong and vigorous man with the prospect of many fruitful years ahead of him, and so it may seem strange, at this time, to write a book about his life. But anyone who reads this book will quickly see that it was a very good idea. This is largely because we have to thank Alan Feinstein for doing it in the right way. For he has done it with an unfailing enthusiasm for his subject, sharing with the reader all the excitement and the pleasure of the discoveries he has made about Aminu in particular and Africa in general, and, through the portrayal of Aminu's life until now, giving us portraits of Aminu's friends and companions in the struggle for progress, as well as insights into the many problems and challenges they have had to meet and overcome.

Aminu is a man whose intellectual gifts have never obscured his interest in people. He is above all a gifted teacher: a teacher, that is, whose teaching gets across because it stems not only from capacious knowledge and unrelenting study, but also from an acute understanding of, and sympathy with, the human condition. That is why his influence has been formative with so many of those whom he has taught. If I myself appear at the beginning of this book, it is because Feinstein asked me to write a preface, but also because I am lucky enough to be among those whom Aminu has taught.

ix

He may be somewhat surprised to read that; and certainly it involves him in no responsibilities for the pupil's shortcomings. But it was as early as 1952 that he received me in his house at Kano, a small house tucked away in that ancient city's alleyways of clay and timber, and sat me down and talked to me of what Nigerian realities were really like.

Those were days when the moral and political liberation of independence from the traditional or colonial present as it was then, with all its suffocating hierarchy of lords and landowners bolstered by British rule, seemed still very distant. The difficulties appeared enormous; a year or so later they were even greater still. Yet Aminu had no inner doubts, I think, of how things could be made to go, nor of what could be achieved. And in having this profound confidence and vision he opened for the visitor, as for many other visitors, and in due course for Alan Feinstein too, a door to understanding through which they went, and became, in going, less unwise than they had been before.

The reader of this book is invited to the same experience.

London, August 1972

PREFACE

There are three good reasons why explanatory remarks for a biography of Aminu Kano are in order. In the first place, the question "Who is he?" undoubtedly arises in the minds of non-African readers, most of whom are unfamiliar with Alhaji Aminu, and who similarly might wonder why and how a biography about this particular man came to be.

Secondly, the problems an American writer met in the process of rescarching the life and times of a man, still in mid-career, from so totally different and unfamiliar an environment, and the pleasures he derived therefrom, should have relevance for his readers.

Thirdly, to point up a segment of the history of Africa that exists independent of, and pre-dates any colonial influences or that of the Western world; to show that Black Africa has produced and can continue to produce leaders of stature and dignity, would seem of value. Blacks the world over are awakening and looking for charismatic figures who can help along their burgeoning self-esteem and the realization of a worth that the Western world oriented historians have denied them for ever so long.

Nevertheless, to try to use the introduction of a book to give the essence of a man about whom a biography is being written would be foolhardy; for that is what the book itself is about. In order to interpret this man's contribution, not only to his country but to the rest of Africa and possibly the world, the detail of his origins and how he emerged from the crushing pressure of the successive waves of history should come fiirst.

Aminu Kano* is very much alive at the time of this writing, and, as a political being, is deeply involved in the cross-currents that push and pull Nigeria's ship of state. But if a man's life seems

---

*Until recent times, a Nigerian Moslem man identified himself by his given name followed by "son of," and the name of his father. If further identification were desired it could continue with a series of "son of." Today, for convenience many men have chosen to adopt their home region or city or even trade as a surname. Women will generally use the given name followed by the husband's full name.

to have some effect on the course of history, one need not, indeed should not wait until he passes away and can no longer influence or be influenced by events, to have his life examined.

If an innovator has a new approach, a new outlook, a new pathway for political leadership that could be introduced in one of the developing regions, perhaps some small insights into the continuing contradictions within the family of nations might conceivably emerge. Perhaps men like Aminu Kano can take the gropings of a highly spiritual, moral Gandhi and graft them onto the revelations of the more objective and realistic attempts of a Myrdal or Galbraith to analyze the nature of our other world of affluence and come up with a hybrid model for the worlds of economic underdevelopment on the one hand, and of moral underdevelopment and economic affluence on the other. If we Americans think that the prototype of our future must be drawn up from *our* society, so do the Russians or the Chinese, or the citizens of Scandinavia or India. Might it not be worthwhile to open our eyes and minds, to examine yet another continent to look for new ideological formulations and to see what we have of new forms, with an eye toward the possibility of some universal application?

GLOSSARY OF TERMS

Action Group (AG): Nigerian political party, organized in 1950 by Obafemi Awolowo and other Yoruba tribesmen. It tried to extend its influence beyond the Western Region, where it became the dominant party, but never went beyond the role of opposition in the federal parliament.

Alhaji (Alhajia or Hajia; female): A title of respect used for a Moslem who has made the pilgrimage to Mecca, considered a sacred obligation.

Alkali: A judge in a Moslem court of law.

Attajirai: Hausa term for wealthy, large-scale traders.

Bokwai: The group of seven "true" or original states of Hausaland [Biram, Kano, Rano, Katsina, Zaria (Zazzau), Gobir, Daura]. The *banza bokwai* are the seven "bastard" Hausa states which, according to legend, arose from the original seven.

Ciroma: A traditional title for an appointee of and adviser to the emir; generally considered to be his heir apparent.

Emir: Chief or king of a circumscribed area of northern Nigeria known as an emirate, the most populous of which is Kano, with about five million people.

Fulani: West African tribe, early converts to Islam, who settled in the Western Sudan, including northern Nigeria. They were educated in religious and secular matters and served as advisers in Hausaland until the jihad of Usman Dan Fodio in the early nineteenth century, when they seized power from the indigenous rulers.

Genawa: Small subdivision of Fulani descent, centered around Kano City, functioning as mallams, principally in the legal field. It includes Aminu Kano.

Hausa: Language used by many millions in West Africa, as well as a cultural designation for residents of Northern Nigeria, applying to Habe (non-Fulani) and Fulani alike.

xiii

Hausaland: Used in text to refer to that area that includes the seven
original Hausa *banza* states together with the *banza bakwai* or the seven bastard Hausa states. It comprises most
of northern Nigeria.
Imam: Islamic minister and leader of prayer.
Islamiyya: Literally, followers of Islam, but also used to refer to a
particular type of school founded by Aminu Kano and
followers that combined religious with secular teaching.
Jihad: Holy War of Moslems to crush the unbelievers. The conditions for such crusades were laid down by the Prophet
Mohammed.
Jinn: Moslem term for spirits, good and bad, who are subject to
supernatural control.
Khadiriyya: Followers of Sheik Khadir, one of the interpreters of the
Islamic religion, and founder of the cult bearing his name;
found largely in northern Nigeria.
Kunya: Hausa term for a personal trait in a woman implying mod-
esty, shame, tact, and an awareness of proper traditional
behavior.
Madaki: Traditional title for one of the emir's councilors, serving
under, appointed by, and usually related to the emir.
Mai: Term used for the king in Northeastern Nigeria (Bornu).
Mallam (Mallama; female): Title of respect for a Moslem religious, or secular, teacher or scholar.
Mufti: Member of a council of advisers to the alkali in a Moslem
court of law.
National Council of Nigeria and Cameroons (NCNC): Political
party organized in early '50's to espouse the nationalist
cause; changed to National Convention of Nigerian Citizens (NCNC) in 1961 after The Cameroons voted to
secede from Nigeria. The core of its strength was in the
Eastern Region among the Ibos; leader was Nnamdi
Azikiwe who became the first President of the Federation
of Nigeria.
Native Authority (N.A.): Local government for an emirate or administrative unit; name was changed to Local Administration (L.A.) after Independence.

Northern Elements Progressive Union (NEPU): Opposition party in the Northern Region from 1950-1966, led by Aminu Kano. It was allied with the NCNC during most of its lifetime.

Northern Peoples' Congress (NPC): Party of the northern traditional rulers, and dominant in the Northern Region, led by Sardauna Ahmadu Bello, Premier of the Northern Region, and Abubakar Tafawa Balewa, Prime Minister of the Federation of Nigeria until January, 1966 military coup, when both were killed.

Pagan: Term used to denote followers of any religion in Africa other than Christian, Moslem, or Jewish, and including many indigenous religions.

Purdah: Cultural practice which confines the wives of a polygamous marriage to remain in their quarters at all times, unseen by any man but their husband, except in very special circumstances.

Region: Subdivision of Nigeria when the British occupied it. At first they were ruled as separate entities (three regions: North, East, and West), but they were merged into a Federation. This arrangement lasted (with the addition of a Midwest Region) until 1967, when Major-General Gowon's Military Government sub-divided the country into twelve states rather than four regions.

Sabon Gari: Literally, Strangers' Quarters, referring to the living quarters of a city, where non-Moslem peoples were segregated.

Sallah: Moslem religious festival, entailing much pageantry, once at end of Ramadan, and a second time at end of Id-El Fitr.

Sao People: Literally "Snake People"; original occupants of Hausaland, before the numerous migrations and invasions which swept over the land.

Sarauta: Hereditary traditional status in Hausaland, which granted a title and office, and was passed on from one generation to the next.

Sardauna: High traditional office, granted by the emir or sultan, usually accompanied by role as councillor or district head.

Sardauna of Sokoto was the title of Ahmadu Bello, Premier of the Northern Region where he was the dominant figure. Through the NPC he was able to dominate the federal government as well.

Sarki: Hausa word for chief or king; addition of letter "n" at end (Sarkin) means "Chief of"; plural, "sarakuna."

Sawaba: Word for "freedom"; was used as slogan for Aminu Kano's Northern Elements Progressive Union.

Shari'a: Moslem code of law, defined by the Prophet Mohammed.

Shehu: Leader or teacher; when used alone (The Shehu) it refers to Usman Dan Fodio.

Sudan: That part of Africa stretching from the Congo on the south to the Sahara on the north. Boundaries of the Western Sudan have never been clearly defined, but now "The Sudan" is a country in eastern Africa.

Tafsir: Traditional practice of oral translation of the Koran from Arabic into the vernacular, with an accompanying explanation and interpretation.

Talakawa: Common people, the masses in Hausaland as counterposed to the sarakuna, or ruling class. In between are the mallams, imams, and alkalis, the learned, religious and ethical leadership.

Tijjaniyya: Sect of followers of Sheik Tijjani, interpreter of the Islamic religion and founder of sect extending widely through West Africa, including a high concentration in northern Nigeria.

United Middle Belt Congress (UMBC): Political party more or less restricted to Middle Belt area in the southeastern corner of Northern Region; includes area of the Tiv, one of the larger minority groups in Northern Nigeria.

Waliyi: Guardian (parent or foster parent) of an unmarried child or adult in Hausaland who speaks for his or her charge in decisions of education, marriage, divorce, etc.

AFRICAN
REVOLUTIONARY

1.

WHY AND HOW

I have known Aminu Kano for over ten years. We first met in 1960 in New York City, when he was serving as a delegate to the United Nations from the newly independent federal state of Nigeria. The most populous nation in Africa, agriculturally fertile, energetically on its way toward industrialization and economic development, Nigeria was vaunted by the Western world as its Black Hope, its bulwark against the insidious influence of the Second World of Socialism.

To welcome this infant state to the family of nations, some black American friends of ours were asked by the U.S. State Department to give a private reception welcoming the Nigerian delegation. There we were, my wife and I, together with our thirteen-year-old son, Fred (who had excitedly tagged along sans invitation), at the tail end of the delegates' reception line, shaking hands with a Nigerian gentleman in native garb. He was short in stature and short in neck, almost turtle-like. Everything about him smiled. His sparkling eyes, his mouth, his entire visage exuded warmth. This was Mallam Aminu Kano.

Fred, not one for formalities, cut through the polite exchange of pleasantries and quickly struck up a conversation with him. We had arrived rather late and no one was pressing behind us, so we smiled approvingly and even tried to turn their dialogue into a discussion in the round. He continued to ply Aminu with questions about his country, its climate, his family, and particularly about the life of Nigerian youngsters. Aminu answered with something more than patience, rather with active interest in an accurate response and in asking his own questions. His warmth was disarming enough for Fred to screw up enough courage to ask him if he would address an

1

assembly of students at his Elizabeth Irwin High School. Aminu readily agreed. A few days later we picked him up at his hotel, entertained him briefly, and after his speech returned him to his room. Thus began a long and fast friendship, covering many continents and circumstances.

For several years our friendship was renewed each fall with each new U.N. session. The General Assembly and its numerous committees occupied Aminu's time daily and our household became his home away from home. When he wanted to escape the succession of formal meetings by day and the innumerable and interminable diplomatic receptions by night, he could always retreat to the informality of our home, family, and friends.

He seemed to derive much pleasure from the naive questions about Africa and Nigeria which our supposedly sophisticated friends would throw at him. Rarely did his patience ebb. His curiosity and interest regarding American affairs would often stimulate vigorous heated discussions, but he would continue smiling good-humoredly and never seemed to lose his self-control.

Aminu was relatively comfortable in the Western world, equally at home with the formal diplomatic set of the U.N., the well-informed literati, or the would-be intelligentsia and the eternally curious world of the teenager. I was continually startled—and apologetic—at the woeful lack of knowledge of well-informed Americans about Africana. If he too was distressed at this, he never showed it. He seemed more resigned to this state of affairs than disturbed.

The more I learned of his background, the more enigmatic seemed this man of two worlds. I wondered what "back home" was like for him, and if it was much of a problem to return each year. (You know, "Is it better to leave the farm for the city and return, or never to have left at all?")

In the fall of 1962 we were talking one evening with Mallam Aminu about our plans for a family trip abroad, when he broke in with, "Well, if you're doing so much traveling, why not include Africa in your globe circling?" This had the sound of a sound idea to us, and after serious discussions at several family conferences, we decided to give it a whirl. We notified Aminu that the projected Feinstein family orbit was revised to include Africa—with West

Africa, and more specifically Nigeria, as the last leg of our trip.

We reached West Africa after many adventures in the Far East, the Near East, and East Africa, landing at the Lagos jet airport in August 1963. From that day on, we were treated like visiting royalty—more so, like his adopted family, that we felt we were back in New York City.

Aminu served as our host, and a gracious one indeed, with the kind assistance of the then Prime Minister Abubakar Tafawa Balewa and, unwittingly, of Obafemi Awolowo, the Western Region leader. The Prime Minister, after being told by Aminu how important our New York household was to his U.N. work, agreed to put us up as guests of the government, in a temporarily unoccupied government domicile. This house, which we occupied for about ten days, we discovered, was vacant because its former occupant, Chief Awolowo, had been required to take up residence in the federal prison. Thus his somewhat involuntary contribution to our family conversion into Afrophiles—for that is precisely what happened.

We did the usual tourist rounds; took a look at Lagos' modern buildings, the museum, Parliament, the harbor, etc., but the high point was a visit to Agege to hear Aminu address a group of his party followers. As our car rode into the town, we saw clenched fists raised in greeting and heard eerie shouts of greeting—"Ame-e-en!—Ameen!—Am-e-een!" As we slowed down, upon reaching the meeting place, crowds excitedly hemmed us in, everyone wanting to see and touch Aminu. The clenched fist, it turned out, is an old Hausa sign of greeting supposed to symbolize the spilling of the good earth, and brotherly welcome, and predates our contact with the West's Third International by well over a century.

The meeting was held in a large yard behind a series of houses and backed by the railroad tracks. Aminu spoke in Hausa, and though we understood not a word, we seemed to. He spoke rapidly, pausing only for dramatic effect. He cajoled, he joked, he admonished, and he waved the closed umbrella he carried as though it were a pointing finger. The audience sat and listened quietly. They laughed at times, and occasionally muttered what sounded like agreement and assent, or "Amen." The women fidgeted a bit during the discussion period after the speech, and rearranged the several babies tied to their backs. I thought, "No baby-sitting problems for political females here!" The crowds were even denser as we made our way back to the car, but Aminu waved or raised a clenched fist and returned the people's cries of "Sawaba!" (meaning "Freedom," as we subsequently found out).

My excitement and fascination with this new, up-and-coming world did not wane after our return to New York. In fact it became the focus of my avocational life. I was absorbed more and more in African politics, sociology, and the continent's emergence into the world of independent nations. And as my extracurricular activities in this sphere grew, my curricular activities shrank. After two years, by the summer of 1965, I was ready for another turn at Africa, where again Nigeria and Aminu occupied a significant portion of my travel time.

Reinforced by a little better preparation in African politics and a strong need to tell my fellow Americans about this new continent I had discovered, I wangled a series of interviews with many of Africa's national leaders, including Nigeria's, largely through Aminu's contacts, but not especially restricted to his political friends. At that time it struck me as odd that his political foes should be so cordial and have such a high regard for Aminu, but this simply shows that I didn't know him that well at the time. It was not until much later that I learned of his ability to continue amicable working relationships with his arch enemies.

Later that year, in New York City, during long and intimate discussions with him, I delved more deeply into his attitudes, hopes, and desires. I found myself personalizing my avid interest in Africa, interpreting events as he would see them. My thoughts were troubled by his distress; his moments of despair depressed me; his frustrated desires and his concern for his countrymen confused me. On the other hand, his continued optimism and seeming selflessness through it all, encouraged me. My cynicism about politicians and their motivations began to weaken. Could there actually be an honest and dedicated politician in this world?

In December 1965, Aminu left New York City, after depositing some of his luggage in our home, expecting to return in three weeks for an economic conference. He didn't return for three years. In

January 1966, the first military coup took place in Nigeria. From that time on, news sources, whatever on-the-scene commentaries I could lay my hands on, occasional Nigerians passing through New York, subscriptions to *West Africa Magazine* and the *Nigerian Daily Times,* and cautiously worded letters from Aminu were the sinuous threads through which I kept abreast of events.

Without attempting to predict what role he would play in the future of his country, without even knowing whether he would be able to survive Nigeria's violent upheavals, I found myself examining his life retrospectively, gradually coming to the realization that he had already had a deep, long-lasting and revolutionary effect on his people. I had begun to regard him as a sort of alter ego, as my personal representative on the power front, asking myself how I would act, what decision I would make if I were he. I thought of his continuing need to make decisions which would affect millions of people, and I wrote an article, "The Dilemma of Power," as though I were faced with these problems myself.

It struck me at that point that a biography of Aminu Kano could be a worthwhile project. If only I could manage to convey the belief that so many millions of Africans had in him, and the reasons for their faith, such a work could have profound meaning for a broad audience, whether in my native U.S.A., Great Britain, Africa, Nigeria, or elsewhere in this political and shrinking world, so in need of something, someone to believe in. The more I mulled it over, the more the idea appealed to me.

By happy coincidence it was just at this point in my thinking (at the end of 1968) that Aminu returned to our scene; three weeks in New York City, again at his post in the U.N. Through all the crises, coups, and countercoups his stature seemed greater than ever. Nigeria was still ruled by a military government, and was engaged in a tragic civil war, but the civilians at the top levels were influential and Aminu was now Federal Commissioner of Communications. He remained respected by most segments of Nigeria's population. From his perigee in 1965 as leader of NEPU (Northern Elements Progressive Union), an opposition party in the North that was practically on the ropes, he had emerged as a unifying force for national unity, with extensive support from most sections of the country and most segments of the social spectrum.

After happy exchanges of gifts and greetings, I tentatively broached the project on my mind—writing the story of Aminu Kano. I held my breath during his initial modest reactions to my proposals, and was elated when he finally agreed to cooperate.

We spent the following couple of weeks in New York planning the project—time schedules, and certainly yet another sojourn for me in Nigeria, this time a more extended one. After Aminu's departure, I devoted some months to library research and interviews with American academicians who had done related work in Africa, in order that my projected stay in Nigeria could be most productive.

My personal impressions of Aminu were buttressed by many who had known and written of him. I seemed to have chosen well, but I had vowed to examine his life carefully and as objectively as one could, even the gray areas. The deeper I probed, the more convinced I became that exposing him to the light of international day would show that he was a man of significant impact, whose life could have some universal meaning.

Thus in mid-June, I found myself aboard Pan-American's direct flight to Lagos, preceding my otherwise ever-present wife by several weeks. The next three months were spent digging into Northern Nigeria's past, ranging from pre-Dan Fodio through the colonial era and the pre-independence political times, right on up to the military regime with its accompanying civil strife.

For several months I traveled throughout Northern and Western Nigeria, including Lagos (the Eastern Region was inaccessible because of the civil war), but concentrated on Aminu Kano's land of origin, the North, where his life had taken seed and been shaped.

My ferreting pointed up some salient facts about Nigerians, particularly Northern Nigerians. Though there has been a long history of *oral* record-keeping, the filing of printed materials has been diffuse, limited, and of course in Hausa and Arabic. *Gaskiya,* the first Hausa-vernacular newspaper, as well as the *Nigerian Citizen,* the first English-language newspaper in the North, date back only to the 1940's. Files of these newspapers are sparse and incomplete, particularly for the early years, and I have yet to discover any indexing for those files that do exist. Written histories of local areas are few and hard to find; personal histories and genealogies (with certain royal exceptions) are extremely difficult to trace. Emirs' archives had been closed in the past in order to protect their owners' revered status, and were only recently being opened.

In light of my own culture, so different from the Hausa, I had to lean heavily on oral testimony—a form of recording that has been notoriously devious, often contradictory, and constantly repetitious. Superstition and prejudice were frequently present, and a cultural heritage vastly different from mine always present, but the real confusion arose when I, an American, attempted to familiarize myself not only with the facts of Aminu's life but also the habits and customs of these residents of Northern Nigeria: his neighbors, relatives, friends, enemies, and associates.

Having a library knowledge of Hausa customs helped make me more aware of the difficulties, but hardly lessened them. Most confusing were the so-called "avoidance patterns" and "joking" relationships and their subsequent explanations. For the benefit of those who know not of what I speak, Hausa people have, over the generations, developed familial relationships which fall into somewhat rigid patterns. A firstborn child, male or female, is generally, other children often, "avoided"—i.e., ignored—by the blood parents. They never refer to him by name, nor does he refer to these parents by name. The parent tries to ignore his existence, and frequently he is literally "given away." In Hausa-Fulani culture, this practice represented great sacrifice, that of the most loved one, a kind of stoicism that proved the family's moral strength or religious conviction. This is the "avoidance pattern." "Joking" relationships apply to the extended family, which goes beyond direct blood descent and includes, as brothers and sisters, the children of the father's co-wives and, as fathers, the uncles on the father's side. The joking relationship, in which teasing is an integral part, is an informal one with all restrictions of the avoidance patterns removed, and exists between grandparents and grandchildren, cousins, and even some in-laws.

Needless to say, though these family relationship are traditionally accepted among Hausas, to an American they become perplexing. I spent one whole afternoon interviewing a sister of Aminu's, during which time she told me the most intimate details of her life, only to discover to my chagrin that she really was no more than a distant relative, according to our equally rigid categories. It took me many long hours to sift out family relationships as we know them, only to be given two or three different versions subsequently, from other sources. Information I thought would be available in simple statements of fact took hours to unravel. I would gather extensive data about a particular individual and then find that the interviewee was talking about another person with the same name. In some instances, questions addressed to one individual were referred to another, because of this need to "avoid"; to speak not or think not publicly of the person involved.

My interpreter—gentle, gracious, and ever ready to help in anything asked of him—unfortunately in this respect, was of Hausa soil. He truly attempted to break out of the pattern and explain it, but more often than otherwise he became deeply interwoven in the web I was trying to penetrate and contributed his share to my confusion.

A would-be researcher finds that as modernization makes inroads the traditional patterns are changing. Good? Ultimately, I guess, but at this time even more bewildering. Is the person to whom you are talking avoiding or not?

Further complications arose when dealing with "given away" children. Custom has it that immediately after weaning, at about two years of age, the first born (and frequently other children as well) is given to substitute parents to bring up, usually drawn from those respected in the community, who may be childless or are in a better position to raise the child—perhaps a grandmother or a brother or sister of one of the parents. Also, the act of giving away the child frequently represents the strengthening of a traditional alliance or the payment of a social obligation. Then who is called mother or father? Who is regarded as parent? Where does the child visit when he is grown and returning from school or another town? Where is the first loyalty?

From what I can make of it, there is much variation, depending on the parents, the clan, or the region. Just as foster parents in Western society will sometimes replace blood parents, so in Hausa society, except that in the latter case, it is commonplace, a practice so widespread that it represents a deep-seated cultural variation. This broad concept, radically different from Western family organization, represents another form of the extended family present in many societies, i.e., family love and loyalty reach beyond the line of direct descent to several "mothers," fathers," "brothers," and "sisters."

Aside from this concept, so complex to me at first, there were other familial habits to confuse me further. A proper wife has *kunya*, which implies a social modesty, shame, or tact. She is simply expected to answer only when spoken to, to observe the customs of the area, to respect co-wives, and to care for the children and the household. Thus when approached by a stranger, particularly a male and a foreigner, she is not likely to be too communicative, and when she does communicate she will not necessarily be the most reliable informant.

One other custom should be mentioned if we are to understand the Hausa community attitudes. According to Moslem custom, a man may marry as many as four wives if he can afford to support them and grant them equal treatment. This custom, however, is tempered by free-and-easy divorce and marriage. Either the husband or the wife can state his or her desire for separation, explain it to the *alkali*, or judge, and after one or two attempts at reconciliation, if desired, the marriage can be abrogated. Most Hausas, male or female, are divorced three or four or more times in a lifetime. To complete the picture, the divorced (or widowed) wife is expected to remarry shortly after the lapse of a three-month (approximately) period of grace and celibacy (Idda). If she does not, her friends and neighbors will ordinarily look at her askance. The same Hausa word, *karuwai,* is used for divorcees or widows who leave their household and go beyond the three-month grace period, as for prostitutes, profligates, or women who remain single until late in life, indicating that Hausa culture links all single women with a common thread. She is thought of as deviant, strange and antisocial—eccentric, unless she returns to the household of her *waliyi* (parent or guardian) to wait arrangements for her next marriage. In the latter case, she is a *bazaure* and has achieved respectability.

Many of these unsupervised women become Bori dancers, a phenomenon about which much can be written. Briefly, Bori dancers are thought to be possessed of spirits, either good or bad or both, that are invoked through an uninhibited and frenzied form of dance and trance, to rid any afflicted devotee of physiological or psychological ailments..

It must be made clear at this point that all these social customs, taboos, and restrictions are currently in a state of flux. Many are changed, others modified, and still others thrust aside completely. Not only are standards of individual behavior breaking down, but the walls of social stratification have similarly begun to crumble. In 1920, at the time of Aminu's birth, there were roughly four social levels: royalty, nobility, descendants of slaves, and *talakawa* (commoners).

Although the British had abolished slavery as a general practice by the first decade of the 1900's, Lord Lugard, the then High Commissioner of Nigeria, wanting to upset the social system as little as possible, decreed that only runaway slaves and children of slaves were free. Thus slaves still existed, and do to this day, as lineage groups. But since none are bound to a master by law, by and large slavery has been eliminated. Nevertheless, social origins still cling, as in most countries, and limit people's social status to a considerable degree.

Even within the traditional slave structure, the rigid patterns of Hausa-Fulani autocracy were evident. The slaves had certain rights, and the owners had certain duties toward them. The slaves of the emir were eminently favored and were used in positions of authority. They were the ruler's representatives and tax collectors, and in some instances had much power. An interesting sidelight within this pattern occurred when the British attempted to introduce Western education into Nigeria and the emirs resisted. Instead of sending their own children to school and on to England, thus contaminating them with Western culture, the emirs would sometimes send the children of their slaves. This act of subtle defiance accounts to a large extent for those well-educated leaders of Northern Nigeria who were of humble slave origin. The careers of the former Prime Minister of Nigeria, Abubakar Tafawa Balewa, and Maitama Sule, a Kano state commissioner and former federal cabinet member, started in this fashion.

The Northern People's Congress (NPC), dominant party of the North and federal government until the first military coup in January 1966, based its power on the existing rigid social stratification. From Ahmadu Bello (a member of the royal family of Sokoto and premier of the Northern Region until his demise), on down, the party gained its dominance through the derivative power of the Native Authority, or Local Authority, administrative arm of the Northern emirs. The only region-wide all-Northern opposition party, the NEPU, attempted to represent the socially disaffected classes of young urbanized civil servants, minority tribes, and principally the *talakawa*, or common man—although it was led by Aminu Kano, who was a "mallam," in a category approaching nobility.

So when I attempted to examine a man's life, which started during an era of rigid social patterns and ranges through current deep-seated change, I obviously ran into difficulties. As I pursued my explorations, I became aware that Aminu Kano, the subject of my study, was also an important factor in *creating* and *hastening* this change. He was not only helping to break down rigid forms of individual behavior, what was expected of each person, but also contributing much toward the breakdown of the class structure inherited over the centuries. Modern concepts of civilization and politicization were creating revolutionary changes. Political power was in the process of being modified and ultimately wrested from the feudal domination of many generations. Since the society, feudal in nature, naturally showed some variation from area to area, wherever local conditions were discussed, I tried to concentrate my attentions on the Kano emirate rather than any other, for this was the childhood locale of Aminu and, politically speaking, his local constituency.

From confusion through fascination to analysis would describe my own transition best; for I found it essential to examine and interpret very carefully each event and each relationship I came across in the light of mores so totally different from my own. Snap generalizations had to be eliminated; I had to immerse myself in the Hausa culture and picture myself a part of it. I hope that I can at least partially help cross this gap for those American or European readers who are no more familiar with Hausa culture than I was when I started my opus.

The pleasures of the trip throughout the North and West and in Lagos were innumerable. Always I was greeted with warmth and curiosity: the good humor of the people I interviewed en route was boundless. With only one exception, everyone I approached managed to find time to discuss Aminu and their connections with him. Each had some fond recollection of common incidents in their past. Each had something of interest and worth to contribute. To meet the people in Aminu's life, in their own milieu, with the mixed background of old and new, left me with indelible memories and strong desire to know more about them.

Then there were problems that did not specifically relate to custom. When the life of a man such as Aminu is subjected to close scrutiny, one realizes how closely, deeply, and inextricably it is interwoven into the history of the area from which he derives. Therefore one must go further and further back to find what constitutes the reality of his existence. If a man is as single-purposed as Aminu and if his manifest destiny is to help bring his country "from Then to When," obviously the social circumstances of the "Then" period must be examined.

So where does one start? With the birth of the man or of the country? When analyzing the interrelationship between the two, I realized there was one event in Nigeria's past which could be directly linked to the life and times of Aminu; the advent of Usman Dan Fodio with its observable impact on his country's history. The Usman Dan Fodio story began and ended before Aminu, or his father for that matter, came on the scene, and requires a separate chapter.

The other major event of consequence that predated and influenced Aminu's life was the British occupation. Although it took place in 1900-1910, the British governmental presence continued on up to 1960. In 1920, when Aminu was born, the grip of British dominance was unquestioned. It represented the reality of his childhood, adolescence, and early adulthood, and therefore can be interwoven into the body of my text.

Another general problem not specifically related to Northern Nigerian culture is that of dealing with a political figure in mid-career. My avowed purpose was to avoid as much as possible saying anything that would influence the career of my protagonist, or for that matter any of his antagonists. I have no intention to espouse a political cause or attack individuals. To write though, one must stop the clock at a particular period in history and time, and one cannot readily do this to the far from static political careers involved. Among other things, an antagonist may become a protagonist overnight. Tactics and tact are major considerations. Yet in search for

meaning and truth some facts and events unearthed are found in
political limbo. There are situations when to be "sure" an author
would have to be "sterile" as well. I therefore resolved early that this
work should be as apolitical as is possible when writing about a man
whose whole being is and was expressed through political channels
—obviously a difficult task. I knew too, that in spite of such an
approach, toes might still be stepped upon. I have tried to keep the
pedal clashes to a minimum, so long as my purpose remained intact;
to present to the world the essence of Aminu Kano, who comes as
close as any man I know to this concept of Karma Yogi (the Yogi of
action); part man, part granite, part prophet, "feelingless, yet merci-
ful, and contented; free of jealousy, fear, exultation, and sorrow; an
activist unaffected by the action, who treats friend and foe alike,
renounces all fruit, good or bad, is untouched by respect or disrespect
[and not unduly] puffed up by praise; who loves silence and solitude,
. . . but rarely has it; . . . has a disciplined reason, single purpose, and
remains unattached in order to achieve his dharma [destiny]."[1]

2.

It is for the historians to separate out fact from fiction in the development of Nigeria as a nation—and a monumental task at that; but for our purpose it is not that essential. Myth and corroborated fact (whatever that is) are both integral parts of the history of a people. Together they influence a culture and determine what makes a people. When we talk of ethnic "qualities" and national characteristics, we talk in generalizations, not at all applicable to any one individual. Yet the presence of the culture is encompassing enough to affect the personality of the individual, his interaction with his fellows and his nation. Where this influence, this intimate coupling of the individual with his society, begins and where it ends is indeterminate, but for the telling of a story of one person, we must begin somewhere, and in this instance that somewhere starts beyond written history, in the never-never land between fact and fiction. So we go back to the origins of the region.

Legend has it that one Bayajidda was responsible for the founding of the seven prominent Hausa Bokwai states.[1] Subsequently seven Banza Bakwai, or "bastard" states were formed, which all together have become what is known as Hausaland. Bayajidda, son of Abdullahi, King of Baghdad, quarreled with his father and left home to seek his fortune elsewhere. According to this tale, he and his band of followers set out westward on horseback (introducing horses to the Western Sudan for the first time), and arrived at the well-developed, well-organized, and well-established kingdom of Kanem-Bornu. Either Bayajidda possessed some magical powers or he had an overwhelming force of followers, for his presence was immediately deemed a threat to the mai's (king's) rule.

14

The mai, cunning man that he was, first bought him off by giving him his daughter's hand in marriage. To further cut off this potential Samson's locks, he separated him from his followers by making each of them the ruler of a newly conquered but distant town, thus scattering them and rendering them impotent. But our hero saw through the mai's sinister motive, and fled even farther west, leaving his newly acquired wife behind in the city known as Biram. There she gave birth to their child, who eventually became founder of the state of Biram. Bayajidda continued his journey until he reached yet another city, Daura. Upon his arrival, he was informed that a snake inhabiting the town well permitted the people to draw water but once a week (undoubtedly reflecting pollution and/or drought conditions). He obligingly killed the snake, married the queen, became king, and lived happily ever after.

His new queen bore a child named Bawo, who took over when his father died. Bawo in turn had six sons, each of whom became king of one of the surrounding cities and founded each as a state. These six—Daura, Kano, Zazzau, Gobir, Katsina, and Rano, together with the above-mentioned Biram— constituted the original seven Hausa states, the Bakwai. The seven Banza Bakwai states (Zamfara, Kebbi, Nupe, Gwari, Yauri, Yoruba, and Kororofa) grew from these.

The consensus of opinion among historians is that this legend is a folk tale which telescopes events that took place over a long period of time into a convenient, popular version of how Hausaland achieved its common culture.

Historically speaking, during the period 900-1500 A.D., Hausaland was beset by incessant wars and waves of immigrants sweeping from the East—where were Egypt and the powerful Bornu-Kanem; or from the north, where nomadic Berbers, Tuaregs, and Arabs swept down out of the Sahara; or from the great Western Sudan kingdoms of Ghana, Mali, and Songhai; or even to some extent from the Nupe and Jukun (Kororofa) kingdoms to the south. The indigenes at the time were known as Sao, or "snake people." A residual reflection of the Daura Bayajidda legend is seen in the various snake symbols on Hausa staffs, flags, and walking sticks even to this day.

Ethnologically speaking, the direction taken by the immigrants of those years was probably east to west. It was out of this nebulous period, sometime before the start of the second millenium A.D., that Bayajidda and his predecessors came to Hausaland. The *Kano Chronicle*,[2] a document written by an unknown author in 1883-1893 lists the genealogy of Kano's royal family, starting back at that time (1000 A.D.) with the first king, Bagoda, son of the aforementioned Bawo, and grandson of the snake-killing Bayajidda.

The *Kano Chronicle* refers even further back to Dalla, the founder of Kano in the era preceding Bayajidda, and his sons. Dalla's origins were unknown, but it seems he was of Paul Bunyanesque proportions, able to slay an elephant with a stick and carry the carcass on his head for miles. He lived on a hill which can still be viewed today in Kano and which of course is referred to as Dalla Hill. He was the head of the blacksmiths who congregated in this area to be near the iron ore at the base of the hill. He had several wives, and seven children. The eldest son was Garageji, and his son was Barbushe, who when his turn came was chief lord and high priest, too.

Each year, when the special days for the sacrificial rituals arrived and people brought black dogs, goats, and fowl to the idol atop of Dalla Hill, Barbushe would emerge from his hill house with his drummers to march with the people to the *shamuz* tree, sacred to their god, Tchumburburi. (This date tree would live out its 500-600 year lifetime, it was said, and when it expired, so would Kano.) They danced around the tree, and the chief told them what would occur that year—the quality of the crops and degree of rainfall—and what history-making events would come to pass, good or bad.

Only Barbushe could enter through the wall surrounding the tree, after the sacrifices had been made. He then would return and report the oracle-like messages from within. And it came to pass that one day Barbushe emerged to tell of the imminent arrival of a stranger who would destroy their arborial shrine and dominate them all. It was then that Bagoda from Daura, grandson of Bayajidda, and of the stock of Ham and Noah, arrived to become the first Sarki of Kano.

Until modern times, the Dalla Hill section of Kano was considered to be unlucky territory, inhabited by the spirits of the gods. As a result, the land there could be acquired fairly easily, making it possible for Aminu Kano to piece together a few small inexpensive parcels of land on which to build a house and a modified compound, in the year 1968.

Iron foundries were known to have existed in both Kano and Daura prior to Bagoda's reign. In Kano the ore and iron foundries in the Dalla section are still being dug up and can be viewed by anyone choosing to take the trouble. The first palace of Kano's ruler was thus on Dalla Hill; the second now houses the Kano Museum; and the third one is occupied by the current Emir, Ado Bayero.

For much of the period between 1000 and 1500 A.D., the small city states of Hausaland were able to retain their independence, probably because they were located far from the centers of power of the large states that surrounded them. At various times, their powerful neighbors would penetrate into the periphery of Hausaland, and would extract their tribute for as long a period as they could exert long-distance control. Each of these distant kingdoms had internal struggles of accession and succession and at various times had to fight off their own invaders. Such distractions served to protect the smaller independent Hausa city-states.

Helping them survive, too, was an apparent division of labor among the city-states. Kano and Katsina were the center of an extensive trading net, a connection between North Africa, with its trans-Saharan trade routes, and South Africa, with its need for ivory, slaves, and other products. Gobir was the northernmost center of resistance to the invading Tuaregs; Daura retained its function as spiritual center of Hausaland; Zaria was used for slave raiding and trading from South to North Africa; and Rano was developed as an industrial center.

These independent city-state functions tended to support one another in a general sense, but were tempered and altered by internecine struggles for power, in which one Bakwai state would dominate one or many other states and then in turn would be dominated themselves.

It is thought that these struggles, particularly between Kano and Katsina and Katsina and Gobir, were essentially efforts to dominate the trans-Saharan trade caravan routes. Through these routes, and through invasions from Mali on the west and Bornu on the East, came the penetration of Islam into Hausaland. Apparently

the indigenous populations were sufficiently developed to absorb
the immigrants, invaders, and infiltrators along with their religion.
Islam was vitiated upon arrival, whether accepted by the royalty or
no. The newcomers made accommodation to the local customs and
catered to the desires of the indigenes. What emerged was a com-
posite of people, made up of both invaders and invaded.

This rapid adjustment, the assimilation of the Moslem invaders
by the native occupants of Hausaland, was attested to by a strange
annotation in the *Kano Chronicle*. A man defiles the mosque built
by Yaji and then is struck blind in retribution. In order not to
alienate the local citizens, though, he is then made Sarki (Chief)
of the Blind—a rather grim concept of justice!

The religious seesaw this evoked in Kano, as well as surrounding states, seemed to represent a continued struggle for conquest and
control of the trade routes across the Sahara rather than missionary
zeal. It went on until the time of King Yakubu, 1452-1463, when the
Fulani migration began to make its mark. Up to that point, Islamic
influence had been spread principally through the Koran and books
on law and tradition. The Fulani, coming from the western kingdom
of Mali, brought with them books on divinity and etymology, in this
way broadening the concept of learning, from the mere implementation of religious rites and traditions into the world of philosophy,
ideas, and conceptual thinking. Yakubu permitted the Fulani to pass
on through Hausaland to Bornu, as many did, or to remain and settle
if they so chose. It is reported that Yakubu's reign was also free of
wars, indicating a generally enlightened diplomacy on his part.

Yakubu was succeeded by Mohammed Rumfa (1463-1499),
the most famous of Kano's kings. It was in this latter part of the
fifteenth century that Islam secured its roots in Hausaland. One
story has it that Abdu Rahman set out from Medina, urged on by a
vision of the Prophet, to proceed until he found a soil comparable
with that of Medina. He and his retinue marched westward, testing
the soil as they went. Like Prince Charming with Cinderella's slip-
per, when he reached Kano, he found the soil matched that of
Medina, and stayed. Mohammed Rumfa welcomed him, built a
mosque for Friday prayers, tore down the old pagan sacred tree,
and built a minaret in its place. Whether it was through the influence
of Abdu Rahman or the Fulani arriving from the west, books and

learned men multiplied and the Islamic faith was firmly established as a state-wide religion, with all of its manifestations.

Rumfa extended Islam beyond its religious confines and tried to run his state according to Islamic principles and law, innovating extensive city walls, marketplaces, and much grandeur. His introduction of ceremonial slippers decorated with ostrich feathers and of riderless horses following him into battle, as spares, are customs that have survived in ritual until today. In the following centuries, Arabic influence spread throughout northern Nigeria through the teachings of Hausa and Arabic scholars, which, however, was restricted primarily to the aristocracy and mallam* class.

The political structure of the Hausa states approximated that prescribed in the Koran, but was also modified to conform to local custom. The king had much power, though he had to deal with the aristocracy at all times, trying to play one group off against the other to maintain his position. Mohammed Rumfa and others after him tried to offset the influence of these aristocrats by granting titles to eunuchs and slaves and appointing a hierarchy of village heads as administrators and tax collectors, but the resident hereditary officials and clan heads remained powerful nevertheless.

Before the superimposition of the invader dynasties at the time of the end of the first millenium A.D., the political and social structure that had been developed was apparently based on vocation. The division of labor necessitated by city living was well developed by that time, with probably over 75,000 residents within the walls of the city of Kano. Each trade was organized for its own defense and was passed down from father to son. Marriages were generally arranged within these clanlike groups—to the point where gradually, over the years, the trades and their specialized governmental functions and social status overlapped until they were indistinguishable. Each evidently chose its own leaders for life. There were the chiefs of the blacksmiths, the brewers, the doctors, the miners and smelters, the dancers, the archers, the salt workers, and so on. Eleven pagan clans of this nature were supposed to be the basis and original stock of Kano. Whether this was literally so or not, the social and political structure of today's emirates of northern Nigeria was carried down

---

*The educated class of imams (priests), teachers, and judges: see page 20.

through the ages, more or less, intact, until independence in 1960, with everyone remaining in their preordained professions and trades.

The mallam class developed quite differently, as a group apart from the seat of power. They were the thinkers, scholars, judges, and priests; they had the final word as to what was correct and moral in the society, though without the authority to impose it. Much in the manner of the early Talmudic scholars of Judaic tradition, they spent their lives in contemplation, discussion, and teaching, devoid of any political influence, except in isolated instances when specific political rulers were influenced by their thinking. With no societal means of their own to implement their judgments, they were totally dependent upon the kings and courtiers.

One of the first records of this relationship was the story of Umaru, son of Kanejeji, who ruled Kano from 1410 to 1421. In addition to being king he was a mallam in his own right and an earnestly religious person, thus creating a conflict in the traditional attitudes and power relationships. When his friend Mallam Abuba-kar returned from Bornu after a ten-year absence and found Umaru still Sarkin Kano, he likened him to the lover of a fickle woman who would live to regret his transgressions, but too late. Umaru, unable to resolve the conflict of sovereignty vs. ideology, resigned shortly thereafter to live the rest of his life in quiet solitude and guilty regret for his eleven years as sarki, in this way reflecting the mallams' contempt for worldly government and rule, and the respect Hausas have retained for learning and learned ones. One might think that Usman Dan Fodio's separation from political authority after his successful *jihad* in the early 1800's was another reflection of this same tradition. So too were the strong-willed, independent Aminu Kano, his father Yusufu, and their relatives in the Genawa Clan, all steeped in reverence for learning. The major difference was that Aminu consciously tried to join politics and education in his attempt to alleviate poverty and introduce modernity—and this without the guilty regret of Umaru.

From 1500 to 1800, Kano and northern Nigeria again were afflicted with repeated incursions of warriors from east and west, as well as with constant internal struggles between the Hausa states themselves. As horses and armor and even guns were introduced, the

The regions of Nigeria

capacity to wage war over longer and longer distances increased, permitting conquest on a more grandiose scale.

To the west, Mali was succeeded in power by Songhai, starting with the rule of Sonni Ali and Mohammed Askia I, in the late fifteenth and early sixteenth centuries. Incursions eastward were common. Hausaland became the battleground between Songhai and Kanem-Bornu to the east. These two nations fought each other and the local warriors, extracting booty when successful and fleeing when unsuccessful, but the battleground was almost always devastated and its inhabitants paying tribute and slaves to someone. There were times when Katsina and Kano rode high in the saddle and other times when they suffered destruction, slave raids, fire, and ruin. But through it all, they emerged with a cultural unity and some degree of organization and learning, drawing from the invaders within Hausaland or from foreign lands some of their physical characteristics through intermarriage, and some of their customs, language, and attitudes. At the end of the eighteenth century, two of these Hausa states, Gobir and Zamfara, grew in power and vied for dominance. The stage was set for the great changes of the nineteenth century, on which much of modern Nigeria is based.

The latter half of the eighteenth century found the Hausa states locked in their perennial struggles. Gobir, perched astride the southern border of the Sahara, was under severe pressure from the nomadic desert tribes to the north. Though remaining aloof for a good part of its history, it had begun looking toward the fertile fields controlled by Zamfara to the south. The ensuing offensive penetration was an admixture of trade, treaty, royal intermarriage, and open warfare. Through constant military pressure southward, Gobir succeeded in defeating its rival Zamfara in battle but, as one might suspect, had ended up severely weakened from long years of war.

It was in this milieu that the great jihad of Usman Dan Fodio was spawned. The man who was to revolutionize this sector of the Western Sudan was born in 1744 of Fulani stock, and raised in Gobir. As was the wont of the more affluent Fulanis who had migrated from the west some fourteen generations before, Usman was educated extensively in the traditional Islamic fashion. He studied grammar, law, theology, and prosody (the art of rhyme and verse), gaining his inspiration from his teachers and from the reformist ideas which prevailed among the learned of the day. It was all in the tradition of his forebears, the leading proselytizers of Islam in all of West Africa.

Armed with the strength of the knowledge and religious fervor of his school years, Usman returned to the city of Degel, where he took up the habits and vocation of mallam: preaching, teaching, and study. He traveled from Degel up and down the land, spreading his ardent interpretations of social and religious reform, attracting larger and larger crowds as his fame grew. These itinerant mallams would set themselves up in market or public square, or merely in front of the compound of a friend. Word would get out that one of them was in town, and interested people would congregate in great or small numbers depending on his reputation.

Although Nafata, then King of Gobir, thought well enough of Usman to have him tutor his son, Yunfa, he recognized that Usman's presence and teachings were a threat to his sovereignty. According to the mixture of Islam and Animism which prevailed at the time as a state religion, the king and his descendants were considered holy, divine incarnations of the supernatural. The strict interpretation of the Koran promulgated by Usman Dan Fodio would obviously raise questions about the king's derivative role on earth, undermine his executive status, and strike at the very core of the monarch's divine right to rule. Mohammedanism crossed national boundaries and gained adherents from many lands, both far and near, again threatening the heart of the monarch's position at the center of the universe. He wanted royal monocentrism, not a social or religious polycentrism.

In spite of the king's apprehensions, Usman remained in favor at the court and among the nobility, for Islam and Islamic learning were still flourishing, even if in this bastard form. Not until Yunfa succeeded Nafata in 1802 as King of Gobir did the issues begin to sharpen, and the royal prerogative invoked to try to discourage and suppress Dan Fodio's influence.

Yunfa started with more subtle means that gradually assumed overt forms. He forbade the wearing of the turban for men and the veil for women. He even tried to prevent proselytizing by decreeing that only those born Moslem could practice Islam.

The struggle between the two men, although usually couched in religious forms and terms, was really a struggle between the Ins and the Outs; the defender of the status quo vs. the radical crusader. It was essentially political, with Usman looking for converts to his cause in secular areas. He attacked the unjust illegal and oppressive taxes; he exposed the extensive open corruption and bribery and military conscription. The cattle-raising nomadic Fulanis, in addition to being religious Moslems, were particularly distressed by the cattle tax and consequently vulnerable to anti-establishment agitation. The Hausa talakawa, the peasants, who were attracted to Usman found common ground on these economic issues rather than on the religious heresies supposed to be the basis of his call to arms.

Yunfa reached the point where he forced Usman to leave his court in disfavor. Usman returned to Degel, his home town, but continued his agitation against the current regime to the point where it is thought that Yunfa was preparing to have him killed. Just at that time, Abd Al-Salam, a disciple of Dan Fodio, refused to bless some traveling soldiers, who in turn arrested Abd Al-Salam's Moslem companions to sell them into slavery. Some of Usman's followers released them and open hostility broke out.

Jihad, or holy war, could be waged if three conditions were met, according to Dan Fodio's understanding of the Koran: (1) when there is an enemy attack on Moslem territory; (2) when captured Moslems must be rescued from the enemy infidel; and (3) when holy war is ordered by the Moslem ruler. Two of the conditions could be interpreted as having occurred already. All that remained was for Dan Fodio to declare himself leader of the Moslems and order the jihad—which he did.

In 1804, Yunfa marched on Degel, forcing Usman to flee to Gudu, performing the hejira in the tradition of Moslem holy wars since Mohammed. It was in Gudu that Usman wrote to his former pupils and disciples scattered throughout Hausaland to proclaim that the jihad was on and the revolution set in motion.

Islamic religion has always been tied closely to government. Mohammed's precepts had defined the moral basis on which the state should be run, so that any attempt to launch a jihad had to have a secular as well as a religious base. In any case, religious reform could not be achieved without a shift of power. The original

Islamic model of the state had a rigid form of social and legal justice, enforced through devout rulers and the Shari'a law as set down by Mohammed and his followers. This return to the early state model, with a purification of the religion and its observances, was the theoretical basis of the jihad.

The practical implementation was another matter. There were many who had personal opportunistic or tribal or class motives as well as religious. The Habe-Hausa* talakawa supported the revolt to rid themselves of the onerous tax burdens and immoral, oppressive administration. The Fulani cowherders had ethnic as well as economic ties. Many of the Fulani townspeople were wealthy and wanted to protect their threatened status. Many still had large herds of cattle in the countryside, and maintained contact and some degree of control over the "Cow-Fulani."

The leadership of the jihad cleverly exploited all these grievances to gain adherents, even using the neighboring Zamfarawa as temporary allies. It was a profoundly popular movement, differing from the pattern of palace revolutions or foreign invasions which up to that point had been responsible for most governmental upheavals. Usman Dan Fodio quickly retired to the protected status of religious leader, assumed the title of Amir al-Mu'minin (Arabic), Sarkin Musulmi (Hausa), and Leader, or Commander, of the Faithful (English), and left the prosecution of the wars and administration of government to Abdullahi, his brother, and Bello, his son.

From their first military victory over Yunfa in Gobir in 1804, the jihad warriors rapidly and triumphantly spread to the other Hausa states, one by one. By 1808, in a brief four years, they had conquered all the major states of Hausaland with the exception of Bornu. Through superior unity and organization, and clever utilization of the issues of the day, the Fulani had been able to establish effective hegemony over most of northern Nigeria. As the jihad progressed, it became more and more political and less and less religious. The purification of Islam and the elimination of corruption and decadence which were the orginal motives for the revolt had become

---

*Habe is the name given to the habitants of northern Nigeria, before the Fulanis arrived. Hausa is the language employed, but has come to be used as a generic term for northern Nigerians including Fulanis and some other minority tribes, either in this simple form or hyphenated as Hausa-Fulani.

a naked struggle for power. Yet even when a state already Moslem, reformist, and modern was attacked, purification of the religion was still the incongruous excuse to eliminate the former Habe rulers in order to install the local Fulani as leaders.

These local Fulanis in each state merely went to Gobir to secure the blessings of Usman, now the Sarkin Musulmi, in the form of a flag to be carried into battle. The possession of this flag denoted central authority's firm support of a jihad in the name of God and his earthly representative, Sarkin Musulmi. In a number of instances, two or three flags were given to conduct the jihad in a particular area, thus leading to local conflict and confusion. In Katsina, where three flags were doled out, on-again, off-again fighting between the contesting rival groups continued, interestingly enough right on up to the establishment of a Franco-British border between Niger and Nigeria—one emirate above the line, another below. Kano fell to Sulemanu in 1807, Zaria to Mohammed Musa.

One day during this early period Usman Dan Fodio was holding court. It was crowded and people jostled about. Everyone was pushing ahead to gain audience with the Great Shehu (leader), to ask a favor or a flag. For seven days, an elderly gentleman stood quietly in the corner, gently observing the proceedings. While in the process of settling a dispute over the issuance of such a flag, Shehu Usman noticed him and approached.

"Dattijo (old man)! Why do you stand there in the corner?"

"I'm waiting for the others to finish their business," the old man replied.

"But where are you from? What do you want?"

"I am from Kano, and I ask nothing, sir. I merely wish to pay my respects and send you salutations from one of my kin, Abdulazziz, who schooled with you in Agades (today in Niger Republic)."

"Of course, I remember him well—a brilliant student of the law. And what is your line?"

"*Fik* (law), too."

"Will you not then undertake to be Kano's chief alkali?"

"This, sir, would be a great honor and a weighty responsibility, but there are others in my family who are more learned, perhaps Abdulazziz?"

This, it is reported by word of mouth, was the first occasion on which a member of the Genawa Clan, from which Aminu derives, was mentioned in association with the law. Since then, many alkalis have been chosen from among the members of this family. There are currently at least thirty Genawa employed as alkalis or muftis.

Apparently Aminu's maternal lineage also had many learned men and women dating back to the days of Dan Fodio. One of them, a very learned mallam, was singled out by Sulemanu, the first of Kano's Fulani emirs, to live within the palace walls and serve as his personal adviser. Mallams never had private means and therefore had to augment their meager pickings as best they could. This particular mallam was a pigeon-fancier, of all things, and sold them when necessary to augment his income. He was therefore referred to as Mallam Mai Tattabari (the mallam chief who raises pigeons), a title that has been used since then for his successors as the emirs' personal imams and advisers on Islamic law. Each has resided in the same compound within the walls of the palace, pigeons or no.[3]

Although the wars continued sporadically for many years afterward, the jihad was considered to have ended in 1808 with the death of Yunfa, the last Hausa King of Gobir. With victory came a modicum of unity. Each of the city-states functioned semi-autonomously, continuing to pay homage to the Shehu, using him to settle some disputes, and the force of arms to settle others. Dan Fodio remained the philosopher of the movement while the fighting, and subsequent administration continued to be the domain of his brother Abdullahi and his son Bello. The question of which of the latter two would be supreme ruler was resolved by dividing the new empire into three areas: East, West, and Adamawa. The East was ruled from Sokoto with Bello as sultan; the West from Gwandu by Abdullahi; and the smaller Adamawa in the far East by one Adama and his successors.

When Shehu Usman died in 1816, the touchy matter of his successor was settled when his son Bello quickly assumed the title of Sarkin Musulmi. Bello's uncle, Abdullahi, who was in Gwandu at the time serving as emir, was reluctant to accept this unilateral decision; but he did so after Bello helped him quash a revolt within his home terrain. As the split control gradually weakened during the decades which followed, the Sultan of Sokoto emerged as sole Leader of the Faithful.

The essential achievements of the Fulani jihad were to create a unified system of government throughout Hausaland; to enforce and establish something resembling peace, permitting something resembling the free flow of trade; and to foster a significant revival of learning. The fact that the Fulanis used the basic political structure of the original Habe governments did not lessen these contributions of political unification and judicial standardization. They were, however, affected by certain distortions which developed after the initial spurt of reformist impulses that had moved minds and armies.

The Fulanis had kept the centralized power structure that preceded them, with the emir in each state ruling by means of an extensive fief-holding and clientage system. The administrative machinery was much the same as it had been, though some attempts were made to conform to Moslem concepts of justice through the Shari'a courts and allegiance to the sultan. But even these attempts to limit the emir's sovereignty were quickly nullified. The emirs ignored admonitions from Sokoto up above, and dictated their decisions to alkali judges and local administrators down below.

On this already existing reactionary and oppressive state apparatus the British superimposed their "indirect rule" in the first decade of the twentieth century. By the time they arrived on the scene, Fulani rule was autocratic and stagnant. Slave raids, slave-selling, and corruption were rife. But it was this structure that the British pledged to perpetuate, not the original reformist government of Shehu Usman Dan Fodio. His ideas were based on a rigorous, consistent application of Islamic justice. All people should have some privileges, but many more moral responsibilities to their fellows. They were expected to behave in a consistent, considerate fashion toward one another. Women as well as men should have an education and a fair degree of freedom of movement. Purdah, the custom strictly restricting one's wives to the confines of their quarters, was condemned as a pagan practice.

These tenets of Usman Dan Fodio are what Aminu Kano fought for. The subsequent distortions of these principles are what he fought against. If we scrutinize Aminu's thinking closely over the years, it becomes evident that he conceived of the Koran in non-fundamentalist terms, attempting to give a modern frame to the moral thinking contained in the Good Book. Hence his emphasis on those portions of the Koran that dwelt upon democratic precepts, women's rights, equality, and freedom.

Aminu also seemed to cast himself as a man of destiny brought upon the scene to liberate his people—not in the stereotyped manner, but in a general way nevertheless. He was educated, single purposed, and willing to dedicate himself and his entire life to that purpose. The strong moral, religious pattern that had been impressed upon him in his youth and childhood shaped his later thinking.

He felt strongly that the emirate system—although its adherents professed to be orthodox, fundamentalist followers of Mohammed and the Koran—actually had sunk into the same heresies committed by the Habe dynasties of Gobir and the other Hausa states around the turn of the century, in 1800. They were using the Koran to justify and bolster their own hierarchical status quo, but nowhere in the Koran was there justification for maintaining such authoritarianism. Aminu felt, and stated so many times, that correction of these injustices was not possible through reform of the existing governmental framework. That framework had to be cast out.

During his early adult years in Bauchi, Aminu chose to function in an atmosphere conducive to struggle. There he felt that he was not alone, and that around him there was a nucleus of thought and action which could launch the great liberation battles and create the upheaval necessary to bring his people out of the middle ages, into the modern world. Thus he could set in motion his own brand of jihad.

Tradition and Hausa beliefs called for a great redeemer to arrive and free the people, rather than for an organized mass struggle. Aminu Kano believed that a strong man was essential for the job and at times even toyed with the ideas of Mussolini and Hitler, but he soon realized that these did not fit the mold in the North. Strength, yes, but it had to lie in moral fortitude, the ability to remain true to the goal, not in brute force. Another leader, Mahatma Gandhi, came closer to fitting this pattern, and Gandhi's teachings and writings and very existence profoundly influenced Aminu's early thinking.

He never forgot the socioreligious background that tied him to his people, no matter how far away the winds blew him. Though he waged what was essentially a political crusade, much of his early criticism and struggle constituted a religious challenge and were even couched in religious forms and terms, as we shall see. His early years found him functioning as perhaps a Dan Fodio might have done, his middle years strongly reflected the Gandhi influence and his political maturation seemed to carry him beyond the self-denial and moral strength of Gandhi's nonviolence, into the more modern, yet deeply rooted African experience of "selective violence" and self-protection, void of offensive aggressive action.

3.

THE BEGINNING

There was a hubbub in the compound of Mallam Yusufu, for his wife Rakaiya was with child. It would not be her first blossom, but the two that had come before were both girls and everyone was hoping for a male issue. It was the eighth day of Rabini Awal, in the year 1338—according to the Islamic calendar, that is.*

Rakaiya's grandmother was busy preparing for her midwifery chores. There was the water for washing the expectant mother being heated in the yard. Another fire had been built indoors with the wood that Yusufu and his relatives had collected during the previous two or three months, so that Rakaiya's room was warm, albeit rather smoky. All her female kinfolk—her mother, mother-in-law, aunts, and sisters-in-law—were gathered in the yard just outside her door, some whispering, some laughing nervously, and one or two praying quietly.

Rakaiya herself was absorbed in her rhythmic contractions and the accompanying pain and fear. She was not thinking of the child's gender or any of the details with which the people about her were busying themselves. All she wanted at that point was to feel the soothing warmth of the hot water that was to be applied to her body immediately after the birth. This prospect, and the thoughts of the piping hot baths she would be taking twice daily, and the taste of the hot highly spiced broth and meat and peppers with which they would be plying her sustained her through her travail.

---

* 1920 A.D. The Islamic calendar starts with Mohammed's hegira (flight), 622 years after the birth of Christ. Its year is shorter than the Gregorian calendar used by most of the Christian world, making an additional Islamic year every 32½ Gregorian years.

She had been listening to the women in the background muttering and murmuring just outside the door, when suddenly she felt a sharp, shooting, intense pain that caused her to gasp and cry out to her grandmother. Gogo Umma approached and, with an understanding nod, started to help her out of bed and onto the floor on all fours in the traditional delivery stance. The moment had come.

Afterward, Rakaiya relaxed into an exhausted, semi-conscious state, with her eyes and head covered, asking nothing. At this stage it was not for her to cast eyes on her new offspring. Now her grandmother would be washing the baby with warm water. She herself had already been washed thoroughly, and a cloth had been tied around her midriff. The added warmth of the fire built in the hole under her bed seeped through to her muscles and bones. She was about to open her eyes and steal a look at her most recent production, when her grandmother called out in a loud voice to the women outside the door, "Allah be praised! It's a boy!" A woman *magudya* uttered the shrill cry (*guda*) which trumpeted the arrival of a child.

That was all Mallama Rakaiya needed. Allah had been good and at last permitted her to bring forth a male offspring. As she dozed, she could hear vaguely the faint scraping noise of the hole being dug behind her quarters to bury the afterbirth and umbilical cord. Wafting through her mind were dreams of the young lad sitting at her feet, dutifully reciting Koranic verses to her. This was to be the brightest, the finest, the most upstanding of Moslem scholars in the finest traditions of the Genawa clan and their Fulani ancestors. The smile on her face lingered as she fell off into a deep sleep.

Three days later, Rakaiya was feeling rejuvenated. Her husband Yusufu, she had been told, was pleased in his own austere manner, and was busy preparing for the Naming Day ceremonies three days hence. There was no need for the barber-doctor, who would normally appear at this point to imbed the facial markings of tribe on her son, for the Town-Fulani would have none of this. She had finished the spiced broth and special *ganda* meat dish served to women who had just given birth. The ganda had been prepared in the courtyard from cows' legs that had been cleaned and cooked all night, and samples had been sent to her kinfolk and neighbors. The milk pulsated in her breasts; she was feeling warm and pampered. Her turn to bathe would come in due time. Yes, everything had been done properly according to tradition. People could feel cozy and secure inside when they knew just what was coming next.

One week after the birth, the gray of dawn was beginning to appear on the horizon, and people were bustling about. Rakaiya was strong enough to move around the compound, but until her son had a name she was not expected to show her face beyond the family's quarters (though on rare occasions the mallam permitted her to emerge into public streets). Outside the entrance to the compound, all the relatives, friends and neighbors had begun to gather. One or two arrived on horseback; the rest came on foot and sat comfortably on the goatskins and mats spread in the narrow alley-like street. Some were jesting and laughing; others looked sleepy and only mildly interested in the event of the morning. There were two other Naming Day ceremonies that morning in the Sudawa section of Kano, and these were busy people.

Finally Yusufu's brother Mazadu emerged, carrying a large calabash filled with kola nuts, which he began distributing to the men gathered around the entrance to the compound. Three or four bedraggled-looking "praise singers" had mysteriously appeared at about the same time and began to sing praises to Mazadu and Yusufu, the court scribe. They were the learned ones, the blessed, the arbiters of justice, etc., etc. Inside the courtyard, a ram had been led in on a tether and meekly awaited his classical fate. Yusufu leaned over and whispered something to the mallam who was presiding over the ceremony. He in turn murmured prayers appropriate to the occasion. Suddenly his murmuring became a shout—"And the child shall be known by the name Mohammed Aminu."

"Mohammed Aminu!"

"The boy's name is Mohammed Aminu!"

"May he live long to follow the path of his parents!"

The shouts rapidly passed through the unlit halls and rooms of the compound into the street. Sing-song chants and vocal blasts came from a praise singer inside. When he repeated them to the women within the compound, he received their pennies saved for the occasion:

"May he follow the path of his father and spread the light of Islam!"

"May he do work useful to the people for all his days!"

After the slaughter of the ram, Yusufu came out of the doorway, accompanied by the mallam of the prayers, and all crowded around to congratulate him. He acknowledged their good wishes graciously and soberly, taking time out only to give kola nuts and a piece of meat to the praise singers and the invited guests. Though the traditional parsimony of the Genawa was passed down in an Arabic song about Abdul Salam, one of their ancestors, the praise singer of those years was not likely to complain about meager almsgiving.

The proper prayers were offered to the Prophet and for the newborn child. The mallam passed his open palms over his face, and the others gathered in the street did likewise, signifying that the procedure was coming to a close. The new and latest entrant into the line of Fulani scholars would take his rightful place as a servant of Allah in Hausaland.

As the streaks of orange and blue that had dominated the eastern horizon faded and the ball of bright sunlight peeked its leading edge over the nearby rooftops, the assembled men filtered away. They went off to work, passing between the high walls of mud houses, huts, sheds, and leantos, through the narrow, winding alleys and pathways, past the confusion of donkeys, goats, and sheep; past the stagnant borrow pools and clay-terraced dye vats that dotted the landscape of Sudawa Ward. The dye craftsmen were already stirring the indigo and even dipping a shirt or two in the dye pots. This day had begun.

In dealing with a birth and then a life, the further back in history one goes, the more fully the mantle of legend and myth casts its protective shadow over the life. All sorts of magical qualities can be attributed to a noted man, the more so if much time has elapsed. If at the other extreme, the man still lives, the qualities in him have not had time to mellow and ripen into semi-history in people's minds. In addition, these can be checked and verified to some extent by exposure to the cold light of modern "now" memory. Though one comes across many noteworthy tales of Aminu Kano's childhood that are of the stuff from which myths are made, they haven't had time to fully mature. The faithful however, already regard him as a kind of soothsayer and the embroidery process has begun.

The stories of Aminu Kano's independence, stubbornness, courage, and defiance go all the way back to his earliest years. It was in July 1969 that Abubakar Naillalla, smiling and toothless, lifelong friend of Aminu's father Yusufu, reminisced about Aminu's early childhood in the 1920's. He dismounted from his tall white steed, one of the few horses still used for personal transport in Kano, removed his tropical hat, wiped his brow with the wrinkled, dirty sleeve of his gown, squatted on the ground, and started.

Gogo Umma, one of Aminu's "grandmothers," had told him how Aminu the toddler would wake up at night and cry for a drink of water, knowing that his mother would lead him into the courtyard to drink from the calabash used for water storage. He would then wailingly insist on staying out to watch the stars. His mother quietly permitted him to remain and tried to explain the heavenly bodies to him as she understood them. Night and day she would spend much time with him, patiently teaching, proudly listening to her mite as he recited the first verses of the Koran, symbol of learning for all the Islamic Hausa-Fulani faithful.

The aboriginal traditions had relegated women to second-class citizenship for centuries. Usman Dan Fodio, in his day urged the up-grading of the Hausa woman. He condemned the practice of purdah, or of isolating wives, and urged the faithful to educate their women. Although Hausa traditions lingered persistently, the Kano Genawa clan, a judicial branch of the mallam class, was among those who staunchly supported these principles of Dan Fodio and his licu-tenants, Abdullahi and Bello.

In this tradition, Aminu, as infant and child, was taught by the learned women in his life: his mother and grandmother. But the story goes that when his step-grandmother Umma, learned though she was, tried to teach the five-year-old Aminu, he rebelled. For one reason or another, he didn't like her. When she beat him with her grass fan, the young rebel had not yet absorbed enough of the centuries-old culture to cower and run away as quickly as his little legs could carry him. Horror of horrors! Instead, he took the drink-ing-water calabash in his hand and threw it at her! The entire compound was in consternation. When Yusufu returned, he sternly beat away at the child with a cudgel. Aminu stoically stood fast, with silent tears rolling down his face.

"Is this a way to show your respect for an elderly woman?" the father asked.

"Is that the way she should treat me?" sobbed the uncomprehending, frustrated child.

His mother had watched the entire proceeding. Her culture told her that the child should suffer and accept his fate; her motherly instincts and pampering love told her to intervene on his behalf. But instead she listened and did nothing.

Although Rakaiya was deeply religious and insisted on *ladabi*, or politeness in her child, she was permissive in many respects. Half a dozen people remembered how the boy Aminu would mark up the walls with chalk or charcoal. He drew figures with loads on their heads, and overseers with whips in their hands, interpreted by the myth builders as oppressing Native Authority policemen and talakawa (worker-peasants) who Aminu was going to free some day. Aminu himself sets no store by these recollections, but he does refer to the drawings as evidence of his mother's permissiveness. She looked upon his scrawls and scribbling as a first precocious groping for writing skills, marvelling thusly, "What kind of boy is this? Everything he sees he draws, everything he hears, he memorizes!" She imposed relatively rigid discipline on him only when it came to his recital of the Koran by rote.

Nevertheless, Aminu at age five seemed to be stubbornly in pursuit of knowledge, already pushing against unopened doors to examine where they led. When an old man teasingly pointed to the sky and asked, "What is up there?" Aminu answered, "I don't know, but I'll go see." He was, in his childlike way, questioning the superstitious concept of Kismet, the unknowing acceptance of the unknown. He seemed to seek to know, to explain the unknown, rather than accept its inevitability.

Yatakko (Hajia), an elderly aunt of Aminu's, tells how, on one bright starry night, the six-year-old Aminu approached her with a sad face and asked solemnly for three white cloths. The following day, his mother gave birth to twins, and all three died in childbirth. In light of Hausa custom which decrees that upon death the body is laid to rest covered with a white shroud, Yatakko could only marvel at the boy's prophetic request.

Since the lack of modern medicine had denied Hausas the most elemental privilege of knowing the cause of death of their loved ones, they attributed all deaths to the same etiology; God's Will. Aminu is the sole survivor of his parent's union, though there were six births. The five other children died before the age of fifteen, three in infancy. How else could Yatakko and her generation explain the frequent early childhood and childbirth deaths? Sorrow and remorse were strong, but society had forced them to accept these as an inescapable part of their day to day existence.

Aminu's living admirers, old enough to remember back to this early stage, regarded the bright, hyperactive child with awe, as a sort of boy-to-become-man-of destiny. What sort of destiny they could not comprehend, for he seemed always to walk an unbeaten path. But to them he had been chosen in some yet unknown way, to lead his people out of the current wilderness, even as others had been chosen before him.

Aminu's explanation of his seeming clairvoyance in prophesying his mother's death, is this: he knew, from the whispers and the long faces of the women in the compound, how seriously ill his mother was. Indeed it was quite apparent, even to a six-year-old, that she was dying. Although he was very close to her, he cannot recall experiencing any severe emotional trauma at the time. The protective shield of the extended family in Hausa society made it quite normal for a child to move into the home of a close relative, even when both parents were alive. Thus, when Aminu began to bed down in the compound of his maternal uncle and grandmother in Madati Ward, the move upset his life much less than would a similar move into a foster home in Europe or America.

Aminu's father, Mallam Yusufu, was a wise and learned man, as were his brothers, his father, grandfather, and great-grandfather before him, for this was the foreordained path of the Genawa. He was proud and independent and looked up to by the community. He and his fellow clansmen had been alkalis (judges) and teachers of the Koran as far back as memory and mouth-to-mouth history could take them; perhaps as far back as the Fulani migration into Africa's Western Sudan.

The Fulanis had come as nomads and herders of cows, morally supported by a single-minded code of ethics that unquestioningly accepted the teachings of the Prophet Mohammed. They arrived in search of the temporal world of sustenance, of fertile pastures for their cattle, but in their quest, they carried with them the learning and religion of the Arabs of Supra-Saharan Africa.

After they had settled in the rural, pastoral areas in large tent colonies, they sent the more learned among them as urban representatives to barter for their herds and protect their interests. As their history developed, a gap began to grow between the rural and the town Fulani, until today they have gone well beyond the country-cousin relationship and are now but ancestrally distant relatives. The king and his courtiers took many of these town Fulani into the court as teachers for their children and as advisers in affairs of state. Eventually the jihad of Usman Dan Fodio in 1800-1810 placed them in a dominant role at the hub of power.

While all this was happening, the need for teachers, imams (ministers of Islamic faith), and alkalis continued. These were a class by themselves, the so-called mallams. They were learned and respected, and their right to perpetual study was unquestioned; yet they had no place in the power structure save in a judicial capacity. It was from this select group, however, that legal, religious and political advisors were chosen.

The Genawa clan in Kano were among the most respected of the mallams, and Yusufu was among the most respected of the Genawa. His puritanic adherence to the rigid ethical code of the Koran, theoretically accepted by almost all his co-religionists but practically applied by few, gained him his reputation as learned mallam. He was strict, compromised but rarely, and carried his code to consistent conclusions with his wife, children, and pupils— and just as naturally into the courtroom. He insisted that his children be properly tucked away at night, but permitted them their usual daytime pursuits—swimming in the waterholes or borrow pits, catching rats, and acting out scenes from plays.

When Yusufu's first wife passed away in 1926, he was a court scribe (i.e., court clerk) in one of the outlying districts of Kano emirate. Two years later, his brother-in-law Jafaru was appointed chief alkali, and invited him to become chief mufti in his court. There Yusufu's task was to consider all the cases before the court, discuss them with the other muftis, and then, as part of a sort of council,

Remnant of past glory

make recommendations to the alkali, whose decisions were based on these recommendations.

His profession he inherited; his education he acquired. It was his God-given duty to pass that education on to others—in the form of dispensing justice according to the Shari's legal code of the Prophet Mohammed and in the form of teaching others. Among his students were some children, but most of them were adults who wanted to learn the law. The literal translation of *mufti* is "one who opens doors," and Yusufu was a literal man.

Normally, when a mallam was teaching, he would seat himself on a mat in front of his compound, with the children (and some adults) squatting in front of him in a semicircle. He would intone the scriptures and write them down for the students to copy on their wooden tablets. By the time a child had completed his education, he was able to recite in Arabic, by rote, some sixty verses from the Koran. The equivalent of a graduation would be granted first in a ceremony called *sauka,* and then eventually in the form of the right to call himself mallam. But Yusufu's job was in the court, and when he sat himself down in front of his door with his books spread out, it was to discuss the contents of the *Maliki* or other of his judicial books with his friends.

Aminu describes his father as a man who was orthodox but not conservative, seemingly a contradiction. Yusufu adhered rigidly to the fundamentalist interpretation of the religious ritual of the Koran, but equally consistently to its moral code. He taught his son in every way he could that God's gifts were found in three places: (1) in the palm of the hand—the material things in life; (2) in the head—the ability to think and to apply one's thoughts to life; and (3) suspended in heaven—the spiritual in life. Unless one properly used the first two gifts, he would never achieve the third, and none of the gifts should be used to the exclusion of the other. One should hurt no one, but go out of his way to help three categories of people—children, women, and the aged, or, as he saw it, those least able to help themselves.

Yusufu regarded simplicity and humility as the symbols of a good Moslem and tried as he was able, to pass on these basic beliefs as the family tradition. He could stand up firmly for women's rights, against personal acquisition of wealth; for all his principles with stubbornness and courage, though he might suffer the loss of God's gift, Category I, i.e. from the palm, as later developments proved. He truly believed the old Fulani tradition that one must inherit only books, for in order to use them, one must become learned.

Aminu's reverence and concern for private property is similarly restricted to his much cherished library, indicating that though the the apple rolled far from the tall tree trunk described, at all times he remained an apple. His total monetary inheritance was five pounds, but he lauds his father's Moral Will and Last Testament by relating the story of the sultan who told three young men brought before him that unless each could justify his existence, he would be jailed.

The first said, "I am the son of a great king."

The second said, "I am the son of a very rich man who has distributed much largesse."

The third said, "I am the son of a very learned man who has taught many, from far and wide."

The sultan responded, that none of these justified their existence, for self-justification must be earned, not inherited. He proved his own worth in the process, however, by concluding, "All of you are young and have this lesson and much else to learn, so I must spare you imprisonment. Now go out in the world to prove yourselves"— as did Aminu, the teller of the tale.

Rakaiya, Aminu's mother, had begun before her death to teach her son about life and the Koran. It is reported that just before she died, she said to Yusufu, "I leave him in your care. We named him Aminu, meaning trust. I trust that you will supervise his upbringing. You trust in him, and all of us must trust in Allah." Whether she actually spoke these words or not, Yusufu did watch over the lad as though she had.

The husband of Aminu's paternal aunt was appointed chief alkali in 1928; a maternal uncle was Mai Tatabari, or imam in the emir's palace; and many other relatives were alkalis—a very illustrious family. Though a child was customarily farmed out to the grandfather or grandmother in his early years, Aminu was never "given away." Instead, for the few months it would take for Yusufu to find a new wife, he was placed in the competent hands of Umma, Rakaiya's mother, in the domicile of her son Halilu. Thus the lad had several compounds in which to lay his head: his father's, where he visited at least weekly, on Friday before prayer time; his grandmother's and uncle's; and those of his many other relatives.

It was his uncle, Halilu, who was subsequently responsible for most of Aminu's Koranic studies, building on what the boy had already learned at his mother's side. Since so much of the educational process in Kano was simply memorizing the Koran, Aminu amazed those around him with his seemingly keen memory. The real reason was that he had learned to read and write very early, thus eliminating the laborious, painstaking memorization and writing of each verse, ordinarily not completed until age 15-18.

He did not reach *sauka,* or graduation, until after his mother's death, but she undoubtedly would have been proud of him when he did. He had proved his worth by his ability to read and write the entire Koran. People were sure that the mallams must have cooked up for him an unusually powerful medicine to impart learning. (Concoctions of this sort usually consisted of honey and water and the washings of chalk from a slate with verses from the Koran on it.) Because Aminu reached *sauka* without writing the verses on his slate, he fulfilled the requirement by confidently reading and translating a private copy of the last page of the Koran before the invited guests. They were all seated on mats spread out in the inner court of Mallam Yusufu's compound, some facing the rooms of the women's quarters opening directly and individually onto the inner court; others facing them looked at the cooking fireplace, right in the courtyard. Part of the eight-foot outer mud wall that enclosed the entire compound served as a third side of the courtyard. The last wall was broken by an archway leading into a dark interior maze that included bedrooms for the men, two yards for goats and chickens, sitting rooms and toilet, and eventually led to the narrow alley in front of the house.

The typical house had floors made of dried mud reinforced by termite-resistant, bound short lengths of palms and walls that were made by setting tubali, or mud cones wetted and dried for several days, into the wall, points up and buttered over with mud mortar. The builder would sit on top of the wall, without scaffolding, and was handed or thrown the mud material. The stagnant pools or borrow pits that grow between the otherwise closely placed mud houses, functioned equally as supply for this mud construction material and as swimming hole for children and Anopheles mosquito eggs. The exterior parapets were usually topped with traditional phallic symbols of fertility, or geometric designs cut in relief.

Admiringly, the guests examined the pages of the Koran and listened to Aminu's flawless rendition of its contents. He went from one mallam to the next, demonstrating his prowess. Finally he came forward, hair shaved and immaculately dressed in a fine new gown acquired for the occasion, ready for the formal aspect of the ceremony. He sat himself quietly in front of his teacher, his uncle Halilu. The guests listened as he read a portion of "Bakara," the longest chapter of the Koran. Then the teacher read a short prayer, followed in reprise by the guests, and each of the other mallams repeated the process. The youngsters who had not yet achieved sauka crowded around Aminu, passing their hands over the graduate's head and then over their own, in the traditional manner, hoping in this way, by osmosis and God's will, to absorb some of the student's wisdom so they too would one day reach sauka.

Aminu spent a little over a year with his Uncle Halilu and grandmother Umma. By that time Yusufu had remarried, and took his charge back into his own compound. But Aminu continued to study the Koran with his uncle, whose learned status was attested and given official recognition some years later by his appointment as Mai Tattabari, or personal imam to the emir. When that occurred, Halilu was required to move into the quarter reserved for the "mallam who keeps pigeons," within the palace walls.

Throughout his childhood, Aminu loved to dramatize his thoughts and dreams in play. From his early years—when leadership qualities first began to manifest themselves in his childlike desires to be the "chief"—and on through his student years, he often acted out his complaints, criticisms, and aspirations in dramatic form. In his aggressive attempts to represent himself as the leading figure, he would compose the play, assign parts to his playmates, and of course reserve the role of Provincial Officer or even Governor for himself: This to such a degree that his grandmother and mother too, called him "amale," (the lead camel in the caravan). In this indirect form he acknowledged the British presence, the ultimate authority image being the *bature,* or white overlord. He would push his shirt into his trousers, Western style, a pan on his head, and declare himself "education officer," or an equivalent authority. Only when he came down out of the clouds to more realistic levels would he deign to accept the role of emir, or chief alkali.

While he and two other youngsters were in the midst of such play one day, they were approached by Mallam Balarabe, son of Jafaru, the Chief Alkali of Kano and Yusufu's sister, and asked if they would like to go to English school. Although the mallam was educated enough in the traditional sense to eventually become the alkali of Garki, at that transitional period in Nigeria's history he was aware of the value of European-style education. He felt he was beyond the stage where he could acquire one himself, but he did not see why the more ambitious youngsters should be denied it. These three eager children, including a younger brother, a nephew of Jafaru's, and Aminu, could and should be given this advantage. They were to be sent to the Shehuci Primary School as children of Jafaru. He was to recommend them himself and provide them with uniforms, thereby insuring their acceptance. Aminu, aged ten, and thirsty for knowledge, was elated. He would learn the English language, customs, and, most important, modern ways.

Nigeria was founded as though it were a collection of individual but pyramided building blocks with small families organizing at first into villages and clans. These in turn grouped into larger kingdoms, emirates, or principalities, though not all under centralized control. This consolidation continued through indigenous conquest followed by the advent of the British, who added their regional administrative units and subsequently joined them into a greater whole, a nation, Nigeria. Since a nation defines itself through its historical development, only time will tell whether it holds together or breaks apart into separate units, with the Nigeria-Biafra civil war as its severest test so far.

But regional administration under the British was the status-quo in the 1920's when Aminu Kano began his life. There was a cultural cohesiveness to the area known as Northern Nigeria, in spite of its many minority tribes, large and small. What held it together was the Hausa language and the common heritage of the Fulani Conquest of the region in early Nineteenth Century extending through the British occupation with its indirect rule.

Although the British superstructure totally dominated the administrative apparatus, this was not so evident to the bulk of the population of Hausaland. Their usual contacts with government and authority in general were with the administrative assistants to the emir and his courtiers. In the countryside there were the village, hamlet and district heads; in Kano City proper there were the Sarkin Dawaki (City Administrator), the Madaki (Prime Minister), and the Emir himself, while the alkalis, the imams, and the teachers that constituted the mallam class, sat in legal and moral judgment over the people. Throughout the emirate, the administrative faces of justice were the Native Authority Police, and the alkali courts, rather than the British police and court system set up for non-Moslems. It was only in very very special circumstances that the superior power of the British was invoked, and even rarer that the British countermanded any Native Authority action.

When the British officially took over governmental reins in Kano in 1903, in their effort to make as few waves as possible, they simply reinforced the powers of the emir and the pre-existing administrative structure. In some areas the emir was made Sole Native Authority, even where he had never achieved this status previously. In other cases they actually created a sovereign emirate where none had existed. From the imperial viewpoint, the subtle system of checks and balances between clan heads, king makers, courtiers, and the emir, was too complex and inefficient to continue. They found it more judicious to deal with one authoritarian figure, reinforced by the implied and often real threat of their military might. Thus in many cases the appointment of alkalis, became the exclusive domain of the emir, where discussion, consultation, and recommendation had been integral parts of the process. The British most certainly retained ultimate veto power, but more often than otherwise were very reluctant to use it, lest they undermine the emir's newly acquired and augmented "total authority" status in the community.

The persistently independent Genawa attitudes which had survived up to that point, either had to disappear into submission and conformity, or sullen acceptance, or to find other channels for protest. This then was the soil in which Aminu Kano, the rebel, took sturdy root and began to develop as a young sprout.

4.

THE STUDENT

Out of a background of deeply entrenched tradition, high on the ladder of a stratified class structure which sharply delineated the role of each of its component parts down to the last rung, came Aminu Kano, the upstart, the leader, the groper for knowledge, the revolutionary.

His early school years scarcely reflected what his future role would be, save in the broadest outline. He could never have been accused of being a follower even then, for he was always brash, eager, and aggressively concerned with everything in his environment—including the learning process and how to filter it down to those about him. On the way home from school he would gather the young children around him to show them his books, with their pictures and maps, and enthusiastically report anything he might have learned that day. Often his lunch break would be devoted to the writing of Koranic verses on his slate and then testing the youngsters, at the same time sharing his food with them. From these first school days he was a constant proselytizer for more education, better sanitation, and scrupulous cleanliness for all. This triad later formed a base for his early energetic one-man campaigns for modernization and self-help.

By the time he entered Shehuci Primary School at age ten, he had already begun to sop up the ABC's and the written English language through such diverse methods as copying automobile license numbers and words from cigarette tins. Thus his progress was rapid right from the start. School began each day at seven A.M. and continued for only four hours, but Aminu was involved day and night with study and play related to educating himself. He had the usual childlike reluctance to speak a new and foreign language, but after

46

Homeward bound

buttressing his knowledge of English with three years of study in primary school (ordinarily four or five years), he adapted easily and quickly to the spoken English in Kano Middle School, where it was compulsory.

His avid interest in education showed up in other ways too. Under pressure from the youngster, his father reluctantly agreed that the home of Mallam Baba, eldest son of Chief Alkali Jafaru and Yusufu's sister, was a more convenient abode for Aminu in his new status as student. In addition to having the son and younger brothers of Mallam Baba as play- and schoolmates, Aminu would be only half a mile from the schoolhouse. Thus his concept of home was extended still further. Mallam Baba's mother (Aminu's aunt) was by that time divorced from her husband, Jafaru, and lived within the compound of her son, as did his children and younger brothers. Then on Fridays Aminu would return to his father's house to pay his respects, attend the Friday prayer, and continue to demonstrate progress in his study of the Koran. Boarding at Kano Middle School in 1933 created yet another domicile for the boy and a further loosening of his home ties.

Rebelliousness was not yet an integral part of Aminu's make up. He still paid deference where it was due: to his elders, his father, and generally those above him in the pecking order. However, his brashness and initiative were becoming more and more evident. When Aminu and his two cousins, Inuwa and Abba, were late for school one morning and unhurriedly approached the school gate, the headmaster was standing there, tapping his foot impatiently. He saw that the youngsters were still wearing their shoes, although they were expected to remove them on entering. Aminu, the spokesman, explained their double delinquency—being tardy and being still shod —by stating that they were all wearing tight shoes, which slowed them up. Oddly enough, the headmaster didn't accept this as a valid excuse, and proceeded to give each of them three whiplashes, and even more numerous and severe tongue lashings.

Other testimony to this type of childhood leadership comes from Shehu Sattatima, a childhood playmate, who describes how Aminu would lead him into the remote alleyways and corners of Kano, into strange homes, where he would look around quickly, speak a few words, excuse himself and leave.

Yusufu, Aminu's father, encouraged and favored his child, for he knew that the boy was honest, impatient, and energetic. More than this, he knew that Aminu quickly picked up knowledge, and was ready to pass it on like a true mallam—all qualities revered by the strict, straight-laced scholar. He had hoped that his son would follow a judicial career, but the die was cast when Aminu went to primary school rather than the Moslem Judicial School. Even as an adolescent, the boy had his sights set well beyond Kano and a judicial role. He was to be an innovator, not an interpreter.

To be sure, there was evidence of his future rebellious role, other than a general manifestation of dominance behavior. In 1935, long before our modern-day student unrest, he was a ringleader in a strike of Kano Middle School students against a shortage of soap, poor food, too many restrictions, and too severe a code of behavior. The guile and mastery of tactics which in later years made it so difficult for the British to categorize Aminu came through even then, for although a few others were punished, Aminu's role was never discovered.

Aminu had a healthy youth's interest in athletics, but the kind of mental energy consumed in his quest for knowledge never had its counterpart in physical activity. A little later on, in college, he became absorbed in scouting, but more as a means of attracting youths toward self-betterment and a modern outlook, than for its out-of-doors appeal. He had demonstrated his early orientation toward organized activity, while still in middle school, by assembling students with similar interests, to discuss their lessons and help the weaker members of the class.

Sanitation and personal hygiene had much more significance for Aminu and Kano during his school and early college days than did the repeated admonitions to keep clean that we Westerners heard in our childhood. In Africa, the high mortality rate was directly related to infections and diseases that were already well on the way to being controlled in Europe and the U.S. Smallpox, bilharzia, and malaria, all highly contagious, were the terrible killers of those years, and even today remain a serious threat. Aminu's contacts with the West, principally through books and schoolteachers, led him to devote much energy to imparting his advance knowledge of disease-control to his fellow citizens. To equate the phrase "dirty old mallam" with religiosity, a concept prevalent at that time, was anathema to Aminu, who wanted cleanliness to be considered synonymous with high morality and deep religious conviction. He himself always wore immaculate white, and insisted on neatness and prompt medical care. Mallam Baba used to joke about Aminu, saying that he needed a full kerosene tin containing four gallons of water for his bath, while everyone else needed only one gallon. When, in desperation, a woman from the village came to his father for prayers for her foot, swollen with pus, Aminu assured her that the swelling was not due to jinns or evil spirits contained within it, but to rapidly proliferating microorganisms and the body's reaction to them. Doubt and disbelief was her initial reaction, but when he directed the woman to carefully debride the wound with his "medicine" (salt dissolved in water which had been used to wash a slate with prayers written on it) instituting antiseptic treatment in this way, she agreed and recovery resulted. After that, he became the all-knowing youngster, or even the good counter-jinn spirit. The role of modern medicine would be considered only incidental to the process. Had he brought her to the nurse or doctor, she probably would have rejected treatment.

To this day young Hausa admirers of Aminu point to their spotlessly clean robes and give their leader credit for inspiring them to scrupulous personal hygiene. This has remained one of Aminu's continuing educational campaigns, extending now to urging more utilization of hospital facilities for childbirth, surgery, etc., and universal vaccination against the real scourge of West Africa, smallpox.

Very few people went through the schooling process in Northern Nigeria in the 1930's. Such education was generally restricted to the children of royalty and occasionally extended to those of the aristocracy and the related mallam class. Katsina College, which opened in 1922 and was relocated and transformed into Kaduna College in 1936, was the only secondary school in all of Northern Nigeria. The original concept of this school, as described by the Sardauna of Sokoto in his autobiography,[1] was that of a training ground for princes, similar to those set up by the British in India. Graduates of this sole secondary school were considered to be teachers all. After three years, they could teach in lower schools; after five years, they could teach in any higher school. Many of them stayed with the profession for years; other quickly went over to the Native Authority, the local administrative apparatus for the emirate system.

Thus, a list of Aminu's teachers in the lower and middle schools would read like a *Who's Who in Kano*. The current Madaki, Shehu Ahmed, and the Sarkin Dawaki, Bello Dandago, both taught him geography and history; other teachers were Mallam Jibir Daura, former secretary of the Emir's Council, Mohammadu Gwarzo, the emir's councillor, and so on down the list. Since they ultimately represented the emir and the establishment, most of them later became Aminu's political adversaries. Yet they all testify that he was of leadership mettle and liked by most of his mates; that he was earnest, clever, and hard-working; and that, as the Madaki of Kano says, "He wasn't troublesome—that came later with politics."

The elegant Sarkin Dawaki, speaking with a finely clipped British accent, remembers him well as a persistent questioner who tenaciously held to a point of view either until he prevailed or until what he considered sufficient evidence was presented to convince him otherwise. Although he respected teachers as authorities (up to a point), he resisted paying the deference normally given, and resented doing anything or taking orders without adequate explanation. He was considered responsible enough, however, to have been appointed prefect of Galadima House in middle school, and then again a senior prefect of Lugard House at Kaduna College. In middle school he was in charge of some one hundred fellow students; in college, about forty. The boarding-in arrangements organized the students into "houses," for competition and convenience, and set one boy above the others as prefect. He received a bit more pocket money, perhaps an extra uniform, and a private room for his pains. All the prefects in college together constituted a small governing body, principally for food and uniform distribution.

Young Aminu's probing mind reached out in all directions, at times creating problems for his teachers—when he asked questions a boy his age shouldn't. He wanted the biblical inconsistencies concerning Gog and Magog explained. The heroes of West African history, Askia Abubakar and Askia Ali, whose tales were in the realm of myth and therefore vague and contradictory—all excited him. Through it all, his teachers report that Aminu was a top student,

and that made him Kano's prime candidate for ongoing study at
Kaduna College the year he passed out of middle school at Middle
Four level.

Examining his relationship to the representatives of the status
quo, and his peer groups during his early school years in Kano,
seems to yield few insights for though his leadership qualities were
observable, what forms these would take were not. His rebellion
hadn't started yet, as his family's social position still dominated his
life. Nevertheless, the combination of this particular social origin and
this dynamic personality would eventually be the key, for as quoted
by Bello Dandago, Sarkin Dawaki, "Childhood shows the man as
morning shows the day."[2]

"To become a man," means different things to different people.
Since the becoming is a process not a fait accompli, attempts to pin-
point the period when this takes place, would at once be shown to
be impossible and relatively unimportant. The best one can do is to
try to bracket the approximate period. Objective events, e.g. marriage, vocation, economic independence, and residential quarters, are
a good part of it. Change in the thinking of the individual is certainly
significant too. Normally, the child's world is self-centered and self-
concerned, his time occupied with satisfying the physiological or
psychological needs of the moment. Only when the decisions in his
life are his own can he be categorized as a grown up.

In these terms, there is little doubt that Aminu became a man
between the ages of seventeen and twenty-two, at Kaduna College.
It was there that he began to think in social terms, there that he was
able to put together a strong ego identity, and there that his life's
pattern began to take shape. His career choice, though complex and
changing, was made in 1940 at the completion of three years' training. Two marriages were consummated, but most decisive to the
future developments in his life was the change in his thought processes and his personality. It was during this period that Aminu's
steadfast refusal to accept traditional solutions to social and political
problems became the frame within which he was to paint his life's
canvas. He had yet to decide what was to be the medium of his
creative efforts but so far as subject matter and form went, politics
it was then and politics it remains today.

Abdu Mani, a fellow student of Aminu's at Kaduna, says that Aminu never *became* a politician; he was born that way.[3] But his future was not really foreordained, for his career choice ran the gamut from policeman through lawyer to teacher. In 1940 he could not consider politics as a career choice for the only political opportunity that existed then was in the Native Authority—and that surely wasn't his cup of tea. The alternative for him at the time was social rebellion, followed by religious challenge. Not until the later 1940's was he finally able to put his life into political terms, and not until the 1950's, when he led the first political party in the North, could he totally adjust his career toward politics.

As a rule, Aminu did not take up the gauntlet against tradition and authority solely for the sake of the challenge. He thought many of his people's customs silly, and couldn't see himself conforming, any more than could his traditional mother, who insisted on teaching her offspring herself, rather than sending him off to another mallam and another household, at a time when the latter course was the pattern. Most of these conventions represented an acknowledgment of, and deference to, social superiors—such as the traditional prostration of social inferiors or removing one's shoes in the presence of a parent, teacher, or ruler. In Hausa tradition, an inferior must always be in lower position physically. He must bow or kneel when the superior is present or, in some instances, actually lie on the ground when his superior is seated. Aminu's rejection of such stultifying mores extended through the field of religion and right on into politics, his area of greatest effectiveness.

Aminu's noncompliance with convention was universally recognized, and by and large accepted (though sometimes reluctantly), by those who encountered it. Not always, however. One day E. L. Mort, the British principal at Kaduna—an elderly, mid-Victorian gentleman, quite inhospitable to any defiance of rigidly established social patterns—invited Aminu to meet a visiting dignitary. Aminu was standing under a covered veranda, waiting for one of those unbelievably heavy tropical downpours to let up a little, when the principal beckoned to him from an automobile. Aminu reluctantly left his sanctuary and approached the principal's car. But before introducing the student to his honored guest, Mr. Mort looked down at the muddied and puddled ground, with rivulets flowing rapidly over his student's feet, and said, "Aminu—what about your shoes?" The response of the impatient and incredulous youth was, "Yes sir, what about my shoes?" This didn't exactly endear him to the school head, who drove off angrily without further comment. Although Aminu's modernism prevented him from bowing to constituted authority, he was almost always able to retain a tone of civility, permitting him to continue working relationships with those accustomed to symbolic traditional humility.

This same E. L. Mort ended up as a tutor at the University of London, in 1947, where he was responsible for the academic conduct of the seven Northern Nigerians, including Aminu, who were sent to study in England as a second small batch of students from the area. He tried, probably unwittingly, to continue holding the colonial reins he had first taken up while back at Kaduna College, but Aminu (and several of his friends) rejected such treatment, as he had done back at Kaduna, while still maintaining a cordial relationship.

The four corners of the aforementioned life frame of rejection of traditional solutions, within which Aminu built his life, were; (1) A basic revulsion to injustice, whether he was protesting a bully's behavior toward his intended butt, or a child's thoughtlessly cruel treatment of a hapless animal; (2) The courage to combat this injustice when visible; (3) An innate need to communicate, convince and to lead, whether it was through the back alleyways of Kano City, in the dormitory of Galadima House in Kano Middle School, as a teacher or a politician; (4) and his peculiar social position between regal might on the one hand and its victims on the other. For a person with this combination of qualities, breaking out of the old Native Authority patterns was the only promise for meaningful change. But Aminu had not yet reached that stage in his thinking. When injustice was wreaked by what he called "Native Autocracy" he continued to accept the system, thinking that if this particular emir were changed things would be different. It was during his later years at Kaduna and thereafter, that his radicalization took place.

At Kaduna College, while Aminu was still young and subject to the pressures of family and society, his drives to communicate, to convince, and to lead took several forms. He organized a Science Society with about ten other interested students, giving the word "science" a broad enough interpretation to permit ventures into areas not usually associated with science. He became chairman of the Photographic Society, whose members augmented their pocket money by snapping and developing photos for sale, using the school's facilities. He made the varsity teams in hockey and football (soccer) but was far from an outstanding athlete.

On the other hand, he achieved some eminence in physical training. While at Kano Middle School, he had become interested in physical fitness and, with characteristic energy, was soon leading the calisthenics. When he reached Kaduna College, the drillmaster in charge was one of only two Nigerian teachers, a Mr. Onimole. Being a Yoruba, he led the activities in the English style. At Kano, Aminu had drilled Hausa style, in Arabic, with a drum rhythm that was quite different. When Mr. Onimole saw him leading a group in this latter fashion, he suggested that Aminu try it with the entire school. Evidently it was a successful attempt, for Aminu was then made drillmaster and adapted the local-style rhythms to the English language.

Here he was issuing commands and evoking direct responses, which must have given him some satisfaction, but drilling did not invoke his moral convictions or permit him to challenge the onerous social strata. Dramatics, however, did. Here he could compose a play, using his natural libertarian bent, in developing its themes; all his cunning to couch this in terms which wouldn't alienate him from his potential audience; his leadership qualities in directing it; and finally he could act in it, thus gaining popular recognition and staying in the public eye.

This segment of his college life occupied much of his extracurricular time and must have been highly effective, for without exception, everyone who knew Aminu during this period spoke of his successful efforts at drama—often with an accompanying chuckle. Aminu knew how to make his plays humorous, in spite of the touchy nature of their subject matter. Shakespeare, who knew how to appeal to the masses of people, served as his model. With characteristic intensity and originality, he was able to combine the ideas of Rousseau, Voltaire, Jefferson, and Tom Paine with Shakespeare's popular approach, to synthesize dramatic works with which Hausa people could identify closely.

The students built a little stage in a field at the school, and the actors would emerge from behind a straw-screened shelter when it was their turn to appear on the stage. The performances were usually associated with one of the religious festivals (Sallah), and would serve as a diversion from prayer or to fill an interlude when nothing else was scheduled. The audience would assemble in a natural but improvised amphitheater, sitting on scooped-out steps. A broad spectrum of the populace attended—from the emir and his district heads and administrators to the townspeople, teachers, students, and lowborn talakawa. The plays were usually performed in the Hausa vernacular but occasionally in English, depending on the intended audience. Aminu was generally the playwright as well as actor and director—sometimes drawing upon literature and converting prose into drama, at other times using strictly original material.

The students permitted him to take almost total responsibility for he dared to do what no one else would. The others participated, not reluctantly, but a little fearfully, for they were well aware that when Aminu wrote he was usually treading on toes, sometimes lightly, sometimes not so lightly. A former classmate, Abdu Mani, put it: "He is the engineer, seated in the locomotive, pulling the rest of the train, us conservatives with him. Whether we agreed with him fully or not, we appreciated what he did, said, or meant and inevitably got dragged along with him."

One of the plays the boys performed was entitled, "Kar Ka Bata Hajin Naka" (Alhaji, Don't Spoil Your "Haj" [trip to Mecca]), later changed to "Alhaji Ka Iya Kwanga," roughly translated as "The Alhaji Knows How to Dance the Conga." As the latter title hints, the theme warns Nigerians not to be taken in by the superficial lures of modern Western ways. Imitation was doomed to fail. Instead, through education, they should change their own customs. He ridiculed the old traditional way of life, of turbans and long, flowing robes whose pockets bulged with good luck charms. Through gross exaggeration he indicated that a simpler daily costume would be very much in order. Nor should the old rigid mallams be relied on as authorities.

He attempted to make each play entertaining and amusing, and yet with a piercing point of view. Another drama broadly satirized the pomposity of the British district officer (D.O.) by presenting him onstage with pillows tucked into his belt and covering them with flowing robes. He was announced by the town crier, who ordered that all the dogs of the village be prevented from barking, the children from crying and shouting, and the donkeys from braying so that the visiting D.O. could have peace and quiet. As a sop to the British in the audience, he had this same D.O. join in the dance in the closing scene. One of the players relates that his expatriate employer berated him after one such performance, warning him away from Aminu and his plays.

Yet another vignette, among the first that Aminu wrote (in conjunction with one Garba Kano), was entitled, "Who Are You That You Can't Be Deceived by the Market People?" It satirized the big-city chauvinism and cosmopolitanism of Kano people by portraying a Kano merchant as full of guile and cunning and warned the audience, particularly the peasants, not to be taken in by the city slicker.

The plays continued to be put on at the college even after Aminu left for his teaching assignment in Bauchi. Maitama Sule reports that though he personally arrived as a student at Kaduna College after Aminu had been graduated, almost all the plays in which he acted were written by Aminu. He remembers that on one occasion the students swarmed to the railroad station to greet Aminu when they heard that he was enroute from Kano to Bauchi and would stop for a short time in Kaduna. The train was delayed for several hours, so they all trooped over to the field to perform a play of his on which they had been working. Aminu, when he arrived, joined the cast, greatly impressing the admiring students with his impulsiveness and vitality.

These short plays—or "revues," as they were called—were among the first to be performed in Northern Nigeria. No one in that rigid and unbending society was too sacrosanct for Aminu's ridicule; yet he scrupulously avoiding attacking any individual. He carefully carried this principle into his political years, learning to attack what he considered evil ideas rather than the people who promulgated them.

Down through the ages, Hausa-Fulani culture, lacking a written language, utilized the dramatic form to convey thoughts. Even after

Arabic letters were eventually applied phonetically to the vernacular, only the most learned, miniscule fraction of the people were
able to read. Mallams entered a village and lectured to all who would
listen. The masses remembered and comprehended more readily if
meter and rhyme were employed, much like songs and in many instances the presentations were actually chanted. Here too one should
mention the so-called "praise-singers," who functioned in a manner
not unlike the epic poets and wandering minstrels like Homer, in
Greek tradition. Aminu, a total product of the Hausa soil, instinctively utilized all these accepted traditions to sway the people, becoming well known as a Hausa poet in the process. He never returned to
Kano from college without organizing some dramatic presentation
or delivering lectures on the subjects he felt were important. This
he did to such an extent that at a reunion of his Kaduna College
class in '49, Aminu was dubbed "The Praise Singer" by one Mallam
Dan Mati.

The students needed rather long holidays if they expected to
return home, for travel was slow and arduous—and could be expensive. One holiday lasted forty-two days, another twenty-eight.
Since secondary school students were rarities in Kano, whenever
Aminu returned home and announced that he would hold a lecture
in City Council Square, or the library, or a hall, always crowds
flocked to hear him. He was fluent, had a good sense of humor, and
usually had something absorbing to say, for he was one of them. He
was learned in the Koran and interspersed his comments with religious allusions, which made him more persuasive to devout Moslems.
He was the first to combine his close ties to the people with a wisdom
culled from beyond their society's usual sources in order to struggle
against the established order.

At one time, he applied for and received the customary permission from the emir to hold his open lecture and discussion, this
time on health care. Invitations had been sent, giving time, location,
and topic. The audience was large and assuredly all male, for the
Kano women had *kunya* and knew their proper place was at home.
The discussion turned to the ever-present danger of venereal diseases. Aminu had indicated that these were transmitted by body
contact with women, and consequently warned the men to avoid
promiscuous relationships. When a questioner asked, "What hap-

pens if the man is the source of the contagion?" he didn't answer but, calm and unperturbed, went on to other questions. People thought he didn't hear the question, but Nasiru Kabara, present at the time, interpreted his silence as an admission that he didn't know the answer and that when he learned it, he would perhaps bring the information back to the gentleman. To a Westerner, this evasion would seem to show an inability to admit ignorance, but Nasiru Kabara, respected head of Kano's Judicial School and an Islamic scholar of some note, interpreted it differently, in light of the old, conservative Hausa culture. He said that normally a learned mallam faced with a question he could not answer would not admit his lack of knowledge and would try to answer. To him, Aminu's silence and change of subject was an admission that he could not answer the question. Nasiru recalled an old tale about one Imam Malik, who could answer only nine of one hundred religious questions put to him and admitted it in a similar fashion. This imam is reputed to have said, "He knows best who knows what he knows not." Aminu, said Nasiru, must have known the legend, for he was aware that Aminu knew his teachings well.

Whether Aminu lectured on sanitation, education, or politics, his goal was always to transmit information. He is remembered fondly by the people of Kano, from the emir on down (so long as he avoided controversial subjects), for these energetic efforts to bring light to his neighbors and friends. The people listened and agreed, though some, like Inuwa Wada, teacher in Kano Middle School after Aminu was graduated and Federal Minister of Works in the 1960's, thought him too impulsive and revolutionary, always impatient for faster change. Inuwa thought that when people are just awakening to problems, they should be given a chance to stretch their muscles over a period of time and eventually to begin to take steps, always very slowly—the view of a true gradualist.

The first really momentous decision Aminu faced in life was in 1940, at age twenty, when he had to decide on his career. Decisions had been made before that, of course, but none quite so profound. Of the twenty-seven boys who graduated after three years from Class VI of the secondary school, those who planned to continue their schooling were automatically expected to become teachers; that was the way it always was. But not Aminu. He shocked Mr.

Patterson, the Resident of Kano, when he announced that he wanted to study law. (There were no lawyers in Shari'a court, and all Moslems were expected to use this court rather than the parallel magistrate's courts.) "But, Aminu, you are a Moslem! What would be the point?" Aminu doggedly stuck to his choice, to no avail. When he had finished middle school, he had rejected the pressure of his father, his relatives, and fellow clansmen to study Shari'a law in the Islamic Law School in Kano, but at this point in his secondary schooling he seriously considered studying for a legal career through the British educational system. Interested primarily in getting justice through law, not in the law itself, he set his sights toward that which would place him above, or at least outside, the aegis of the emir and the local jurisdiction. Though of patrician parentage, on the fringe of aristocracy, his political inspiration and life style derived from the young educated few and from the lowborn talakawa at the other end of the spectrum. Unfortunately, in order to escape the talons of the tradition-drenched, strongly entrenched establishment, he needed the cooperation of the British. Lacking it, he had to turn in other directions.

His next choice was medicine. Yaba Higher College, located in southern Nigeria, trained dispensers, or pharmacists, who could go on to England for a degree in medicine, if they so chose. However, the long-range prospect was discouraging. Aminu would have had to spend a year more at King's College in Lagos before being admitted to Yaba, and there were fewer than a handful of such potential students. What with much student unrest at that time (1940), the principal of King's was not eager to enroll someone of Aminu's ilk.

After rejecting what he considered a flattering offer to serve as head of the Kano Emirate Library, Aminu surprisingly turned to the army. But here too, he was rejected and then subsequently by the police force for the same reason—his height. He was five feet four, an inch shorter than the minimum requirement. The principal of Kaduna College continued to strongly urge, push, and cajole him into the teaching profession, but Aminu, though convinced of the importance of imbibing and teaching knowledge, resisted.

It was a Dr. R. E. Miller, the science teacher at Kaduna, who finally persuaded him to join the other thirteen students for advanced teacher training. Dr. Miller's argument went thus: "Look, I'd advise you to join the teaching class. With the war going on, and the Germans advancing on all fronts, it isn't inconceivable that Hitler may temporarily take over Nigeria. In such a case, you would need a professional hiding place, and what better place than teaching? Besides, I would take you as the sole teacher-in-training for science —one of your great loves, right?"

By this time the inter-session was almost over, so Aminu hastily reported for the beginning of the September term. His special status in science was rather short-lived, however, for Dr. Miller was drafted into the British Army by December and, lacking a science teacher, Aminu had to join the others in social science, geography, and history. He backed into the profession of teaching in this way, squeezed into the mold that the British and Fulani aristocracy had formed for all young educated Northerners . . . or so they thought.

The first year of advanced teacher training was much the same as the preceding three years, but the second year consisted of practice teaching in middle schools; five months in Bauchi, five months in Zaria, and two months visiting schools in the south. This final year served as a kind of decompression chamber, or transition to his politicization, but in the process one event had a major impact on his thinking. This concerned his father, Yusufu.

In 1941, while Aminu was student teaching, back home in Kano the local political machinations had been continuing apace. Chief Alkali Aminu of Kano (uncle of Aminu Kano and brother-in-law of Yusufu) had died, and his replacement had to be chosen by the emir, subject to the British administration's approval. Aminu's father, then chief mufti in the Chief Alkali's court, was the logical successor, with his learning and Genawa background. Evidently Emir Abdullahi Bayero had his reservations, though the British clearly approved such a choice. As mufti in the Chief Alkali Court, Yusufu had never attempted to curry favor from the emir's advisers, nor for that matter from the emir himself. He would not modify his advice to the Chief Alkali to suit these courtiers, nor had he joined the others to pay homage to them during the Sallah festivals, and as a result was unpopular in court. To gain time to consider an alternative, the emir appointed Yusufu as "Acting" Chief Alkali. As a Genawa, Yusufu preferred the relative independence of the alkali courts to a subordinate role in the emir's court, so Yusufu the traditionalist accepted his new responsibility unquestioningly. That was the way it had been done and so it remained. The British ambivalence showed itself clearly here; on one hand they encouraged modernity and judicial independence, on the other they wanted to function through their sole Native Authority, a direct contradiction —so they resolved it by conceding to authoritarianism, a path they had trod many times before. Mallam Yusufu's consistently inflexible concern for justice as he conceived it, placed him in direct conflict with the emir. He knew that his own permanent status lay in the emir's hands. Yet as Chief Alkali, acting or otherwise, when called upon to make daily decisions, he was incapable of adjusting these decisions to suit his patron, the emir.

One of his cases dealt with a favored servant of the emir, whose compound was within the palace, a thirty-three-acre network of buildings encircled by a wall twenty to thirty feet high. He had invited a mallam friend of his to share his household. Over the years, this mallam had made many additions and repairs, improving and remodeling the entire house. But he fell out of favor, and was summarily ejected by the emir's servant. The mallam felt he had been dealt with unfairly and appealed for justice. The emir referred the case to Yusufu's court, as was done traditionally in cases involving the emir. At the same time he let it clearly be known that he wished it to be dropped.

Yusufu decided that the plaintiff had clearly developed equity in the household and either had to be permitted to return or be paid compensation forthwith. The battle over this case was further blown up when Aminu, the *ciroma* (the emir's favored son), and the rival royal family contending for the throne were drawn in. After the defendant was jailed for nonpayment, the emir himself angrily gave the full sum to the aggrieved mallam. Thus the already tenuous relationship was severely strained by Yusufu's decision in this and yet another instance, not quite so directly counterposed to the emir, but which distressed him nonetheless.

During World War II, imports from Niger on Kano's northern border were prohibited. When a trader was caught by the Native Authority bringing in ten tons of salt, the cargo was confiscated and the merchant jailed by the emir's Native Authority police. According to Yusufu's concept of the Islamic code of justice, this constituted double jeopardy. Either the salt should have been seized and impounded *or* the man should have been arrested, not both. He stoutly maintained, despite strong pressure to the contrary, that if another interpretation was to be forthcoming, it would not come from his Shari'a court, but that the case could be taken to the parallel system of magistrate's courts, administered by the British authorities.

These two decisions just about shattered all possibility of any continuing cordial relationship between Aminu's father and the Emir of Kano. When the opportunity came, Emir Abdullahi passed Yusufu by on the basis of advanced age (he was in his sixties) and appointed someone else to the supposedly lifetime job of Chief Alkali—Bashir, son of Yusufu's elder sister. Thus by appointing a Genawa, he conformed to the letter of the traditional system, if not the spirit. When he turned to Yusufu at the installation ceremony and condescendingly said, "I hope that you, as the eldest member of the court, will remain to give guidance to our new and inexperienced chief alkali," Yusufu, consistent with his pattern of accepting his fate as God's Will, replied, "I cannot do otherwise, for you dignify me by choosing for this honored position a son of mine, whose mother suckled at the same breast as I."

These events represented the apogee of Yusufu's productive life. He was given the honorary title of *wakili* (chief assistant), and continued to read, study, and teach, but the spark had left him. By 1945, his eyesight had begun to fail, and he wanted to retire, but at Aminu's insistence he traveled seven hundred miles to Lagos for the eye operation he needed. It was successful, and he ultimately returned to the Kano court, continuing there a few years longer until his retirement in 1948. Whether he ceased working because his hands were tied or to clear the way for his rebellious, ever-vocal son was not important. In keeping with his rigidly defined role in Hausa society, he was effectively put out to pasture for his remaining years, until his death in 1967.

For Aminu, with his deep-rooted hatred of injustice, the rejection of his father as chief alkali had a profound effect. He regarded these judicial decisions as the end of his father's turn in an unending

relay toward justice and the beginning of his own. He was ready to
seize the baton, and carry it at an accelerated pace.

Although he personally doesn't consider these events as a turning point in his life, some investigators have seen it in that light.
C. S. Whitaker in a significant article, "Three Perspectives on Hierarchy,"[4] comparing the political lives of the three leading figures of
northern politics* at the time, traces the roots of "the deep enmity
between Aminu and the Kano Native Authority" back to the months
when Yusufu "acted" as Chief Alkali. Aminu's first literary attempt,
the angry pamphlet entitled *Kano Under the Hammer of Native
Autocracy* was written at this time. In it he struck out vigorously at
the injustice he saw around him and at those who he felt were the
perpetrators of this injustice. "Native Autocracy" was his term for
the type of conniving, scheming rule of personal opportunism that
prevailed. He later realized that this was a heritage of the traditional
hierarchical emirate system that existed throughout Hausaland and
even predated the Fulani royal lineage. But at the time, the emir,
his family, and cronies were the more obvious targets of Aminu's
politically immature attack.

Counterposed in his mind's eye to the internecine machinations
of the royal court were the sparse in number, up-and-coming educated young people of the north. These were the worthy ones who
deserved recognition and status, who would bring relief to the
talakawa. Yet it was inconceivable that a democratically elected
representative leadership could take over the reins of government.
Rather he perceived that justice would come through a change in
accession, to the descendants of Aliyu, the emir deposed by the
British when they took over in 1903, and now a rival royal clan.
"The emir rules . . . with despotic power. . . . Under Native Autocracy
. . . cruelty and disregard of human life became manifest . . . [they] . . .
think people exist for the emir, not . . . [vice versa]. The throne is
ripe for the Aliyawa."[5] Because the dispossessed descendants and
relatives of Aliyu were educating themselves while they were the
"outs," they would be the "good guys," if given the chance. How
much the dispute between the emir and his father colored and inten-

---

*Northern Premier, Sardauna Ahmadu Bello; Federal Prime Minister
Abubakar Tafawa Balewa, and Aminu Kano (prior to the first military coup).

sificd his indignation, it is hard to say, but active resistance to the society existing beyond school and immediate environs, apparently began at this time. The only leaders of any prominence in Kano that were spared from his biting criticism were the Ma'aji (treasurer) and the Alkali (judge), both somewhat removed from the seat of authority, but also incidentally relatives of young Aminu. *Kano Under the Hammer of Native Autocracy* is pertinent for Aminu's sullen, frustrated disaffection with the emirate system and his relationship to that system, rather than for the childish declamations and immature attacks on individuals.

Thus, the student seemed to be stepping from one stone to the next, inexorably in one direction. Perhaps a stepping stone may have been slightly off to the left, but this was the general direction anyway, and didn't really represent a change in compass point. In addition to reinforcing a preestablished direction these events added a few nails to two of the four corners of the frame for his life's canvas; notably, his revulsion to injustice and a reinforcement of his social stance between the royalty and the talakawa whose cause he chose to champion.

In the Western world, one's family relationships are an obvious and eminently meaningful part of one's life. They may be good, bad, or indifferent, but they are ever-present, and usually worn on the sleeve. If this applies at all to Hausa culture, it is perhaps buried in the individual's internal emotional make-up, for most overt behavior seems to deny the impact of the family. Interrelationships in the immediate family appear to be less personal, determined to a much greater extent by more rigid societal norms, than in Europe or North America. There is less room for individualism, initiative, and intrafamilial byplay. The woman's role is rather strictly defined. Her specific family tasks include child rearing and maintenance of the home but exclude the husband's or child's social life or its intellectual family planning. The girl ordinarily leaves the household to marry shortly after reaching puberty. Hence, at age thirteen or fourteen, she removes herself from parental guidance, though the process may be delayed by frequent and early divorce, at which time the girl returns to her parents' household until her next marriage. The boy child's fate is decided by his father, who uses social tradition as his guide, whether applied to vocation, or avocation, or educational plans. Thus there is little room for any direct influence of parent on child or of wife on husband. If Aminu's (or any Hausa-Fulani's) life varied from this pattern and escaped from the accepted social limits, it is only to the extent that he has recognized the validity of applicable Western ideas.

Although Aminu and his mother, as we have seen, were unusually close, her early death was not too shocking an experience for him, because the cultural norms permitted and even expected an early severing of the umbilical cord. Though he similarly respected and observed proper decorum toward his father and elder relatives, they did not really exert continuing control or influence over his life. Until he reached adulthood, he conformed to what society expected of him, not necessarily what his family wanted. It was under the combined impact of his Fulani-Mallam family background and the influence of Western culture that eventually Aminu's particular personality, goals, and capacities emerged as an explosive mixture quite different from that expected of him by society and by his family as part of that society. Through it all, however, the Hausa-Fulani societal modes rather than family emotional ties retained the strongest influence on his approach to his own life and that of his nation. He continued to conform in most respects, rejecting only those patterns which he felt were undemocratic or which retarded modern social and economic development, the vehemence of his opposition changing with his mood or circumstance.

This conformity-with-modifications applied to his marital relations and his attitudes toward the seven wives in his life (still a normal number for Hausa men and women). He was more radicalized later during his teaching years in Bauchi, but back then in Kaduna (1939) when he took his first wife Umma, he remained within the accepted social limits. Even so, he was not the choicest of bridegrooms for his father was not wealthy and though deriving from a learned family, Aminu himself was known as an unpredictable non-conformist. To avoid the long, complex ritual required when a man married a maiden, Aminu chose a divorced woman.

Had Umma not been married previously, there would have been seven days of celebration. The bride would have been taken to the home of a friend and smeared with henna (a red dye) for five days. On the fifth day, the groom would similarly go to the home of his best friend, where he would be hunted out by an old woman representing the bride. When she found him she would smear him with milk and make *guda*, a shrill, weird cry of discovery. Friends of the groom would spend the next two nights playing games of chance forbidden at other times, and the women would occupy themselves with Bori dancing and drumming. On the sixth night, the groom would be dressed up, friends would stuff small gifts of money in his pocket, and the bride would be brought to him with further celebration.

On the final night, the groom and his friends would ride around the city until they reached the thousand-year-old baobab tree in Dalla where the groom would circle the tree several times, corresponding to the number of children he desired. The bride and her friends would also go to Dalla and rap on a piece of metallic stone representing the dowry and wealth of Fatima (the daughter of Mohammed), in order that she follow in Fatima's footsteps.

The men would then return to "buy the tongue" of the bride by placing money in front of her and trying to make her talk or laugh. When successful, they would leave and the marriage was consummated.

Though Aminu avoided all this ritual by marrying a divorced woman, he did perform the minimum required of him by giving the proper number of kola nuts, calabashes of rice and millet, locust bean cakes, etc., to the bride's parents. They were royalty of sorts, and were greatly distressed by Aminu's open anti-royalty stance. Though the marriage did take place in Kano, they succeeded in having it dissolved while he was away at Kaduna College. Umma, however, resenting her parents' decision, took the only path of resistance open to her and ran away. Oftentimes a young girl in that position, lacking an alternative, would flee to another city to become a prostitute. But Umma had a better solution. She ran to Kaduna where she was remarried to Aminu. Unfortunately for her, this was just prior to Aminu's return to Kano on holiday. When the young marrieds arrived, Umma's parents had the local alkali dissolve the marriage a second time. That was enough to discourage the career and education oriented Aminu, but young Umma ran away once again, this time to Ghana. The entire relationship lasted less than one year and seemed to mean little in Aminu's life.

It was his second wife, Hasia, who came closest to fulfilling the role of ideal wife envisioned by male Westerners at that time in history—monogamous, deeply attached to her husband, always struggling to keep up with his pace, dreams, and aspirations as well as his conception of her proper function in life.

Since Aminu was only halfhearted about his first marriage, thinking that marital ties might hamper his ambitious educational plans, he did not rush to find a successor to Umma. However, Hasia's grandmother had a high regard for Aminu and his family. She approached Yusufu, his father, on Hasia's behalf, and the two of them put their heads together to come up with a *sadaka* wedding. In such an arrangement the groom's parents do not pay a bride price; instead, the bride's family, out of respect for the groom's learning or status, award him the bride as a gift. So, Aminu, away at school, was merely notified that all arrangements had been made and that he had a wife awaiting him back home in his father's compound. When he returned to Kano a month or two later, he brought gifts of cloth and dresses for his bride, picked her up, returned briefly to Kaduna, and then moved on to Bauchi, where he was posted to his first teaching assignment.

Hasia's grandmother, born of royal parentage, had lived in Bauchi as a baby. When her father, leader of a royal clan, was defeated in battle, the nurse in charge fled to Katsina with the child. The family later moved to Kano where Hasia was born. Thus when Hasia and her *kaka* (grandmother) accompanied Aminu to Bauchi they were, in a sense, returning home, and were greatly surprised to find many long-lost relatives— brothers, sisters, aunts, and uncles. When they acknowledged that royal blood flowed through Hasia's veins, Aminu teased her, saying that "her majesty" was married to the greatest anti-royalist of them all.

Although Aminu's mother and grandmother were literate in both Hausa and Arabic, they were extremely unusual Fulani women. Since he was unlikely to find such a well-educated spouse, Aminu became a powerful advocate of husbands' marrying their very young wives to teach them to read and write so they could help educate others. He did this with Hasia particularly, and again, though to a lesser extent, with subsequent wives. Together they went through the Koran, the English version of the three R's, and Arabic modern hygiene. He taught her sanitation, hygiene and to accept modern changes; to look guests as well as her husband straight in the eye, to discuss her problems, and to eat with men. When eventually Hasia insisted upon divorce (for reasons to be explained later), Aminu persuaded the Emir of Katsina to give her a job in a maternity hospital. Without such independence, he felt that she would have been at the beck and call of any man she married, thus wasting her hard to achieve education.

This precaution proved wise indeed, for although Hasia is now with her sixth husband, she has never had to depend on the largesse of any of them. She is still working effectively in the hospital and training and teaching others to do the same. She retains a great reservoir of good will toward Aminu and follows his career closely. With a wistful tear in the corner of her eye, she obviously regrets her unhappy intransigence.

Even at that early age, to the extent that Aminu thought about marriage and divorce and his personal life, he put them in the context of his single purposed direction: to modernize and improve the living standards of his fellow countrymen. Though he had read Gandhi extensively and was greatly influenced by him, it is questionable whether Aminu's simple life, approaching the puritanic at times, could ever be considered self-abnegation. It seems more that the temptation of a life of hedonism—that aggrandizement, lush living, and sensual satisfactions have had little or no meaning for him as an alternative. Hasia speaks of him as one who warmly loves people, be they young or old, high- or lowborn. According to her, he always had a sympathetic ear for the many who came to him for help or money. Though he never objected to a pretty woman in his presence, he consistently avoided close personal attachments which might interfere with his polarized orientation toward his long-range goals.

The last year of Aminu's schooling (1942) was characterized by a shift from a strong personalized criticism of crippling, useless class stratification to a broadened sociopolitical mode of thinking. He was going from random criticism to attempts to find solutions in this his practice teaching year. It was in Zaria, during the latter five months of the school year, that he met Sa'adu Zungur, the man who was slated to become first his mentor and then his closest associate and political compatriot. During this year, too, his father Yusufu was denied appointment as Chief Alkali of Kano, and Aminu wrote his scathing *Kano Under the Hammer*. At the same time he began to use his cutting pen to write for the few existing newspapers and magazines in Nigeria, to spread his ideas as widely as possible. That was the year when he began to think in terms of organization and the year when his politicization started to crystallize.

5. THE MAN—THE TEACHER

Of the fourteen students who were graduated from Kaduna Secondary School in 1942 with higher school certificates, three were from Kano; Shehu Kazaure, Aliyu Gwarzo, and Aminu Kano. Only Aminu did not choose to return to Kano for a teaching assignment, in this way creating the first significant cleavage between himself and the Native Authority and laying himself open to charges of ingratitude. One can only hazard a guess as to why. Several researchers have suggested that his father's conflict with Emir Abdullahi Bayero and rejection as Chief Alkali, together with his bitter attacks on the emir, the ciroma (heir apparent), and the rest of the royal Bayero family, contributed to this decision. Aminu himself merely says he preferred to teach elsewhere, where things were happening.

Probably all these reasons have some validity, but the sum total seems to point to the simple fact that Aminu Kano had bigger plans than were realizable in his home town. Traditionally one returned home upon completion of higher education to discharge one's obligations, but by this time he had decided that the solution to the North's problems had to be found outside the established limits of an autocratic emirate. If Aminu had returned to the domain of the Emir of Kano, he would have had to submit himself to the machinations and internal political struggles of the emir's court, and if he was a "good little boy" he might become Chief Alkali of Kano, a niche that had been preserved for him and his Genawa forebears over the generations. If he was not such a placid lamb, the best he could hope for was a minor official's position as librarian, court scribe, or some such post. Obviously, none of these alternatives would satisfy Aminu's drives.

During his final year at Kaduna College, he divided his practice teaching between Zaria and Bauchi, which had become cultural centers for the slowly burgeoning corps of young educated elite. Among the men he encountered was Sa'adu Zungur, who was to influence Aminu's thinking prcfoundly and the two together were destined to affect the thoughts and actions of millions of other Nigerians. In 1941 Sa'adu was head of the School of Pharmacy in Zaria, training sanitary inspectors, while Aminu was practice teaching in the same city. It quickly became apparent to both that they saw eye to eye on many matters, and they became tight friends; soulmates. Sa'adu's home became Aminu's refuge after school hours, and their discussions there, the sounding board and jumping off point for Aminu's ideological and political development. Sa'adu was some years Aminu's senior and had formulated his ideas earlier. He had also had contact with the "outside world" while a student at Yaba Higher College (Lagos) in Southern Nigeria, where nationalist turbulence had already begun bubbling. His age and greater sophistication established something of a master-disciple relationship at the start, though as the years went by this was altered to that of the philosopher-ideologist counterposed to the activist. Aminu had of course come in contact with the ideas of Western ideologues of the French and American revolutions as well as those of Ali Jinnah and Gandhi in India, where the national independence struggle was considerably further along. Though these ideas helped mold his own in relation to Nigeria, he had never been in personal contact with any leaders of political thought.

Sa'adu and Aminu had originally met in 1935 back home, while Sa'adu was visiting in Kano. Though Aminu was still a schoolboy, the magnetic qualities of this Islamic scholar had impressed him sufficiently to establish a sporadic continuing correspondence over the years—until they remet in Zaria and then again in Bauchi. Sa'adu's staunch defense of modernization, including the unprecedented step of wearing European dress, helped to channel Aminu's volatile adolescence into his first outlet for rebellion: social nonconformity and ridicule of royal pomposity.

The presence of Sa'adu Zungur and other intellectuals in this triangular cultural nidus of Bauchi, Zaria, and Kaduna strongly influenced Aminu's choice of locale for his activities in the 40's. His

School age Hausa-Fulani children

attacks on the Kano local administration had cut him off from home base. During his five months of teacher training in Bauchi, this community had struck him as a likely locus for his educational activities. Since he had never regarded teaching as an end in itself, his reasons for entering the profession at this point were twofold; to earn a living and to gain access to the minds of northern youths so as to expound his pan-Nigerian plans to them and educate for modernization. It was clear at this early stage that his sociopolitical orientation would dominate his activities; all else in his life would be relegated to a subordinate role. The time had not yet arrived when he could ignore the need to support himself, but its secondary status was evident even then.

He had met the teaching staff at Bauchi Middle School when he had been assigned there for training. Among them were such men of stature as Abubakar Tafawa Balewa, ultimately Prime Minister of Nigeria, and Yahaya Gusau, future member of the Federal Cabinet (Commissioner of Economic Development). Sa'adu Zungur, stricken with a lung disorder, had returned to his native Bauchi to recuperate. These men, and others resident in the area, were to provide a nucleus for the formation and spread of the first northern organization of any kind, outside the native administrations.

When Aminu moved to Bauchi to start working as junior teacher in Bauchi Middle School, he and his wife Hasia were assigned a mud hut with a thatched roof that had been set aside for him as a junior staff member. Parenthetically, this hut had been used prior to Aminu's arrival, by a Mallam Ilm, who had been appointed Chief Alkali of Bauchi. He had reported that the house was infested with jinns and as a result the one room without a thatched roof could not be occupied. Aminu and Hasia did live in all the rooms, and somehow never encountered any other occupants, supernatural or otherwise. Perhaps the three windows Aminu had built into this particular room may have helped the jinns to escape.

He had been imbued with all the vigorous ideas of a student fresh out of school regarding the world of education, politics, and social revolution. It was peculiar to the North, at this juncture in history, that the brunt of its nationalist fervor was to be directed not so much at the colonial overlords as at the feudal organization of their own society. Only secondarily were objections raised to the British practice of propping up and perpetuating this archaic governmental structure through Lord Lugard's inviolate, not-to-be-questioned "indirect rule." In the southern half of Nigeria, the indigenous governments had lent themselves much more readily to the modernization process, so that nationalism was turned directly against the colonial power. This difference was partly due to Lugard's unfortunate pledge not to interfere with the northern emirate structure in any of its complex ramifications, including education and religion. Christian missionaries who penetrated the south had been prevented from doing so in the north, for there Islam was dominant and interwoven with the state apparatus. Keeping the European religious proselytizers out meant keeping modern forms of education out as well, for missionary schools brought with them the three R's, English, and training for the modern professions.

This was the time of the birth of northern nationalist thought, and Aminu consciously set himself up on the outer limits of the nationalist circle, where he could gain maximum speed when rolling. Others who were to join him in the struggle were to distribute themselves closer to the center of the circle, so that, when set in motion, its centrifugal force would not spin them off into indeterminate space. In 1950, when Aminu withdrew from teaching in favor of total politics, he put it thus: "I have seen the light on the far horizon and I intend to march into its full circle, either alone or with anyone who cares to go with me."[1]

The Islamic schools were set up principally to teach only those skills necessary to the proper knowledge and understanding of the Koran and its Islamic law. The emirs were reluctant to educate their constituents or even their own families for fear of establishing social criteria outside the traditional ones of birth and divine right. Aminu, in one of his early works (1941),[2] accused the Emir of Kano of creating all kinds of barriers for the existing elementary school in Kano. He objected strongly, for example, when the emir set up a school for the members of his royal family—not out of an interest in spreading education, but out of a desire to separate the royal offspring from all other children.

In 1942, when Aminu and Hasia arrived in Bauchi, there was only one secondary school in all Northern Nigeria and a mere handful of middle schools (4 years elementary were followed by three years of middle school, thus essentially still elementary education). Standards were such that if a person could quote a line of Arabic from one of the Islamic commentaries, he was considerably more impressive and convincing than if he attempted to use reason and modern logic.

To change this educational pattern required a herculean effort, unlimited stamina, and courage—Aminu's strongest traits, as most of his opponents have testified. The problem for him was how to be most effective in achieving his goals, not whether he could "stand the gaff." In the Bauchi Middle School he rapidly made a niche for himself, upsetting the balance of some of its longer term inhabitants in the process, but it was in his after-school activities that he made an immediate impact.

Aminu believed that one should be proud to marry a young unschooled girl and, while so doing, raise her educational level. Hasia had begun her studies prior to their arrival in Bauchi, and he continued her education as private tutor. She learned to read and write English and Hausa, and in turn, willingly taught the other women around her all she knew. Aminu was monogamous and pledged to remain that way in order to be able to give the time for continuing her education. It was his personal contribution to social modernization, for he felt that the polygamous habits of his fellows degraded the women involved, perpetuating their lack of social status and education. Classical Islamic law permits a man up to four wives, not because of sex or physical attraction, but because a community's honor must be protected by assuring a home to bereft women. For example, if a man has a close friend who passes away and leaves an unmarried daughter or a young wife, that man might feel obliged to marry her. In addition, each of the wives had to be treated with equal consideration. His ardent advocacy of monogamy in these early years reflected a balance between his radicalization on the one hand and the influence of his traditions on the other. But in his personal and political life he did rationalize the degree of militancy to fit his needs of the moment; for example, though he ordinarily permitted his wife to wear her shoes in the house, on at least one occasion, after a domestic quarrel, he temporarily withdrew the privilege. Nevertheless, in spite of such minor aberrations, he continued to push for greater social equality; in this he was consistent.

When he first arrived in Bauchi, he greatly revered the formal education he had just completed, and the modern world it revealed. He wanted to spread it far and wide in all its aspects, teaching youngsters, politicalizing the adults and liberalizing human relationships. Part of this elevating and liberating process was a break with the old tradition of purdah, wherein the wife was hidden from public view except under the most extraordinary circumstances. His insistence on Hasia's exposure was the first obvious stir created by their presence in Bauchi. On festival evenings, Aminu would deliberately take her out to visit friends, to view the fireworks, or just to stroll through the wide dirt streets, thus shattering all precedent. It was the first time Bauchi had witnessed such flagrant disregard for tradition. The British government representative, the Resident, was shocked and consulted the emir about Aminu's behavior. The emir indicated that as far as he was concerned Aminu was a mallam and a son of mallams, with very learned antecedents, and surely knew what he was about. The Resident, thinking the matter too serious to rest there, sent a report to the administrative center in Kaduna. It was returned via Aminu's Senior Education Officer, who put him on the carpet and asked, "Isn't this against Moslem law and custom?" Aminu answered, "Most certainly not. Is it not true that in many Moslem countries the women move about freely in the streets? When the Koran speaks of male and female Moslems, is it not granting them equality? Did you know, sir, that from as far back as Emir Mohammed Rumfa in the fifteenth century, right on up to 1930, there was a woman minister in Kano whose office was in the public marketplace?" The issue was never resolved to the satisfaction of the Resident, and Aminu continued his shocking behavior, taking his cooperative wife out unmolested. He never told her about these difficulties, for he felt that might have frightened her.

Abubakar Imam, currently head of the Federal Government Statutory Corporation and a man of some note in Nigeria's intellectual circles, reminisced with amusement about a visit he and his wife had with Aminu Kano in the early 1940's. He was doing some research for a few days in the Bauchi area, during which time he left his wife in the women's quarters with Hasia. When he returned, he was startled by the vivid and excited picture his wife painted of Bauchi's shops; the palace with its high mud wall and large vaulted rooms painted in bright white; the mosque and the market; the public buildings and private compounds, all in the classic red clay; the bicycles and horses on the wide unpaved streets. When asked how she knew all these things, she demurely responded that they had all visited the town. Had the relatively conservative Abubakar Imam been consulted, he never would have permitted his wife this daring exploit. After the fact, however, what could he do? Aminu good-humoredly shrugged his shoulders and said with a smile on his face, "How could I have done otherwise with such a gracious guest to entertain? Circumstances have willed it."

Several years later, while studying at London University, Aminu set down his ideas on "The Problem of Girls' Education in Kano" in a term paper. He urged universal public education, for both sexes, including high- and lowborn. His was a practical approach, not exactly conforming to that of the current movement for women's liberation, but one that he felt could work in contemporary Hausa society; one that taught women how to function in their own environment. A simple, basic knowledge of domestic science, infant care, personal and social sanitation, even the why and how to use a latrine would help to combat the initial problems of ignorance, apathy, and fatalism. As he saw it, the populace, long tolerant of autocratic rule, could easily accept such quickly attainable goals as compulsory education, a required Islamic marriage register, and a legal prohibition of child marriages.

Aminu called for a Department of Public Enlightenment which would put pressure on the educated clerk or administrator to teach his wife, sister, or female relative to read and write. He insisted that enlightenment must penetrate into the purdah circle. The lifeless, arbitrary, static, bookish type of information taught in the Koranic schools merely made mentally stultified children and passive adolescents and adults. He asks, "How many creative people has Kano produced in its schools?" The women produced by this lopsided system were ignorant and full of superstition; they accepted infant mortality fatalistically; in illness, they resorted to medicine men, witches, and prayer.

He believed that the education of women should not be restricted to the classroom. It should be all-encompassing, ranging from the propaganda apparatus of radio, libraries, cinema, etc., to the formation of clubs for continuing studies after graduation, for "mothers are the teachers of tomorrow." He insisted that reforms need not be gradual, that what was necessary was an internal revolution in philosophy and psychology to release the people from their political shackles.

His approach was prophetic too, since he felt that social psychology was even more important than developing the economy. Giving people more money to spend during World War II, without educating them toward self-betterment, had merely endowed them with the ability to support more wives, buy more clothes, and have more elaborate ceremonies. (Are not today's sociologists in our consumer-oriented economy pleading for a social orientation and an upgrading of spiritual and moral values?) Aminu, the radical but practical politician, never permitted his ideas to separate him from the immediate needs of the people. Whether or not he kept his shoes on when he was expected to remove them, both feet inevitably remained firmly planted on Hausa soil.

At Bauchi, Aminu took his role as teacher seriously, interpreting it as encompassing the total training of his charges, both during and after school hours. He rapidly established himself as a sort of ferryman on the River Styx, bridging the chasm between pupil and teacher—to the delight of the boys and to the consternation of the faculty, whose training inclined them to keep that gap wide and deep.

Most of the boys came from royal and aristocratic families. In Hausa-Fulani society, those with royal blood ties were *sarakuna,* an inherited status which ranged from ruler or emir to honorary titles and high positions in administration, regardless of merit. Though titles and position were not inherited in Hausa-Fulani culture, status appointments were made from among those born with *sarauta,* making them eligible for certain traditional titles—this in contrast to *shigege,* an achieved status and the next step down the ladder. Then there were the commoners themselves, from whom those with *shigege* were chosen. These could be further subdivided into freemen and former slaves, and the latter into *cucanawa,* many of whom had extensive power delegated to them by the emirs, and *bayi* (slaves who could be bought and sold). Though slavery had been abolished by the British at the turn of the century, the social stratification had carried over and evolved into dependency and patronage relationships with their former masters. Vocations are to this day still determined to a great degree by social status, with most of the former bayi (no longer identified as such), as butchers or musicians, usually at the bottom of the social structure.

But at this stage the majority of these Western educated boys regarded the modern world of the European-style schools as superseding their sarauta in importance. In some instances, this was translated into an odd influence on their fathers as well. The Emir of Katagum, noting the Katagum boys' admiration for Aminu, including the son of his Waziri (vizier or prime minister), offered him one of his many relatives as a wife, in order to establish a blood tie. The marriage actually lasted only a month or so, for Aminu reports that the girl turned out to be very disturbed and hence was shipped back to her point of origin—another unprecedented act.

The students flocked to Aminu's house after hours, where they would discuss extracurricular matters well beyond the daily curriculum. They were joined by students from Bauchi Teachers' Training College and others on Friday and Sunday, their two days off, at sessions serving as a sort of lesson for the boys. They all came with questions or ideas to develop and talked into the wee hours of the morning, discussing the future development of education, how to bring about change, or how to improve existing practices. As they spoke, they projected dreams of what the future would bring.

To this day, Aminu is still highly regarded as a teacher and as a moral and ethical guide for youth. When he is at home, be it Kano or Lagos, the young, including many of his former students and political adversaries, congregate in a wide circle of easy chairs in his always-open living room to partake of the dialogue, ask advice or guidance, or just to sit and listen to the little man with the round head and short turtle-like neck, seated alone on the central sofa, with a foot tucked under him picking at his broad feet, nose or ears . . . They stay far into the night and freely share his bed and board when the occasion arises. One current state commissioner, a former leader of NPC, has said, "He is my father, teacher, and leader."[3]

In those Bauchi days, Aminu pulled no punches. He spoke uninhibitedly about the behavior of other boys throughout the world. He used original materials from Western sources, or directed Abubakar Imam's plays and stories, to involve the students in dramas

Aminu Kano: Still the teacher

directed and slanted to ridicule old canards and traditions and illiterate top administrators. Scout troops were organized by him in his role as Bauchi commissioner of scouts; similarly, a debating society to teach public presentation of issues was formed, dealing with all kinds of controversial questions.

His innovative approach to the teaching of English included the use of a long, original thousand-line poem or song entitled "Song of the Changing Times." By design, it encouraged progress, calling for institutional changes and the abandonment of archaic customs, such as elaborate modes of dress (with turbans which he likened to bandages for a broken head) and too many horses and wives. It advocated the elimination of superstition; the strengthening of the family unit by giving women greater freedom and better education, with an accompanying clamp down on free and easy divorce; and preservation of, and pride in, the art, history, poets, mallams, and heroes who represented the true democratic and moral traditions of their ancestors. The song was popular with the students who memorized it and sang it in the classroom and the streets, to the chagrin of the ruling traditionalists. Twenty-five years later, two members of the foreign service, former students of Aminu, were still able to recite the lines and chuckle in reminiscence, even though the poem was never formally published.

Aminu would set up a stool in front of the class and ask each student in turn to mount it and orate, with gestures and meaningful content. A small stick in his hand, referred to as a "persuader," aided the process. Aminu was an indefatigible instigator of any activity that made for original thought, that taught people to speak up, to question, to act independently. He was able to apply relatively high standards and evoke a severe discipline from the boys, who followed him admiringly and would perform at these high levels out of love and respect. His youth brought him particularly close to the senior boys, his radicalism was a quality appreciated by students of all ages.

Though all this made Aminu a heroic focus for the student body, the faculty and administrative staff were far from happy with him. They interpreted his ideas as disruptive. How could this display of independence be controlled? Traditional homage to men of stature no longer could be assumed or imposed; the students were learning to be skeptical and rebellious. Everything the teachers said or did had to be justified. They were imitating Aminu. At one point, the staff members complained to the education officer that Aminu was too friendly with the students and was usurping all the positions of leadership in the school—only to be told, "Why don't you take the initiative out of his hands? If you do the organizing, they'll follow you instead." They tried it with some degree of success, and despite their refusal to dress in shorts and perform calisthenics with the boys, they were gradually able to assume the leadership in physical training and games. Even the leadership of the literary society Aminu had organized was taken from him, leaving him only the scoutmaster job. The education officer had called the staff together upon Aminu's arrival to bid him welcome. Although he didn't remove his shoes, Aminu did conform to the extent of sitting on the floor with the other teachers. In introducing him to the others, the E. O. said, "Here we have a little lamb. Watch him carefully to see that his horns don't grow too long!" The staff certainly was doing that. However, in the very process of trying to reduce his influence they were being pushed in the direction he wanted them to go.

The older men on the staff, who were trained at Katsina College before it moved and became Kaduna College, tended to be more conservative than those of Kaduna. Although the alumni of both colleges all professed to be advocates of modernization, they differed in their notions of how long it would take to attain their common goals. At that time this did not seem an insurmountable difference. In subsequent years, however, rifts widened between them, varying with the degree to which each was ready to challenge the native administration and the extent to which traditional methods could be incorporated in modern governmental structures.

The headmaster, one M. Baraya from Gombe, was evidently a conformist, even to the extent of incorporating the evils and excesses of early British school administration. Under him as senior teacher was Abubakar Tafawa Balewa, a quiet-spoken advocate of mild and gradual reform whose sincere attempts to moderate the two extremes over the decades gained him great respect from all sides. Warring forces found it expeditious to make use of his competence, intelligence, and imperturbability in determining a middle way. These traits unfortunately also proved to be his undoing, but back in these school years, he was thoroughly respected by staff and students, albeit in an aloof way. Yahaya Gusau was the science teacher, followed by Aminu, the junior teacher. Coincidentally, these four of a total of nine teachers eventually placed in this same order on the political spectrum.

The fascinating relationship between these two outstanding northerners, Abubakar and Aminu, began at Bauchi Middle School and spanned two and a half decades of political in-fighting. Abubaker came of a slave lineage in Bauchi Province, and owed his advanced educational status to a quirk in the relationship between the emirs and the British overlords. The emirs at times would send lowly representatives to the British school in order to placate the British and shield their own royal sons from its insidious influences at the same time. Several outstanding Northern Nigerians owe their education to this unusual development, including its most outstanding product, Abubakar. As a lucky, lowly, yet worthy representative of the status quo, he did not feel impelled to challenge its totality. Modern Western education taught him the need for change and updating, but in his mind's eye he saw an integration of the old and the new— a stance which permitted him to question and to try reform on the fringe but never go beyond the pale. This even when much later, in the Northern House of Assembly, the Sultan of Sokoto in response to Abubakar's famous defense of reforms, was to say, "This is what happens when you let loose your servants! This is our reward!" He was the first plebian non "sarauta" member of the Emir of Bauchi's Council, and wasn't likely to jeopardize his "shigege," or acquired status.

Aminu on the other hand, deriving from a patrician yet power-less lineage, turned his Western education into a direct sharp challenge to the entire society: "power to the people" and strip the emirs of their aristocratic heritage.

The personalities of both men fitted them for their chosen roles —one a moderate, the other a radical. Yet they found a great community of interest and developed a warm relationship of mutual respect and trust, though they were almost always on different sides of the fence. Their essential goals were the same, but they had radically different approaches to the manner and tempo by which these could best be achieved. When Aminu and his fellow student-teachers came to Bauchi in 1941, Abubakar welcomed them, invited them to his home, and conducted active discussions, an approach quite advanced for those years. Aminu, less inhibited than the others, struck up an active friendship with him. True, Abubakar was among those staff members who complained to the education officer about Aminu's activities and usually defended the British or N.A. position. Yet he always maintained a hearty respect for his ebullient junior. He was half-amused, half-tolerant of his doings, and continued to regard Aminu as a true friend of the North. In the relationship, there was perhaps a hint of a father's attitude toward a son who had learned his lesson too well and applied the morality of his parents a bit more militantly than they would have liked. When he would later good-humoredly refer to Aminu as "Molotov," implicit in this humorous reference to his political stance were respect, admiration for Aminu's courage, and a warmth dating back to their friendship and struggles during their teaching years.

The students found Aminu the teacher unique and eminently approachable. His home was always open for them to break bread, congregate, or just talk and argue—an unprecedented attitude. Up to that point, no teacher had ever been available after hours, and here was an authority figure who mingled with them as though he was one of them, stimulating them to ask questions and answering them straightforwardly, with respect for the questioner. He was constantly sparking their internal struggles for self-identity in this key period in their lives, whether in school, in his home, or on one of their scouting expeditions.

His associations with them were so close that when an occasion arose to take social action, they did not have to consult him. They knew he would support what they considered a just struggle. When one day they complained bitterly to the headmaster that many of them had never been issued uniforms or blankets, that pocket money had been withheld, the food meager and hardly edible, they were sure of the support of at least one member of the teaching staff. At four A.M. the following morning, the entire student body went on strike—five classes, with approximately thirty students in each. According to the best information available, only one student remained behind. He was the head boy, an appointed student leader (by coincidence Abubakar Tafawa Balewa's younger brother) who had been requested by the others to stay at school as a spokesman. The senior boys (among them Sule Katagum, present head of the Federal Public Service Commission) led the pack on a march down the road toward Maiduguri, with several teachers and the Emir of Bauchi in hot pursuit. They caught up with the students about nine miles out of town, where Abubakar and the emir tried to dissuade them from their militant actions. The only response was a shout, "We want Aminu!" When Aminu arrived at last, accompanied by Yahaya Gusau, he reassured them that their complaints would get proper airing and that they had best return to their dormitories.

When they followed his advice, he was understandably accused of having instigated the walkout in the first place. The furor aroused by the event became academic, however, when an investigation by the education officer revealed the validity of the students' claims and the headmaster was removed. Each staff member moved up a notch. Tafawa Balewa became headmaster and righted the pre-existing wrongs, though still remaining the mild reformer and reluctant defender of the status quo. Aminu continued his active proselytizing for rapid change, in the debating society, the drama society, the science society, and the boy scouts, all directed toward stirring the pot of national awakening à la Aminu Kano.

While all this activity was going on at school, Aminu was not exactly permitting the rest of the world to pass him by. Sa'adu Zungur had become ill and returned from Zaria to convalesce at his family home in Bauchi. Sa'adu remained bedridden, weak and feverish with his lung disease (probably tuberculosis though no one seems to specifically identify it as such). The two men renewed their earlier friendship, with Aminu at Sa'adu's bedside daily, for long discussions about the fate of their country Nigeria, and their first love, the north. They talked far into the night though the area was infested with hyenas and Aminu had to walk home afterward. Sa'adu spent his remaining years in and out of bed, never really able to function fully for any extended period.

His physical incapacity did not in any way slow his thinking processes, which had taken a radical turn in northern Nigerian terms, dating back to his year at Yaba Higher College in southern Nigeria, where the intellectual ground rules were for a different league. The Zaria Friendly Society, his first attempt to raise the north out of its centuries-old intellectual slumber, was initiated in 1941 while he was still teaching at the School of Pharmacy in Zaria, then a center of the educated elite of the North. Other intellectuals in the area, including men like Abubakar Imam and Nuhi Bamali (Federal Foreign Minister in the 1960's), were willing enough to consider mild reform in a tangential way but reared back when Sa'adu attempted to use the organization as a forum for attacking the North's system of local administration and the "indirect rule" of the British which buttressed it.

Aminu Kano, still a student at Kaduna College, was then practice teaching in Zaria Middle School. He spent much of his time with Sa'adu but because of his junior status the relationship was that of the teacher and his disciple. The Friendly Society became moribund when Sa'adu was politically isolated and frequenty hospitalized.

Aminu divides his life into three stages. The first ended at the point when he met Sa'adu Zungur. He had not yet projected himself into the social and political spheres, beyond his studies, his students, and his immediate environment. In Sa'adu Zungur he found an inspiration for his ideas and their implementation. When Sa'adu was stricken ill and returned to Bauchi, they both flowered in each other's presence. Aminu began to express his ideas in letters and articles to newspapers and magazines, including the first Hausa-language newspaper, *Gaskiya Ta Fi Kwabo* (Truth Is Worth More Than a Penny) and the *West African Pilot,* published in southern Nigeria by N. Azikiwe, the first President of Nigeria. Men like Yerima Balla, former Secretary General of NEPU and now a commissioner in the North Eastern State, read his articles from as far away as India, where he was serving in the British army, and started a correspondence. Aminu began organizing and thinking on a region-wide basis, consulting and planning with Sa'adu. The interdependency between them shifted subtly and gradually to that of equals—the one the ailing strategist and eventually an elder statesman; the other, an acti- vist-tactician. Under the sharp pens of this duo the educated youth of the North began to stir.

Sa'adu seemed to develop an attitude of leaving ideas for Aminu to apply, perhaps suggesting a course of action or drawing Aminu's attention to a particular tactic. They played back and forth, often agreeing, often disagreeing. He had discovered in Aminu a kindred spirit, and learned to lean heavily on him. Sa'adu wrote equally fluently and frequently in English, Arabic, and Hausa, persistently attacking colonialism, indirect rule, and Lord Lugard (the British administrator credited with conceiving and applying this notorious system), exposing its fallacies wherever possible. Illness limited his activities but not literary efforts which continued apace. He is generally considered the first northerner to think of, and agitate for, pan-Nigerian and pan-African unity. He abhorred those traditions and customs that stifled the people, warning continuosly that lack of modernization and education would permit the southern half of Nigeria to dominate the North and to eliminate all that it cherished.

According to Aminu, the second stage in his life ended and the third began when he left teaching in 1950 to enter the political arena full time to range through the whole of the North, with Kano once again his home base. In a sense, subdividing his life in this way testifies to the role Sa'adu played in helping to mold his thinking. He served as an alter ego, one to whom Aminu could continue to turn to for strength again and again when venturing into unchartered waters. Together they lit the fires of nationalism, democracy and anticolonialism. Aminu fueled the fires, trying to build them up to a conflagration, while Abubakar Tafawa Balewa, Abubakar Imam, and many others tamped them down to smoldering embers.

One of the first logs thrown on the small blaze was the Bauchi General Improvement Union formed in 1943. Men like Abubakar Tafawa Balewa and Yahaya Gusau steered clear of its emphasis on rapid, thoroughgoing change and reform, but Aminu's vitality and boundless energy was an added ingredient that made for a degree of success. He and Sa'adu wrote letters and articles to any publications that would print their denunciations of the British "directed labor" policy, in their eyes merely another form of conscription. Great Britain, fighting for its life in World War II, needed people to grow large quantities of food crops, such as corn, and needed tin miners as well as soldiers. So pressure was put on the Native Authorities to "direct" prescribed quotas of food and men to each category, though Nigerians in general felt the effects of World War II only peripherally.

The union members discussed modernization and attacked the "indirect rule" that stifled it. In the process, they attracted about twenty or so to each of their meetings, but their principal effect was to stir the British rulers to action. The senior political officer, a Mr.

Knott, read an inflammatory unsigned article in the *West African Pilot,* attacking the British method of inducting Nigerians into their army. When he asked at the Bauchi General Improvement Union about its source, Aminu readily admitted his role as author. Thereupon Mr. Knott, thinking to contain these eruptions, suggested a new organization, officially sponsored, which could be used as a forum for debating any and all ideas. Since the Union had become so vocal, there would be an opportunity for the British to use it as an escape valve.

The weekly forum which grew out of this suggestion became well known as the Bauchi Discussion Circle. It attracted a broad membership including department heads, administrators, merchants, and teachers. They held debates on economic development, democracy, medicine, war, and religion. Aminu was selected as secretary, with a Mr. Ibiam, a medical dispenser, as his assistant. The moderates joined this time, since the Circle had official government blessing, swelling the number of participants to well over one hundred per meeting. But with Aminu more or less in the driver's seat, sending out the invitations and choosing the topics for discussion, it didn't take long for the organization to run into controversial terrain. Since the meetings were organized either for formal debates, followed by voting, or merely for questions, answers, and discussion, it was not surprising to see debates on such resolutions as "Resolved: That indirect rule is the best form of government for Northern Nigeria" or "Resolved: That the newspaper *Gaskiya Ta Fi Kwabo* should be removed from government control, as its present form constitutes a brake on the wheels of progress." Nor was it surprising to see Aminu and Sa'adu taking the extreme positions, with Abubakar Tafawa Balewa or other moderates defending the British role.

In the debate on the freedom of the press, when Aminu and Sa'adu showed that, on the one hand, the British suppressed and privately condemned the only voice independent of the emirs and that, on the other, they publicly urged independent initiative and thought, the contradictions of the British position became apparent. In the debate on indirect rule, Abubakar timidly defended the dual system, basing his defense on the need for order and a secure foundation from which to launch the desired reforms. Aminu attacked the system head-on. He pointed out that the British had stepped in just as the people were beginning to throw off the tyrannical yoke of Fulani rule and asked, "[though] the so-called system of indirect rule was in the first place a purely military necessity, a plan to extend the influence of an ambitious power and to win the confidence of the oppressed population—may it not rightly be said to have outlived the purposes for which it was originally intended?"[4]

He also pointed out that the regimes existing in 1900, at the time of the British takeover, were autocratic in nature and essentially un-Islamic, despite their assertions to the contrary. Both Mohammed, the Holy Prophet, and Usman Dan Fodio, the founder of the Fulani empire, strongly indicated that succession of rulers should be chosen by the people on the basis of worth, not birth; and therefore the prevailing system at the turn of the century was not at all the traditional system the British made it out to be. The early caliphs were supposed to be chosen by and responsible to the governed.

The day of this particular debate was one of the many when the ailing Sa'adu was restricted to bed. When he could not prevail upon his cohorts to carry him to the meeting in a bicycle basket, Aminu substituted for him. However, after Abubakar's stance was reported to him, he gave Aminu a scathing letter to be read at a subsequent meeting, bolstering Aminu's arguments with a few additional ones of his own. He politely but caustically begged Abubakar to reconsider his ill-conceived defense of indirect rule, directing his vitriolic charges against the "ignorance and evil motivation of the paramount leaders and their advisers" and the "indifference of the political and administrative officers" in charge, which "brings advantages to the rulers of the dual system and exhausts the ruled."

His pen sharpened further with, "The selection of its [the Native Authority's] gutter elite is being made neither on the basis of intelligence nor capacity, but simply by denial of the decent citizen's outlook. Members of the ruling minority have the readiness of desperadoes to gamble, with nothing to lose but everything to gain."[5]

Senior Political Officer Knott was not very enthusistic about the role these two muckrakers were playing, but not until he and his Emir of Bauchi were put on the spot, in one of the question-and-answer sessions, did he give up the ghost. With the emir presiding, the barbed question, "What determines an emir's salary?" was put

to the chair by Aminu. Mr. Knott stumbled through the obvious answer—the extent of his duties and the weight of his responsibilities.
When Aminu retorted, "Why, then, is the Emir of Bauchi's salary
less than that of the Emir of Adamawa, whose constituency and subsequent responsibilities, as well as traditional status, are so much the
lesser?" As chairman, the Emir of Bauchi was not at all displeased
by this discussion, but the meeting ended at that point, somewhat
abruptly. Soon afterward, Mr. Knott announced the dissolution of
the first officially sponsored organization in the North, explaining
that the meetings were just "getting off the rail." It had lasted less
than a year.

The abandonment of the Bauchi Discussion Circle did not stop
the spate of "social organizations," "discussion circles," and "youth"
or "friendly" societies that then began to spring up throughout the
North. There was the Sokoto Youths' Social Circle, the Zaria Youths'
Association (to replace the original Zaria Friendly Society), the
Kano Youths' Association, the Northern Elements Progressive Association (NEPA) in Kano, and so on. Wherever education had crept
in, the educated young were organizing some form of discussion
group outside the Native Authority apparatus. In order to bring
Northern Nigeria out of the past and into the present, a break in the
previous forms had to occur. The emirs and their emissaries saw
clearly what this could mean to their ancient structure and fought it
all the way along the line. At first, any organization of any kind was
banned. Then the British recognized the need for some kind of
accommodation to the shrinking of the modern world and tried to
siphon off the growing nationalist needs by channeling them into discussion societies. But there was no mistaking the growing political
undercurrent in each of these. The more enlightened of the administrators considered their function as a rearguard or delaying action,
in order to hold the reins as long as possible, to steer this upsurge into
more amenable paths.

In this way the internal struggle became one of extent and pace.
Aminu and his ailing ideological partner led the pack in both, push-
ing for "far and fast." Undaunted by the dissolution of the Bauchi
Discussion Circle, they tried another one, this time called the Bauchi
Community Center. It was actually another form of the earlier Im-
provement Union, with a mild name and an innocuous goal: com-

munity improvement. But of course it too was basically a political organization. For the first organizing meeting, with no other place to meet, about twenty charter members gathered in the Native Authority Library, directly across from the emir's palace. They just started their discussions when suddenly they saw Abubakar Tafawa Balewa, often unwilling but ever the emissary of authority (British or emir), approaching with an N.A. policeman at his side. When he arrived, he announced quietly and perhaps a little sheepishly, "As a member of the emir's council, I am hereby requested by the emir to inform you that you are to disband, as all unions (organizations) are forbidden." The assembled members looked at one another perplexed, not knowing what to do. Then Sa'adu spoke up, "Tell me, sir, are you a messenger carrying information, or are you the executor of the order as well?" When Abubakar answered that he was merely delivering the message, Sa'adu continued, "In that case, we ask you to deliver our reply to the emir, that we will *not* disband."

After Abubakar and his escort retired, the assembled discussed their next step, deciding that Aminu, as secretary, was to send a letter to the senior political officer, the resident, telling him what had transpired, demanding that the oft-reiterated right of freedom of assembly and association be implemented, and stating that the Emir of Bauchi was trespassing on their rights.

Three days later, while Aminu was teaching a class, his headmaster—by coincidence, Mallam Abubakar—entered his classroom to inform him that the emir wanted to see him as soon as school was out. As he turned his bicycle toward the palace gates, he noted that the other members of the Community Center were also converging.

The emir greeted them formally from his mahogany thronelike chair upholstered in red velvet, the only piece of furniture in the spacious room. The carpeted floor merged with the severe white walls, which rose into a high, vaulted ceiling, setting the tone for the meeting. They seated themselves on the floor in a semicircle, facing the emir, the traditionally lower stance for social inferiors. "You apparently misunderstood my message," he began. "At no time did I say you couldn't hold meetings. Only the Native Authority Library typewriters and facilities, and of course the time from work is denied to you, nothing else. If you meet in your own time and place, you can function."

At that point, Abubakar, in the presence of all, complained that the message he had delivered had accurately represented the emir's directions. Sa'adu was quite ready to push the contradiction and catch the emir in a lie, but cooler voices prevailed and the modified edict was accepted.

So they filed out to a nearby place in the sun, to consider possible meeting places. The N.A. offices, the market place or stalls, were all official and therefore eliminated, but one elderly gentleman, Mallam Waziri, said he had a big enough hall, but it had no roof. "If you roof it yourselves, you can use it." They emptied their pockets, collecting enough to cover the cost of the roof, and eventually thatched it with grass of sorts, plastered the interior, put a lamp, table, and chairs inside, and a sign reading, "Bauchi Community Center" outside. Thus emerged the first private meeting hall in Northern Nigeria.

These organizational endeavors represented Aminu's avenue for contact with the small but growing group of forward-looking persons emerging from the rigid, stagnant society which prevailed. The student community at the school absorbed another significant portion of his energies. But the third and by far the largest group with which he maintained close relations, was that of the uneducated talakawa, the local administrators, and members of the trading community, who by and large were continuing to stick close to the ways of their ancestors. The subtleties of formal debates or of scientific and academic investigation were not for them. The small gaps in their day-to-day routines of hard work and rest were filled with superstitious rites and the most threadbare of pleasures.

On one occasion, when Aminu was passing through Jos, a mountainside resort and commercial center, he decided to relax by spending a night or two with friends there. He and several acquaintances were wandering through the streets in the market area when they came upon and joined a group of several hundred people gathered around an itinerant mallam. He was inveighing against sinners generally, telling the assemblage to beware, for if he prayed against a soul, it was doomed; that it is written that anyone who takes a journey on a particular day would go to jail; and so on. Young Aminu, whose patience with this sort of thing was short, shouted loudly, "From what book do you quote? Where do you get that information?"

The crowd and the mallam were stunned at this impudence. After a few moments of silence, the preacher recovered enough to go on. This time he started with, "Our book tells of how the preaching of our prophets will be disturbed by a living devil, a Christian missionary who had become learned in the Koran . . ."

"What chapter? What verse? Where is your book?"

When the mallam mumbled a title and sent a child to get the book to check, Aminu responded, "Don't bother!" and proceeded to quote the passage word for word.

The crowd picked up the dispute. "How can this youngster question that elderly imam? Since he is so young, he must be wrong."

"No, he sounds as though he knows whereof he speaks . . ."

The arguments waxed back and forth, becoming more and more boisterous, until a policeman asked Aminu to leave. He did so, heading for the home of Mohammed Dan Karfalla, his host in Jos, followed by about fifty of the most impressed listeners. Never one to waste an opportunity, Aminu harangued them in front of his host's house, discussing this and related events. The outcome was a Hausa Society, the counterpart of the Ibo and Yoruba fraternal unions and the first of its kind in Jos. The next day, the people came to stare at the house of Mohammed Dan Karfalla and the young man who was so right. And the old mallam himself returned to the marketplace to say that he had checked his source and the boy was correct and should therefore be blessed not cursed.

To such people in Bauchi, Aminu was like a man from outer space. He was more of a curiosity than the foreign British *baturi,* for he was one of them and yet not. He was compounded of pure Fulani and its antithesis, and used Hausa-Fulani means to accomplish non-Hausa-Fulani goals. Even a man like Sa'adu Zungur was more understandable than Aminu, for Sa'adu to them was a learned mallam, thoroughly schooled in the Koran and its commentaries; who perhaps because of his illness, did not mingle too freely with them. In spite of the radical nature of what he said, he seemed not unlike the itinerant mallam of yesteryear who preached about the wrath of demons, hellfire and brimstones, and the forthcoming Armageddon.

Aminu in a sense maintained a similar relationship with the masses, but he did not stop there. He had the patience and took the

time to educate the young and the ignorant toward their own legitimate goals. His attraction was not so much his age as that he spoke
to them on their own level. He was of patrician heritage, but approached everyone as an equal, ignoring the centuries-old status
structure that so dominated their lives and thinking. He moved freely
in and out of their homes and welcomed them to his. He could meet
and greet them in the market, in the public square, and everywhere
he went they thought of him as being above opportunism and the
desire for personal aggrandizement. Yet he had emerged from the
heart of a system that accepted these as inherent. He gave freely of his
time to the lowliest, and defied the tradition-ridden and respect-
demanding social stratification. The fact that he still did not get
struck down by it aroused a dormant sense of independence in the
people—something they had never dared acknowledge before. As
the years passed and his consistency and courage were sustained, his
reputation grew. Dozens, even hundreds, flocked to his house—
knowing they would be received respectfully—just to gaze at him or
listen open-mouthed to his oracle-like words of wisdom. In the
political years to follow, his political adversaries could attack his
lieutenants and followers, but usually not him, for they always kept
a healthy respect for him and his goals. Ordinarily, the worst they
could conjure up was that he was too impatient or a dupe.

In an area where Sufism had such a firm hold, many thought
of him as one who could foresee the future: "He can predict what is
to come." "We listen to him, for he knows of what he speaks." His
thorough knowledge of the Koran and the culture and traditions of
his land bestowed upon him the aura of a teacher who interpreted
reality as they saw it. Years after her divorce from Aminu, Hasia,
his former wife, said almost reverently, "He foresees, and *tells*, the
truth. He told a friend that if he continued drinking he would suffer.
The friend didn't stop and was faced with destitution on more than
one occasion. He told me that if I divorced him *I* would suffer, and
he was right, as he always is." Sarkin Mallamai (Chief of Mallams)
of Bauchi put it this way: "He can tell what will happen and urges
everyone to sacrifice time and effort to achieve it." Another man
said, "Events smell, and Aminu can smell them!"

This awe with which he has been regarded by so many is compounded of admiration, respect, and mysticism. Dozens of people

who know him have voiced the same opinion; that however he did it, he has acquired the kind of wisdom which permits him to predict events. One foreign observer quipped, "His prognostications come not from any extrasensory perceptions but from reading *The New York Times*." Aminu himself has always deprecated these beliefs in his supernatural abilities, pointedly telling any who listened, that they too could gain similar powers with application, analysis, and above all, education. Nevertheless, Gogo Nana and Nasiru Kabara in Kano and Ali Agba in Agege will continue to think of him as a soothsayer.

If we carry these references to Aminu's clairvoyance back to his growth years, we can readily see how early he repudiated the Fulani pattern of accepting one's fate with abject resignation, and how he actively sought answers to the unknown. At the age of four, he was determined to find out "What's up there in the sky"; at the age of six, he "predicted" the death of his mother; he pursued medical knowledge and scientific facts, predicting the cures based on such knowledge. Finally, he used his knowledge and experience on the political front to prophesy dire consequences for those who neglected the people's wishes.

It is said that two years before the death of the Premier (Sardauna) Aminu predicted he would not last two more years if he continued his arrogant rule, and that a military regime would replace the Nigerian republic if official corruption continued. But the most whimsical of his predictions did literally come out of *The New York Times*. Sometime during his years in Bauchi he informed the ciroma (heir-apparent) that there would be an eclipse of the sun at a particular time and place (shades of *The Connecticut Yankee!*). The skeptical prince said that if this happened, he would till Aminu's soil for one full year. The eclipse of course occurred as announced. The prince was a man of his word, but since he was also a man of royalty, he had to perform his pledged task in the dark of night, hidden from view.

Perhaps if he truly had these powers of foresight, Aminu should have been able to see that those early years of teaching in Bauchi would end, even though temporarily, with a long odyssey to a distant land where he would meet with strange people and adventures. However, he could hardly have anticipated such a development, for it was brought about by the very people he attacked so vociferously, the British. Abubakar, his headmaster, had gone to England as one of the first five northern Nigerian scholarship students, and that was understandable and predictable. But Aminu could not have realized that he would be next in line. Clearly, getting him out of the country, even for a year, must have had some advantages to the British. It might have served as a bribe, or a brake, but even if that were not so, getting him off their back would give them a breathing spell. (They were to try this tactic again a few years later when they promoted him to a remote school at Maru in Sokoto Province—but, as events unfolded, all to no avail.)

In any event, when Aminu was offered one of seven scholarships for a year's study in England, in September 1946, he was elated, and accepted unhesitatingly. It was to be his first trip out of Nigeria, and he was to make the most of it, though his heart stayed behind in Hausaland.

6.

THE OUTER CIRCLE

The speaker at Free Speech Corner in Hyde Park was waxing eloquent on some religious subject or other. Aminu stood on the fringe of the crowd, listening with only half an ear. It was a chilly, damp London day, much like the many others he had experienced since his arrival, and so unlike the heat and rain of Kano, or even the cool balmy mountain air of Jos. As he pulled his collar a bit tighter around his neck, his attention wandered. He realized that what intrigued him here was not so much what the speaker—any speaker— might be saying, but just the very existence of such a spot. Here anyone with a grievance, crackpot or otherwise, could get up and spout ideas quite unacceptable to the establishment, and yet not get clapped in jail.

This country, where people could think independently, disagree with the authorities, and, most important, *do* something about their fate, was so different from his home environment that he made a qualitative leap in his thinking. Up to that point, government *for* and *of* the people had been his dim, distant goal. He suddenly realized that the revolution he had conceived for Nigeria had to switch onto a new track if it was ever to reach the desired destination. There had to be government *by* the people. But did not his fellow countrymen have to arrive at a state of mind similar to that of the "free" British before they could even begin to achieve significant change? Was it not imperative that they first stand up and fight for their rights, as individuals, to participate in government? Hundreds of years of Hausa-Fulani traditional relationships had never provided a means for the common man, or talakawa (derived from the Arabic word meaning "freed man") to participate in the decision-making process

save as a client of one patron or another, or as a disgruntled dropout
—and the British presence had not changed that one iota.

These ideas were rolling excitedly through his head when his
reverie was shattered by the voice of one of his fellow students.
"Aminu Kano! Of course you are here! Mr. Mort has been looking
for you at the hostel. He wanted you to pop up to his home in the
country this weekend. We didn't tell him you would probably be
here, for you know how angry he gets when he doesn't find you
studying at home like the rest of us."

Aminu made a wry face in response. He couldn't be less interested in such a weekend. He had seen enough of E. L. Mort, both as
a tutor at London University's Institute of Education and as a principal back in Kaduna College. Here in England he wanted to use
every spare minute to learn, to discover, to investigate. That meant
going into every intellectual nook or geographical cranny of London,
wherever he could find something new. He was eagerly devouring the
words of Harold Laski, George Bernard Shaw, and Karl Mannheim,
a sociologist-lecturer at London University and author of *Man and
Society,* the source of many of Aminu's ideas on the ideal human
society.

Although he knew very little about it, socialism was a concept
that attracted him, leading him to join all the socialist groups he
could find: the Socialist Labor Party, the Student Socialist Society,
and the Young Socialists. He befriended some of the left leaning
MPs and quietly admired their Labour Party for its welfare state,
knowing that Nigeria had a long way to go to reach these minimum
requirements and even though at times he baited the party openly
for its compromises and inactivity. The ideological spectrum was
completed when, as a colonial student, he was courted by another
kind of socialist group, the communists, and even met some of the
top leaders.

His head was spinning with all the ideological nuances and
variations he was sopping up, and with his attempts to apply them
to Nigeria and Africa. The other six Northern Nigerians studying
with him were sticking close to their assignments and were not too
helpful to him in his search, nor were the southern Nigerians, like
Jaja Wachuku, who were busy running their own show. But he met
other students from the Asian and African colonies at the Colonial

Students' Office, in the Ministry of Colonial Administration, where all administrative arrangements were handled and student allowances picked up. Many of them have turned up as Africa's leaders— among them Kwame Nkrumah, Jomo Kenyatta, and Seretse Khama.

It was the eve of independence for India and Pakistan—a struggle that united all the colonial students at the time. When Ali Jinnah, Indian Moslem leader, and Jawaharlal Nehru arrived in London in 1947 for pre-independence discussions, they were greeted wildly at the airport by these students, to whom freedom was still a visionary dream. "Forward to Freedom," a united group of students from the colonies, organized a tumultuous welcome at London's Holborn Hall, with Aminu in enthusiastic attendance. He was a young underling with only a few months of Western-world experience. The philosophy and political concepts of early French and American revolutionaries, of Shavian Fabian socialism, became entwined in his mind with his early learning from the Koran and the writings of Usman Dan Fodio. Although he was still influenced by Sa'adu Zungur's radical but parochial thinking, London was broadening his outlook and giving his own ideas a world-wide context. The struggle for freedom from the colonial yoke, with its accompanying Gandhian nonviolence (*satyagraha*), and political leadership through self-abnegation, was stirred into the pot of ideas, which could no longer be put in place quite so easily. "Think, study, and think some more" was the order of the day.

The West African Student Union, a broad organization that included all West Africans, suffered from the plaints which usually accompany broadness—moderation. Since official sponsorship permitted WASU to serve as an open forum on politics and social welfare, but not much else, a smaller, more militant group of students, purportedly more African in style, organized themselves into the West African Secretariat. Under the aegis of Kwame Nkrumah, George Padmore, and others resident in England much longer than Aminu, it pledged its members to go back to their homelands, and to provide the dynamism they felt was lacking in the broader group. By this time, Nkrumah had returned from the U.S., but had not yet gone back to his native Gold Coast. Subsequent struggles in British West Africa found Aminu and Nkrumah seeing eye to eye on many struggles, primarily because of their mutual militant anticolonialism.

Although Aminu was very much taken with his newfound concepts of socialism, he and the leaders in the West African Secretariat were not thinking of mass movements in Marxian terms. Rather, their African experience told them that the masses were not yet ready to move on their own; they needed strong charismatic, Napoleonic leaders who could attract crowds and move mountains. In the process, perhaps they could train people for mass participation. As events developed, men like Nkrumah found this latter course too difficult and hence enjoyed and indefinitely extended the first phase of strong leadership. Men like Gandhi and Nehru actually influenced Aminu more deeply than did Nkrumah, but not until India had achieved her independence, largely through nonviolent techniques, did Aminu think to apply this dynamic, militant approach to the struggle in Nigeria.

Since Aminu's concept of education was modern and progressive, he reached out for information into areas far beyond London University itself. But within its walls he read voraciously and attended lectures by any professor he felt could contribute something worthwhile, whether in the field of education or outside it. Most of all, he used his year abroad to ferret out information that was not available in Nigeria. As he assimilated it, he kept funneling it into, "How can this be applied in Nigeria?"

Around him, all this complex and highly organized society and not a single region-wide organization of any type in all of Northern Nigeria. He gathered together his fellow Northern Nigerians and school teachers—Salihu Fulani, Z. Y. Dimka, Yahaya Gusau, Shettima Shehu Ajiram—and several others, to organize the Northern Teachers' Welfare Association, (which became the Northern Teachers' Association (NTA) when it was transplanted from London to Nigeria). Shettima Ajiram, the headmaster of Bornu Middle School, was chosen president pro tem; and Aminu, secretary pro tem. There were issues enough: teachers' rights and welfare, the need for an improved syllabus, salary differentials between North and South; and the eligibility of teachers in Christian Mission Schools for membership in NTA. Aminu was authorized to send letters to headmasters throughout the North, urging them to attend an organizing meeting in Nigeria the following year. Here in London, then, was hatched Northern Nigeria's first labor union, its first region-wide organization of any kind, and what is generally considered the precursor and "lineal antecedent of most nationalist organizations founded in the North."[1]

How else to apply all this to his homeland? At this point Aminu chose to write the term paper discussed in Chapter 3, "Girls' Education in Kano Emirate." Although it did not represent a tremendous amount of original research, it did reveal some analytical thought, an ability to cast out preconceived notions of the Hausa-Fulani establishment, and an attempt to build something new on old foundations, thus providing a clue as to why he was always the radical back home.

Aminu's course at the Institute of Education included practice teaching in London's elementary schools, where he was able to sense at first hand the vast cultural differences between the two countries. In a booklet entitled *Motsi Ya Fi Zama* (It Is Better to Be on the Move than Idle), he subsequently described the uninhibited English children as "naughty" and "like young monkeys who don't like to stay in one place." However, he eventually learned to control their exuberance and befriend them and their teachers, to the point where the children looked forward to "Mr. Aminu's Day."

Since it was "better to be on the move," at the conclusion of the school term Aminu arranged to extend his experience into rural areas as a guest of the Young Farmers' Club, a self-help community development organization. He spent several weeks in the Welsh countryside, billeted in private homes, observing and running the combine-harvester, milking cows, and so on, always thinking of possible applications back home.

He had skimped on his allowance to save his pennies for traveling in the British countryside and for one big trip to the continent during his vacation, simultaneously serving as part-time Hausa language announcer and translator for the British Broadcasting Company, to augment these meager savings. In August, when he was almost ready to finance his trip, he had a pleasant surprise. Because of his boy scout activities at home, and his present proximity to France, he was chosen as delegate to the forthcoming World Boy Scout Jamboree in Rosny, near Paris. This meant that his fare to Europe would be paid and his living costs greatly reduced while there, since France extended many discounts and much hospitality as its contribution to the Jamboree.

But Aminu was most impressed when, on July 26, 1947, the eve of his departure for the continent, the entire boy scout contingent was invited to Buckingham Palace for inspection and "tea in the Stables" with the king and queen. Of the thousand-odd scouts there, about three hundred represented the colonial contingent—from India, Burma, Hong Kong, East and West Africa, and actually the entire globe. Aminu was amazed and shaken by the free and easy way in which the king and queen mingled and chatted with the boys. Back home the British officialdom was so aloof that a Nigerian did not dare present himself to the resident—not to mention his superior, the governor, who in his turn would not dream of approaching the king and queen. There, the royal couple was untouchable; here, he, a little fellow, was touching them, shaking hands with the very symbol of all the power that the resident represented. His awe of colonial rulers was shattered. In Nigeria, they did not even acknowledge the dignity of man that was practiced here in their homeland, making it obvious that their system was crumbling. Colonial rule had to be thrown out and a government based on socialist ideals set up. There was no other way out.

After this revelation, Aminu's trip to the continent was almost anticlimactic. The spirit of love and tolerance engendered at the Jamboree, where thousands of boys from all over the world were gathered in a gigantic tent city, left him with an exciting hope that this same spirit could be created in his own country. When Mr. Snowsell, the British scout leader of their contingent, complained of the barbaric French continental breakfast, with coffee rather than the tea to which he was accustomed, Aminu jestingly but caustically reacting to his recent experience at Buckingham Palace, asked if tea drinking were a qualification for nationhood. "If so," he continued, "shouldn't we Nigerians abstain from drinking tea until Nigeria has achieved its independence? And how about India's independence? Didn't the East Indians drink tea for centuries, long before the British?" His counterparts, the delegates from the Western and Eastern Regions— M. N. Sagoe and Christopher Mojekwu— laughed heartily. (Aminu saw Mojekwu years later, in 1968, on the opposite side of the peace negotiation table in Kampala.)

From the Jamboree, Aminu was able to manage a trip to Switzerland, Rome, and Paris, seeing all the sights en route. As a gaping tourist, he wandered through city streets, picking up bits and pieces of information and storing them away in the remote recesses of his brain. He preferred London to all other European cities, for the usual reasons: he had made more friends there, spoke the language, and generally felt more at home.

Reluctantly he faced his imminent departure for Lagos, for he had enjoyed his other world life as a student. He did briefly consider staying on to study law, but he had made a commitment to return immediately after completing his course and feared the possibility of being denied readmittance by the British. More than this, he also had a strong urge to go back and put into operation some of the exhilarating new and revolutionary ideas he had picked up in his year in the outer circle—ideas that might effect the changes necessary to bring his own land into the wider orbit of the modern world.

7. PUTTING IT TOGETHER

When Aminu returned to Bauchi after his brief sojourn in England, he knew that political upheaval and social changes were surely coming. Though he did not know where or how he would function, he did know that he was most certainly going to play a leading role. The teaching profession he saw as the anteroom of a labyrinth, leading where he knew not, but into which he was ready to plunge headlong.

The British did not know how he would fit in either. Aminu's year in England had given them a respite, but now they had to put him somewhere. Instead of cooling off, Aminu had come back to the struggle reinforced. They wanted to train Nigerians to help guide the country, but when successful, independent souls like Aminu emerged to create all the problems of conflict that arise within a modern society.

While they were casting about for a controllable post for him, Aminu was not content to wait silently. In his absence, political organizations had begun to bubble more actively in scarcely concealed forms. The Friendly Societies mentioned earlier had taken root in most towns of consequence. In 1946, a group of young nationalists in Kano had attempted to organize a frankly political region-wide organization called the Northern Elements Progressive Association (NEPA), but the Native Authority quickly squelched it through the simple expedient of transferring or sacking all its known members.*

The groundwork for its replacement, the Northern Teachers Association (NTA), destined to be the first successful regional

---

*Included among them were Abdu Rahman Bida, President; Raji Abdallah, Secretary; and Abubakar Zukogi, Field Secretary.

organization in the history of the North, had already been laid in England by Aminu and his colleagues. Aminu's assumption was that if he moved carefully, the authorities would not be able to stop it. All parties concerned knew that the very existence of such an organization, whether ostensibly a professional society or not, would have explosive effects on the political scene. The question was how to avoid giving any excuse for suppression by either the British or the Native Authorities. Although Aminu had all kinds of contro-versial plans for his brainchild, he had been cautious enough to include conservatives like Abubakar Tafawa Balewa and Shettima Shehu Ajiram as founding members, and to approach all teachers regardless of their political positions. The organization's stated goals were to enhance education and to represent the interests of the teachers.

In spite of this circumspection, official sanction was denied them. Undaunted, Aminu continued sending out letters to every school in the North, urging participation of all teachers from the headmasters on down and reminding them of the organizing meeting to be held in Zaria in March 1948. A reluctant education officer who admitted he could see nothing wrong with the project was persuaded to invite the Emir of Zaria to be patron, and incidentally grant them permis-sion to use a convention hall. The emir graciously (though hesitantly) agreed to both, and appeared during the sessions to accept his hon-orary title.

He was not the only unlikely one to attend. The British were keeping a close watch on Aminu's organizing activities. A Captain C. D. Money, formerly senior district officer in Kano, had been assigned to Kaduna Central Headquarters for the North as a sort of roving political-intelligence officer to observe and control ques-tionable activities. In Kano, the captain had something of a reputa-tion as a progressive and a strong man, to be feared by emirs and chiefs, for he had insisted on their opening the doors to change. He had come to know Aminu in Kano and, while in England during Aminu's stay there, had even asked him to spend a weekend at his home in Brighton.

Upon his arrival in Zaria, Captain Money invited Aminu to lunch and greeted him with, "How is my friend Stalin, and how is the meeting of the Northern Nigerian Soviets progressing?"

"But isn't Stalin on his way out? He's so old?"

"You know I was joking. You're just in Stalin's category."

Aminu banteringly ended with, "I wish I *were* in his category."

In spite of their sparring, these two were able to maintain cordiality, so that Aminu ended up inviting the captain to open the meeting.

Captain Money and the British were taken by surprise at the success of the meeting. For seven days, the large number of teachers in attendance managed to hammer out a constitution and an organizational form. All the pro tem officers were elected to regular terms: Shettima Ajiram, president; Abubakar Tafawa Balewa, vice-president; and Aminu Kano, general secretary. Aminu's home in Bauchi was to be the headquarters. There all the rules and regulations were to be published and invitations to form individual branches were to be dispatched. Men like Dr. R. A. B. Dikko, D. A. Rafi, and Abubakar Imam, representative of the only learned group in the North other than teachers, were in attendance, and suggested: "You have succeeded in forming a region-wide organization with general acceptance, but what about people like us? We are not teachers, and we need organization even more. We hope we can count on your active cooperation to help place us all under one umbrella."

Within a year the NTA had twenty-five branches and had been granted official representation on the Board of Education—one of Aminu's first demands upon assuming his role as organizing secretary. But at the very first Board meeting he attended as delegate, he continued rocking the boat. To everyone's surprise, the enigmatic Aminu supported the request of a group of Christian missionaries who asked permission to open a mission school in a Moslem area—even though all previous requests had been denied. In addition, as a committee member he helped work out a complete revision of the current syllabus and successfully negotiated improvements in teachers' salaries and working conditions.

Though there had been a pre-existing Nigerian Union of Teachers in the south, at that stage in the history of the north Aminu felt it was important that the organization be not only region-wide but free of any taint of possible southern domination—nor for that matter had the southerners approached him. Not until a few years later, when politics had been launched full scale and Aminu left the NTA, did the northern group eventually affiliate with the national union.

In the interim, back home in Bauchi, Sa'adu Zungur was still seriously ill but functioning actively—though his thinking was taking him off in a slightly different direction than Aminu's. Rather than continuing to search for an indigenous politics, independent of the south, he had come to regard Nnamdi Azikiwe's National Council of Nigeria and the Cameroons (NCNC), based principally in the South-East, as a possible outlet for national unity and a matrix on which to build a body politic. The first attempt at regional organization, the NEPA, had directly associated itself with the NCNC, openly welcoming its support in 1946, when that group sent a pan-Nigerian delegation to tour the North.

Although the stated aims of the NEPA were those of the majority of the young, educated elite of the north, most of the members were afraid equally of the wrath of the Native Authorities and of the possibility of being dominated by the better educated and far more aggressive southerners. Those with influence, whose cooperation might have made repression difficult, were not ready to have their own heads lopped off with a direct accusation of collusion with the southerners. Thus the guarded and prudent approach of Aminu and others in the organization of the NTA and the subsequent Northern People's Congress (NPC). To the extent that the NCNC had any support in the north, it was largely due to a nucleus of southerners resident in the area or to minority groups living close to the southern border.

The NCNC elected Sa'adu Zungur its federal secretary at a national assembly in Kaduna in April 1948, and after a send-off party in May, he left for Lagos to take up his duties there. Aminu, though close to the pan-Nigerian NCNC* in his radical approach to the north, shrewdly assessed the northern fear of the south as an overriding consideration. Thus, when the time arrived for his newly organized party to align itself with the NCNC, it did so, but only after it had already established a solid base, essentially northern in character.

---

*NCNC: Although attempting to spread its influence throughout Nigeria, the core of the party's strength was in the Ibo heartland in the Eastern Region, and what eventually became known as the Mid-West.

Aminu's characteristic instinctive brand of radicalism enabled him to retain working relationships with all his young adult friends and relatives, even through the bitterest and most acrimonious of times. His antagonists knew that when the chips were down, Aminu would chalk up as a northerner. This northern orientation of his showed through frequently during the next two decades, beginning with the constitutional conferences of the early 1950's. Though he was not averse to dealings with a southern party, at no time did Aminu's party relinquish its independence of action, despite its opponents' accusations to the contrary.

Early in 1948, Aminu learned of the possibility that the NCNC would offer him a scholarship for further study, either in the U.S. or in Great Britain. He welcomed the prospect and waited impatiently for it to materialize, but to no avail. When the offer finally came through, it was equivocal and Aminu did not accept it under those conditions.

During these months, Aminu waited impatiently to hear from the British regarding his immediate future, while simultaneously hunting for his own solutions. His frustration at the slow pace of change was clearly in evidence. He burned with desire to alter the status quo, but was stymied by the reluctance of the British and the emirs to accept any changes not introduced by their own officialdom. His personal life had taken a frustrating turn too. He had been married five years by this time, and was still childless. Hasia, his wife, had been ill with an elusive but somewhat serious and long-lasting spleen affliction, further reducing the possibility of childbearing. Then, in 1948, his hopes were aroused when she became pregnant, only to be dashed again when she miscarried.

Obviously Aminu's political and vocational uneasiness was not relieved by these personal uncertainties. In his diary he listed the following as items still outstanding at the end of 1948:[1]
1. Need for continued development of Teachers' Welfare Association (Nigerian Teachers' Association).
2. Shaping up of Bauchi Community Center.
3. Wanting child (I have great hope).
4. Help father.

His diary also reveals an impatience with his fellow leaders, noting that they were wasting their time attacking one another, and that many were selling out for comfortable positions with the old order. "The mill of God grinds slowly but perfectly well," he complained. "We are determined to fight all imperialists." The Bauchi people were disunited, the talakawa beaten down and immobilized. "Nigeria is doomed if [the] pernicious system of bloodthirsty, barbarous, obsolescent Fulani rulers is pursued." Perhaps a strong leader was the answer. "May God Almighty raise someone who will erase the influence of the chiefs and emirs. Maybe He'll give us a Mustafa Kemal, or a Mussolini . . ."[2] While expressing this disoriented impatience at not finding his niche, he continued to agitate for democratic reform, indicating an overriding, instinctive trust in the power of the people.

In Bauchi, however, Aminu was proceeding full blast. On his return from England, he had gone back to his former post in the Bauchi Middle School, but a few months after his arrival, he was asked to move to the Bauchi Teachers' Training College. The move gave some minimal recognition to the higher status accorded him by his study in England. Yet it did not alter his out-of-school activities in any way. He changed schools smoothly in April 1948, without shifting out of high gear.

At this time, the newly appointed Governor, Sir John MacPherson, was in the process of making a tour throughout the North to survey his realm. His itinerary included all the major cities of the North, but for some unexplained reason he was skipping Bauchi. The group of militants led by Aminu and Sa'adu felt the omission was deliberate. They believed the Governor's northern advisers and representatives knew that Bauchi was the only place where he would have been confronted with a list of demands, grievances, and suggestions for change. Planning their tactics well, Aminu, Sa'adu, and one other person went to the Emir of Bauchi and told him of the Governor's projected slight of his emirate, tying it up with Bauchi's poor school system, roads, and economy. The people of Bauchi, said this committee of three, wanted the Governor to see these conditions for himself. The emir readily agreed to the proposal that they address the townspeople, protesting the Governor's omission.

Had this trio approached the Native Authority police for the necessary written permission to speak to the public, it would undoubtedly have been delayed and then denied. But by going over the heads of the bureaucrats they were able to organize the first mass rally ever held in Northern Nigeria. About a thousand people assembled in the marketplace. They were addressed by Sa'adu and Aminu; resolutions were passed urging the Governor to come to Bauchi to see for himself and a letter to that effect was sent to the Resident of Bauchi to be forwarded to the Governor. There were reverberations throughout the North. The British were shocked that such an unprecedented event could take place without warning. The British head of the Bauchi police asked the committee for their permit two days after the rally, and roundly admonished them and the emir to whom he was referred by the supposedly innocent and naive committee which did not understand such intricate administrative procedures.

The years 1948 and 1949 were notable, too, for the beginnings of political parties in Northern Nigeria. The Social and Friendly Circles that had sprung up were harbingers of change, but not until two such groups—one in Zaria the other in Kaduna—decided to merge did the nucleus for an all-inclusive, region-wide organization develop. Dr. Dikko (first medical officer of northern origin) and Abubakar Imam, editor of *Gaskiya,* the Hausa language newspaper of the North, and other charter members of the Zaria group, had approached Aminu at the convention of the Northern Teachers' Association to help extend such a "cultural" organization throughout the North. Since Aminu's sights were set beyond the teaching profession, he willingly agreed to cooperate. Wherever he went to organize chapters of the NTA, he encouraged the parallel organization of branches of what was to be the Northern Peoples' Congress (NPC), and persuaded the many existing social and cultural organizations to affiliate. From its inception in October 1948—when the Zaria and Kaduna groups merged, followed shortly by the Bauchi group—the NPC spread like wildfire. In June 1949, an inaugural organizing meeting was launched in Kaduna, at Green's Hotel. In attendance were Sa'adu Zungur (though he was general secretary of NCNC at the time), Aminu and Isa Wali, a cousin of Aminu's. Although the spectral political spread and the resultant differences between the organizers prepared the way for future splits, the issues at this initial congress centered around two proposals. The first was advanced by Isa Wali, on behalf of the Kaduna branch: to abolish the Northern House of Chiefs as a legislative chamber and substitute in its stead a council of elders that would include the emirs but give them only advisory powers. The second proposal was to admit women to membership. In this matter, Sa'adu Zungur, as the organization's adviser on Moslem law, ruled that women were eligible, using a long-standing precedent—that Shehu Dan Fodio had admitted women to his classes. The Sultan of Sokoto's blessings were read before the assembly at its opening session but later withdrawn when the sultan objected to the vigorous debate on the elimination of the house of chiefs. Pro tem officers were elected, including Sa'adu Zungur as adviser on Moslem law, Aminu Kano as joint auditor, and Isa Wali as assistant secretary.

Over the years, Isa Wali rapidly became a very meaningful part of Aminu's life, starting back in Kaduna when Isa roomed with Sule Katagum, Aminu's friend and former pupil: There were several limitations to the relationship between these two. Isa was younger, and a member of the civil service throughout his short life. This career of Isa's proved to be something of a barrier to their joint action, for civil servants were forbidden to take open political positions. The cousins (or brothers, as they called each other) were frequently stationed or occupied in different towns; but whenever they could, they put their heads together to project their individual ideas regarding the future of their country. Isa, though barred from active participation in political life, jumped eagerly into the social arena, and became a champion of women's rights.

Aminu, the rebel out to change the essential power structure, could not stray too far from accepted social limitations for fear of cutting off his mass support. If his wife appeared with a woman's group or at a political function (as on one occasion in 1952 when Aminu returned from London), that was acceptable, but the following day she would return to her usual role. Isa, to whom popular personal support was of little concern, insisted that his wife be liberated. She ignored purdah (isolation of wives), went to school, and even drove a car. When Isa received an invitation from the emir to a social gathering, he returned it with a note saying that he could not accept unless his wife was included—a hitherto unheard-of action. In every way he could, he consistently pointed out those Hausa-Fulani and Islamic traditions that encouraged the free intermingling of the sexes. During his several years of foreign service in the U.S. and other countries, his egalitarian view of the relationship between the sexes was strongly reinforced.

The contradictions existing in the North at that time were clearly illustrated by this Wali family. Suleiman, Isa's father, was an influential, religious member of the Genawa clan, related to Aminu both as a distant cousin and as husband of his maternal aunt (parenthetically, another of his wives was a daughter of the emir). As a learned imam, he accompanied the emir on a pilgrimage to Mecca, thereafter becoming his close intimate. When the *waziri* (prime minister) passed away, Suleiman was *ma'aji* (treasurer) but his family lineage would not permit him to be appointed in the waziri's stead. So Emir Abudllahi bestowed the title "Wali" upon his friend and adviser, left the post of waziri open, and permitted Suleiman to function as though it were his portfolio.

In a way, Wali Suleiman reflected the inconsistencies and uncertainty of his times. He came out of the same background as Aminu and his father Yusufu, but when he was shown favor by the emir, those who staunchly defended the traditional independence of the mallam class considered this shift to the side of power as a betrayal. The trust the emir placed in him and his advice reflected Suleiman's allegiance to the traditional power base. Yet this same defender of entrenched hierarchy was responsible for starting the School of Arabic Studies in Kano, and insisted on many modern educational reforms, including the study of English for all his own children, as well as the emir and his councilors and wives.

After having served from 1935-1939, he was removed as wali during a tumultuous inner court upheaval. He and several of his fellow councilors and members of the inner court all died at almost the same time, under circumstances never adequately explained.

As Isa Wali and his brothers grew up and became educated, they disagreed with their father's defense of the establishment. All achieved high status in the civil service as part of the educated elite, and were classed as progressives and modernists. In a general way, at least, they were all in Aminu's camp, and although as civil servants they were prohibited from political activity, there was never much doubt as to where their loyalties lay. After achieving ambassadorial rank, representing Nigeria in Ghana and serving as U.N. delegate,

Isa himself met an early and tragic end suddenly in 1967. To a Western observer, his contributions might not seem revolutionary, but the full extent of his challenge comes into perspective when we see that Zainab, his widow (who had achieved some status as the only woman member of Kano's Consultative Assembly),[3] chose to remarry a prominent northerner, to submerge herself in purdah, speaking to men through a curtain, emerging to view only after rare and specific permission of her husband. This in 1969! The pull of the traditional system is still that strong.

The new ideas regarding change to modernity which Aminu had brought with him from England were frowned upon by the authorities as too radical for the North, but they still didn't know what to do about him. Now his motto was, "What is good enough for the British in Britain is good enough for us." On this basis, Aminu was doing nothing illegal and could not be molested by the British in Nigeria. As a matter of fact, he was doing what the British were publicly urging—preparing his people for entering the modern world—but privately they wanted to preserve the status quo. Their resolution of this conflict was such that governmental policy became not much more than an attempt to brake the growth of political activity, in order to retain the framework of British domination. Aminu was moving too fast and too far for them. They had to find some means of slowing him down.

Although Aminu was not exactly sitting and waiting for their decision, he knew full well that the British were in a dilemma and were trying to find a spot for him. Hence he was not surprised when the education officer approached him one day in his classroom in the Teachers' Training College, to tell him to make tracks to Kaduna to meet the Chief Secretary to the Government, Mr. Knott (the same Mr. Knott who had organized the Bauchi Discussion Circle a few years back and who had since been promoted).

He traveled to Kaduna by train (the principal means of transport available to him in those years), and was somewhat jolted to find the Chief Secretary himself waiting for him at the station. He was jolted even more when Mr. Knott invited him to put up at his residence. Until he left for England he had been totally ignored. Now he, Aminu, a very junior teacher was being met by one of the highest officials in the land and asked to be his guest! In response to the invitation, he could only stammer, "Isa Wali, a brother of mine, is working here in Kaduna and expecting me. Thank you very much in any case." Whereupon Mr. Knott drove Aminu to the flat which Isa shared with Sule Katagum. These two roommates were later taken to task for associating with their friend Aminu, the flaming revolutionary. On at least one occasion the reproof came from the Senior Assistant Secretary in charge of security—further evidence of the contradictions in British policy at that time.

The following morning, the awe-stricken Aminu was picked up by Mr. Knott and driven to an interview with the Queen's representative, the Governor himself. His remarks, though cordial, did not exactly put Aminu at ease, for they had to do with Aminu's sharp criticisms of him and the government he represented. "You have indicated that you think we intentionally keep the North backward, and the North and South divided—that you want us to go so that your country may have independence. You're a man from an important Kano family, young and full of spirit, but you must realize that we don't intentionally prevent changes and keep the country from progressing."

Aminu listened open-mouthed to the highest voice in the land and said nothing. He was dismissed with, "I thought I should meet and exchange a few words of welcome with you, but it's really Mr. Knott who will give you the particular reasons for your visit."

Mr. Knott started in a similar vein, but quickly reached in for details. "You may be critical of us, but we really like men like you, who are ahead of your countrymen. You have attacked our misuse of taxes, claiming we are milking Nigeria for Britain's advantages; yet we are ready not only to show you how our funds are spent but to have you participate. We want you to come to work for the financial section of the government, to see for yourself.

"If you prefer, we can make you the next editor of our Hausa-language newspaper here in Zaria, where you can keep in touch with your people all over the country. You see, we are ready to use your capacities; we have nothing to hide."

Aminu answered, "I will certainly consider your offer, but you of course realize that I am not alone in my endeavors. I would want to discuss it with my friends and will be happy to transmit my decision to you through the Bauchi Resident."

As he concluded, the Chief Secretary remarked that if neither of the two posts pleased Aminu, they would consider something else; for they wanted to place him in a position where he would be happy and could do the most good.

When Aminu discussed it with Sa'adu and the others back in Bauchi, they all concluded that this proposal was merely a ruse, an attempt to disperse the small group of Bauchi activists and render them impotent. So he told the resident of Bauchi that he appreciated the government's offers, but he was really an educator and preferred to stay with the school system. A few months later he realized that the British were more canny and had more resources and tricks up their collective sleeve than he. In January 1949, he was told by the director of education from Kaduna headquarters, while on an inspection visit, that a new teachers' training college was being built at Maru in Sokoto Province, made to order for Aminu. He would be headmaster and could do what he wished, and wouldn't he like that? This time Aminu had boxed himself in, and could not refuse, for the suggested assignment was in education and he had been waiting over a year. Three months later he left with his family for this remote school, far from his hub of activity in the past but still deep in Hausaland.

8.

THE REBEL

When Joseph Tarka, native of the Middle Belt area of Nigeria and currently Federal Commissioner of Communications, first met Aminu Kano, he said that he was quite startled. He was sure that someone of Aminu's reputation throughout the North must be tall, broad-shouldered, and imposing. Instead, a rather short gentleman, slight of build, with curly, close-cropped hair and beautiful straight white teeth, presented himself. In the early days of Maru Teachers' College, too, Aminu's reputation had preceded him, so that Abubakar Gumi, a newly arrived junior teacher, must have been equally surprised to have an unassuming, dark brown-skinned man with somewhat stooped shoulders appear and identify himself as his headmaster.

The British had evidently seen to it that another aspect of Aminu's reputation preceded him too. To the extent that he advocated reform of the old institutions they favored him. To the extent that he pushed for their own elimination from the scene, in order to achieve this, they opposed him. But they felt that they had to separate him from Sa'adu Zungur and from his other companions, get him out of Bauchi and at the same time slow him down. Further complicating the attitude of British administrators was their awareness that he had made extensive connections at the Colonial Office and with persons of influence in England, including left-wing MPs.

If Aminu had not already had ample evidence to demonstrate their ongoing ambivalent concern toward him, he found it a few months later when as acting Education Officer he was inadvertently given free access to certain confidential files. There he found his own dossier, which included a warning to local Sokoto authorities about what to expect upon his arrival. On the basis of this admonition, the

117

Sokoto officials at Maru could have visualized a bearded ogre, capable of starting a jihad, rather than a short, good-humored and unimpressive-looking young man.

Aminu, on the other hand, had his own conflict. He was disturbed at the British role in maintaining the onerous emirate system, yet dependent on them to change it. And in the midst of all of these hesitations and confusion, he was sent into the lion's den, to Maru, this small village in Sokoto Province.

Sokoto was considered the most conservative section of a very conservative North. It had been the seat of the jihad of Usman Dan Fodio, and had remained the center of traditional and religious authority to the extent that decentralized control of the northern emirates hadn't eaten it away. Here Aminu would be isolated, but even so the British were apprehensive, fearful of putting his talents to the test in an area that was still considered religiously sensitive and inflammable. They showed the Native Authorities their confidential reports and asked them to keep a watchful eye on this potential troublemaker. The Native Authorities wondered why, if he was so dire and disquieting a figure, such an upstart was being sent to their area; but then they had not been consulted.

Back in Bauchi, in 1948, Aminu had seriously considered leaving the government service, as indicated by a notation in his diary at the end of that year: "Government people are incompetent and stupid—[I] will resign within two years to join politicians." Instead he evidently decided not to cut back his relatively open political activity and to pass the buck to the government, for up to this point he had somewhat successfully played the N.A. against the British administration and vice versa, utilizing their built-in conflicts and inconsistencies to get things done.

When he arrived in Maru, the new school was still under construction, making it necessary for students and staff to double up in improvised billets for two or three months. On the staff there were the education officer, A. J. Spicer, Aminu as headmaster, one other Englishman, and two or three Nigerians, including the abovementioned Abubakar Gumi. The latter had recently completed his studies in the School for Arabic Studies in Kano and was hired to teach Arabic, mathematics, and religion, while Aminu taught English and the social sciences. Mr. Spicer taught some classes too, but went on leave for some months, shortly after the school opened, leaving Aminu in full charge as acting education officer. While serving in this capacity, he understandably thought that he was entitled to the wages of an education officer, and precipitated a running feud with the authorities, who tried to keep him in check by refusing the increment.[1]

Access to the above-mentioned files revealed that the British had him pegged as an excellent teacher, but one who was "running too fast." According to this report, he was frustrated by a lack of educated people around him, and therefore should have a job where he would be among his intellectual equals. Left alone, he would be dangerous. A job as lecturer in Hausa at Oxford University was offered him, which he quickly turned down.

The many unresolved conflicts in Aminu's life continued to spur him on. Uncompromising in his criticism of whatever injustices he could ferret out, he rashly and unhesitatingly challeged any authority that he thought was perpetuating them. As he says, "I hated government that *sat on* people." At Maru he became embroiled in local activity and controversy almost immediately. Sokoto was the citadel of traditional power, and the Sultan of Sokoto its symbol. All cowered and bowed to him—except Aminu, that is.

In each government department in his area, the Sultan had men assigned to serve as private eyes. Professor C. S. Whitaker puts it this way: "An emir's control over his territory rested to a considerable extent on his superior command of sources of information. . . . Effective rule presupposed the ability to assess accurately the strength of various parties. . . . To this end, the emir employed a variety of persons (Yan Labari, or Sons of Information), whose primary duty it was to inform him of all happenings of potential or present significance."[2] Aminu was apparently unaware of this practice. When greeted by an elderly man hanging about the school site, Aminu extended alms to him, assuming he had some working function there. Not until several weeks later did he learn that this was the Sultan's Yan Labari. Then, when he asked the old man to leave the grounds and threatened to have him arrested if he showed up the following day, the private eye was quite dismayed. He immediately took a lorry to Sokoto to report his difficulties to the Sultan, setting off the first of several eruptions between the Sultan and Aminu.

The repercussions sifted back downward in the form of a letter from the British district officer calling Aminu to task and asking what harm the old man was doing. Aminu's smoldering response pointed out that he was not working for the Sultan but for the British government, and that even if this were not true, he could not tolerate someone sitting in front of him all day to spy on him—custom notwithstanding.

Nor did Aminu, the thorough political animal, permit himself to be isolated. Almost immediately upon his arrival in Maru, he paid his respects to the local authorities, wandered about the streets and the marketplace to talk to the people. He thought of setting up a discussion circle, but there were too few educated people in the area. Gusau, the closest town of any size, was thirty-five miles away, over terrible, barely passable roads. In fact, so bad were the corrugations and ruts that a British district officer passing through Gusau on the way to Sokoto almost got killed while passing over a gorge, one of the worst spots. The following day, a mass of laborers were out repairing it. The day after that, a stinging letter was sent to the newspaper *Gaskiya* by the new headmaster at Maru Teachers' Training College, pointing out that dozens of Nigerians might have been killed on that road in the past, but nothing was done about it until one precious Englishman's life was endangered—and Aminu was on the carpet once again.

And then there was the conflict over the land. Astute Aminu tried not to address the talakawa in regard to the total inadequacy of the system, though he himself believed that to be so. Rather, he spoke of the most flagrant abuses of their rights. About six months after his arrival, Aminu discovered through his many new friends among the local residents, that the land on which the school was built had been taken from about thirty farmers, who up to that point had either been paid only partially or not at all. He took up the cudgels for them in the form of a letter to the authorities urging prompt payment. It evoked an indignant response from the British. By this time they were truly beginning to be fed up with this upstart, always so ready to take on anyone and everyone, big or small. "Before you spout off, please verify your facts. Incontrovertible evidence shows that the Native Authority was paid at the proper time for the land." Aminu was certainly gleeful at such a response, for though the N.A. had received payment, it had never reached the farmers. Where, then, was the money? After much heat, the farmers thanked Aminu profusely, for at long last they got their money, though not without dire threats of recrimination. This little incident did not, of course, further endear Aminu to the Sultan. Although he and almost anyone of consequence who passed the school would normally stop by to pay their respects, the Sultan thereafter gave it a wide berth.

All this local "acclimatization" did not in the least affect Aminu's activities on a region-wide basis. Every holiday he would return to Kano—but not to relax. There were the chapters of the Northern Teachers' Association in Katsina (sometimes enroute) and in Kano itself. And when he arrived home, one of the first things he would do was schedule lectures in the School for Arabic Studies or the local library. There he would attempt to awaken the people to the need for study and learning, or talk of the inadequacies of their institutions and what to do about them. In Kano at that time, people were still encouraged to give lectures, for they were not yet clearly regarded as a threat. When the young students from the School for Arabic Studies, or elsewhere in Kano, heard that Aminu was coming— whether through an official announcement by the headmaster or other sources—they would flock to his lectures.

The political pot was beginning to come to a boil. The inaugural meeting of the Northern People's Congress held in Kaduna in June 1949, with some five hundred in attendance, set the stage for its first general meeting in Kano in December of the same year. In the brief interval of six months, the organization already had ninety delegates, representing thousands. The British approached this convention with much trepidation, but with official sanction. At one of the opening sessions, a district officer, a Mr. Stevens, was sent by the resident to convey his official greetings. He did so in somber terms, warning the assembled delegates that they could accomplish the desired reforms only if they moved slowly and with caution; that one must learn to walk before one can run. This was the first time he had spoken to and mingled with an audience that included merchants and talakawa. His simple admonitions evoked a response whose echo to this day still reverberates throughout the public and private halls in Nigeria, and which almost any "Northerner [of prominence] today will recall with pride and amusement."[3] Aminu rose to ask that the delegates give the speaker a vote of thanks for his words of advice, but that he should report back to his superiors that: "If we go on foot, we will not walk, we will run. And if we fall, we will pick ourselves up and run again. But mark you, we will *not* go on foot. You might tell us to go by camel, or horse, but we will even skip the motor car and go by plane. . . . And the British had best not deny us the choice of our means of transportation, no matter how fast."[4]

Abubakar Imam, a leader of the more cautious element present at the meeting, reports in retrospect that "it didn't take Aminu too long to realize that we were going to walk too slowly for him and he would have to find another vehicle for himself";[5] for to Abubakar that was the principal difference between them—just speed.

But Aminu and his associates thought there was more to it than that. The Kano contingent voted to affiliate with the NPC—thus complicating matters, for they were the more militant group. The "go slow" advocates were essentially saying, "The British will disappear as antagonists if we organize ourselves to maintain the emirate structure," but the radicals within the organization felt that a two-pronged attack was necessary. The British were not the enemy except insofar as they maintained the emirs. "All we have to do is get rid of the autocratic structure, and the British will leave for lack of control or purpose."

When the Kano delegates who had sought the politicization of the NPC were turned down by the December Congress, a regrouping took place. Still pushing for the same goals, seven members, led by Maitama Sule, a Hausa schoolteacher, and Bello Ijuma, a Yoruba resident in Kano, decided to opt for a frankly political organization. Sule, a foundation member and the man who proposed the name of the party, reports that Aminu wasn't involved as a charter member of the Northern Elements Progressive Union (NEPU), but he indicates clearly that Aminu Kano was an active consultant. "It was his brain that made it work and his courage that kept it going." Maitama

Sule himself was summoned to the governor's office with each NEPU pronouncement of a political nature, and was threatened with expulsion as a teacher. He finally gave up when he was accosted in the street, roughed up, and threatenend with further physical violence if he continued. "I couldn't stand the victimization,"[6] he said much later (1969). He went over to the NPC when it eventually became political, and later rose to cabinet rank (Minister of Mines and Power).

Aminu's role in the organization of NEPU was slightly hazy. As a government employee, what he did had to be done surreptitiously, in light of General Order 40 (B) which explicitly forbade government servants to take part in political action. Not until he left Maru several months later could he openly participate in NEPU activities and take over the dominant role in the party. Nevertheless, it is an open secret that he was deeply involved prior to that. His diary notes various meetings with NEPU people, and in his files a copy of an NEPU manifesto over his signature, dated 1949, was unearthed. The manifesto advanced eight basic principles, which not only were used for NEPU but were also advanced as basic principles urged upon the historic Northern People's Congress meeting at Jos in December 1950. Aminu, in his initial attempts to form an organization, even thought of forming a "Socialist Party of Nigeria" and wrote to the Independent Labour Party in England for help.

Apart from these organizational endeavors, the impact of Aminu's ideas was felt throughout the region. He kept up a constant barrage of letters to individuals and to any newspapers that would print them. Among these were Dr. Azikiwe's Southern-based newspaper, the *Comet,* which had begun issuing an edition in Kano, printed in Hausa and English; *Gaskiya,* the government Hausa-language paper; and the English-language *Citizen.* Since they were the literate Northerner's only source of current information, Aminu sent his vigorous letters to all of them. His rash attacks covered a broad field, stopping at nothing. A letter[7] written from Maru in 1949, captioned, "Is the Government Awake or Asleep?", complained of administrative inactivity in the face of a drought that was gripping the region. "Is the government going to say, 'Let us wait until another year'? Why not dig huge [irrigation] wells if the Niger or Benue [rivers] cannot be utilized? The money? You could borrow it from

England or [the] U.S. . . . Anyway, let the country see that something is [being done]."

The only chance Aminu really had to travel through the region,
attending meetings and organizing, was during the school holidays.
After these trips he would return to Maru and take up the struggle
on a local level once again. But he never stopped burrowing. Once
he returned to the school, his letter writing would start up again. At
one point, every emir in the North, every important religious mallam,
and many of Aminu's friends received copies of a communication
questioning whether the Islamic religion permitted the emirs to
accept specifically Christian awards from Christian countries. More
pointedly, he inquired whether the C.B.E. (Commander of British
Empire) award of the Cross of St. George, which had been bestowed
on some of the leading emirs, should be worn. Since the emirs all
fancied themselves religious leaders, one can imagine what a stir that
created. The only responses came from friends who agreed that such
actions were unacceptable in Islamic tradition, but the rumblings in
the remote back rooms of palaces and government offices assumed
the proportions of an earthquake—and Aminu had another demerit
to his name.

In Sokoto Province itself, Aminu came into his first significant
contact with Ahmadu Bello, the Sardauna of Sokoto, who was to
become the chief proponent of cautiously and slowly maneuvering
the established traditional rulers into positions of control in a modern
society—and from that vantage point, Aminu's arch antagonist. In
1943, the Sultan's court had convicted Bello of misappropriations of
jangali, or cattle tax. Yet as a direct descendant of Mohammed Bello,
son of Dan Fodio, and as grandson of the eighth Fulani sultan in
Sokoto,[8] the Sardauna was a potential choice for Sultan when the
occasion arose. An ambitious, young, educated, competent climber,
he was a formidable antagonist in one of those traditional power
struggles at the top of the ladder. The jangali trial was part of that
struggle, and in spite of his total immersion in the traditional administrative apparatus, the Sardauna won his case by an unprecedented
action. He went above the head of the Sultan and appealed to the
British superstructure. His resulting acquittal strengthened his hand.

During this prepolitical period, Aminu had been teaching at
Bauchi and had been jumping into every controversy in which he felt

a principle was involved. He knew that the conflict between the Sultan and the Sardauna was moving along traditional lines, but he had two reasons for coming to the Sardauna's defense. First, the young man was being singled out for victimization, and, second, he was pursuing the goal of modernization that Aminu sought uninterruptedly throughout his life. The first meeting between the two to-be lifetime adversaries, was through the College Old Boys Association, the alumni association for Katsina and Kaduna College and the source of the bulk of Northern Nigeria's leadership. Aminu thought enough of the Sardauna's struggle at the time to contribute an inordinate proportion of his meager income toward a defense fund for him, a fact which greatly impressed the Sardauna.

In the continuing rivalry between himself and the Sultan, the Sardauna recognized the rash young headmaster of Maru Teachers' Training College as a potential ally. Frequently, when passing the school en route to nearby Gusau, or to Sokoto, he would stop to visit and have tea with him. When, in turn, Aminu came to Sokoto as a representative chosen by his district to participate in a provincial constitutional conference (a procedure outlined by the then Governor MacPherson), he stayed at the home of Sardauna Ahmadu. It was on that occasion that the Sultan made one of several conciliatory overtures to Aminu. He sent one of his close councilors to invite him to a private audience; but since he didn't want this to be known to the Sardauna or anyone else, he asked Aminu to come at two A.M. On the night preceding this appointment, while Aminu was being taken to the Sokoto Middle School to deliver a lecture, he told the Sardauna about the impending meeting. When the Sultan heard this he was furious, and canceled the audience.

This type of traditional rivalry at the top, exemplified by the Sultan-Sardauna conflict, had a religious aspect, too. Over the centuries, there have been interpreters of Islam who have gathered large numbers of followers around them and their interpretations, into sects that in many instances have crossed national boundaries and been carried on from one generation to the next. In Northern Nigeria there are two such major religious fraternities. The great Shehu, Usmand Dan Fodio was a member of a group called Khadiriyya, as are his descendants in the royal line of Sultans of Sokoto, their relatives and clients, and most Sokoto Province residents. The

current leader of the other sect, called Tijjaniyya, is based in Senegal, but in Northern Nigeria its high priest has been the Emir of
Kano; and consequently the area of Kano is a bedrock of this sect.
Since the lines between religious and secular leadership in Hausaland
overlap considerably, it is not surprising that a rivalry has grown up
between the two groups.

Many of the people of eastern Sokoto were Tijjaniyya followers,
so that when Aminu arrived, the British, the Sultan, and his courtiers
were concerned. They associated him with Tijjaniyya because of his
Kano origins and worried lest his abrasive presence might arouse
smoldering rivalries. This geographic, religious and sociological
juxtaposition did give Aminu fertile soil for his attempts to politicize
the backward north, but he was not interested in stirring up religious
differences in the old style traditional areas of conflict. Nevertheless,
a few years later, his party NEPU found great strength in areas like
eastern Sokoto, that already had a history of simmering challenge
to authority.

In 1949 and 1950, however, politics per se had not yet begun,
so that Aminu had to make his presence felt in other ways. He moved
cautiously, planning step by step. He knew Sokoto history well, and
guarded his moves. Though he joked informally with the laborers
and local residents, he was a strict disciplinarian with the students,
regardless of their parentage—sarakuna or talakawa, high- or lowborn (a welcome change from past practices). He took them to salute
and pay their respects to the village head, the district head, and the
local alkali and then on Fridays, he and his teacher of religion,
Abubakar Gumi, accompanied them to the mosque to pray. Usually
the two men waited outside the building, but on one occasion during
the rainy season they were forced to go inside. There they noticed
that the imam who led the services was omitting the ablutions normally performed each of the five times prayers are said during the
day.

According to the ritual prescribed in the Koran, the exposed
parts of the human anatomy—the hands, feet, and face—must be
washed prior to each prayer session. When absolutely no water is
available, one may place the palms of the hands on the ground, then
shake and wring off the dust. Should no water be available on Fridays, one must stay at home to say the required prayers. But Aminu

and Abubakar saw that the imam was merely placing his hands on the ground—this in the mosque and within easy access to water. When they confronted him with his ritualistic errors, he refused to alter his behavior, saying that was the way his father had done it. So Aminu, after careful consultation with his authority, Abubakar Gumi [some years later to become the Grand Kadi of the North (equivalent to an Islamic Chief Justice)] withheld his students from attendance at the Friday service. The ensuing flurry of excitement resulted in a promise from the district head that the imam would either change or be removed. But when the boys returned to the mosque the following week, he was still repeating the same errors. The Chief Alkali of Sokoto, the Education Officer, and the Sultan himself were all consulted several times, but the only decision the Sultan could reach was that the imam could not (or would not) be moved because he was ill. Although this was no affair of the British government, since only the Sultan could appoint or remove imams, the British feared that a Khadiriyya-Tijjaniyya religious feud was in the making. They associated it with Aminu's Kano origins and though Abubakar Gumu was Khadiriyya and from Sokoto Province, wasn't he trained at the Kano School of Arabic Studies? Could Aminu be trying to displace the Great Shehu Usman Dan Fodio? The tempest raged, involving Kaduna central headquarters and the highest government authorities. It did not die down until Aminu and Abubakar Gumi devised an acceptable compromise: They would send the boys to the mosque, and do their own prayers privately, back at the school. Aminu felt satisfied that the Sultan's infallibility had been effectively challenged and that an individual's right to determine right from wrong had been established.

This doctrine of free choice has represented Aminu's approach to religion over the years. He was religious because he was moral on a gut level, rather than because of an overwhelming belief in the power of the supernatural and the fear of retribution. As James Coleman puts it, he felt that, "Although Islam like Catholicism isn't necessarily conservative, the political elite used certain interpretations of Islam to impose—hierarchy—political deference and subordination."[9] And his profoundly religious background gave him the capacity to protest against these interpretations in an Old Testament style.

Aminu related his religion to the welfare of man. His stated belief in God implies a gratitude for the good things in life, including an essential feature called *isalah,* or doing good for others (the group). To share is the highest goal. The ultimate in self-gratification, he feels, is self-denial for the common welfare. Although God knows what is right, it is incumbent upon man to be able to choose right from wrong, act accordingly, and find freedom and release in the correct choice.

Armed with this enlightened approach to religion, he was able to apply it in situations where a religion rigidly imposed from above was used as a weapon of oppression. For every moral challenge, he could find quotations hidden away in the Koran and its commentaries to fortify his case. This knowledge, coupled with an indifference to self-aggrandizement frequently bordering on asceticism, usually made his case strong and unassailable. The primary weapon left to his opponents was repression and victimization, or perhaps derision.

It wasn't until some months later that Aminu left Maru, but this seemingly trivial religious conflict and the Sultan's uncompromising reaction to it was influential in determining Aminu's ultimate path. Of course, the Sultan had once again stopped coming to the school, but he did make several tangential attempts at reconciliation, including gifts of native cloth for the education officer who was leaving, a cow for the students, and a turban for Aminu. These were all received politely, without any rancor, but the die had been cast.

There was yet another explosive incident before Aminu left Sokoto. The Sokoto boys according to Mr. Spicer,[10] the Englishman who served for a time as education officer, were not as motivated as the Bauchi students. They were indolent and difficult, particularly those from the city itself, whose residents were stifled by a heavy cloud of religious and traditional conservatism. Since Aminu's clashes with the Sultan became easily evident to the boys in school, several of them felt they had to take action in defense of their traditional ruler. The action they chose was to complain to the Sultan that he was being abused in the classroom. They also refused the food served them by Abubakar Gumi at one point. In the ensuing conflict, Aminu proved that he had not spoken ill of the Sultan in class (at least not obviously). A strict disciplinarian, he insisted on dismissing the five students who participated. Two of them returned later, but Aminu had won his point.

Why did Aminu leave Maru? Usman Bida, who had been a classmate of his at Kaduna, said it was his impression that Aminu was forced to resign. Similarly, Sule Katagum, a close friend of Aminu's who had once been his pupil at Bauchi, agrees. He feels that Aminu's ideas were incompatible with those of traditional Sokoto, and the education authorities simply put on the pressure.

But whether he was forced to resign his last tie to the establishment or whether he arrived at this decision through his own free will and staunch decision, would that have altered the meaning of this decisive act? There is little doubt that he himself considered the choice his own. Notations in his diary in April and May 1950 reveal that his inner need to resign grew stronger and his course of action clearer and more determined. When the Deputy Director of Education for the North told Aminu that he could not be reappointed if he continued his political activity, Aminu noted in his diary, "All right, that's his problem. Mine is to resign by next year."

Then on Oct. 12, 1950—"One can't realize difficulty arriving at a momentous decision until one comes to do so. Date still undecided. The 15th or 29th."

Friday, Oct. 13—"Stand firm in submitting resignation on 16 Oct.! May God be with us all!" Fasted to dusk.

(penny stamp was affixed in diary on 16th to mark it a red letter day)

Sun Oct. 15—"Fasted all day to get greater moral courage . . . eighty-three letters to all parts of the world!"

Oct. 16—"Resignation letter to education officer early morning —one month notice!"

Nov. 1—"Farewell address to students. They collected 39/9 for me to buy souvenir—Hmmmm!"

And finally, he wrote happily on Nov. 4, "Left Maru for the last time." *Gaskiya* published a short notice of his resignation with an accompanying warning to the country to watch this dangerous man carefully. On November 11, 1950, an explanation entitled "The Cause of My Resignation" was printed in Kano by the *Daily Comet:* "I resigned because I refuse to believe that this country is by neces-

sity a prisoner of the Anglo-Fulani aristocracy—I resigned because
I fanatically share the view that the Native Authorities . . . are woe-
fully hopeless in solving our urgent educational, social, economic,
political or even religious problems—

"My stay in England . . . has hardened my soul in elevating truth,
freedom and above all human rights for which the world fought off
fascism—

"I had twice been threatened with the merciless fangs [of General Order #40 (B)] . . . while all around are piled corruption, mis-
rule, political bluff, slavery under another garb, naked nepotism,
tyranny, poverty . . . unnecessary retention of hereditary parasites,
naked and shameless economic exploitation. . . .

"I cannot tolerate these things because of their awful smell. . . .

"I am prepared to be called by any name. Call me a dreamer or
call me a revolutionary; call me a crusader or anything this imperialist government wills. I have seen a light on the far horizon and I
intend to march into its full circle either alone or with anyone who
cares to go with me. . . .

"To these same suppressors of our people, I say this: 'Look
Out! Africa is a sleeping giant no more! She is just about to shake off
the stupor. . . .' "

9. CRUSADER-POLITICIAN

In January 1966, when Major General Aguiyi-Ironsi took over the reins of government from what was left of the leadership of the first Federal Republic of Nigeria, all political parties were abolished and remain so today. A discussion, therefore, of the birth, growth and demise of these parties would be superfluous, if it were not for the fact that the leaders and people who participated in the building of these parties during the pre-independence decade are still very much alive. When the time comes for democratic rule to return, they will again emerge into the political arena in one form or another. The movement for Nigerian independence which launched the political parties is no longer a factor—at least not in its original form. However, the leadership of tomorrow (those who will have survived) and the shape of political things to come will all bear a direct relationship to the dynamics and the political configuration of the 1950's, when these parties blossomed forth.

When Aminu gave up teaching in November 1950, politics in Northern Nigeria was still in its birth throes. The first political party, the NEPU (Northern Elements Progressive Union) had been formed just two months previously. Aminu had not the faintest idea where his next meals would come from, but he was ready to start organizing a revolution from a point where there was hardly such a thing as organization and independent political action was *verboten*. In essence, he was undertaking not to lead a revolution, but to create one. The people had been totally subjugated to the autocratic emirate system for centuries, wherein a gathering of any kind, whether for acquisition of knowledge or for a wedding, needed the express approval of the emir. No protest movement had emerged since the great jihad of 1803 save a palace war here or there, in which a ruler or two may have changed, but not the ruled.

There was fertile ground for change in 1950, however, both at the top and bottom. At the top there were some educated people, competent to assume leadership and aware of the need for it, but who somehow lacked sufficient courage, consistency, or sincerity of purpose. On the bottom there were undoubtedly people with these qualities, but they lacked organizational know-how and orientation. Aminu Kano seemed the only leader on the scene at the time willing to try to combine the two.

To the extent that this dual capacity was within him it was enhanced by his awareness of the gap between the old ways and the new, and by his continuing urge to speak to the people in their own terms. Emir Jafaru of Zaria summed it up by remarking, "The damage done by Aminu Kano was to let the talakawa know they could say NO"—after generations of acquiescence. By giving up his teaching position, he was saying figuratively to anyone who would listen, that one could thumb his nose at the established order of things, do something about his fate, and yet emerge intact. He be-came a symbol of successful defiance for the young modernists in the cities as well as for a significant group of tradespeople and the talakawa, urban and rural. Instead of sullenly grumbling over their problems without the least effect, they now could hitch their star to Aminu and NEPU and dream and hope for some solutions. Aminu, on the other hand, consistently reaffirmed his confidence in the integrity of the common man. There were times when he saw only listlessness around him, but he continued to recognize the need for a leader figure who could behave in the spirit of their legendary ancestors—one whom they could emulate—and he saw himself as that leader. He started with this deeply imbedded concept of the importance of charisma, modifying it somewhat as he was forged in the fires of organizing politics.

Aminu left Maru, which was little more than a tiny hamlet, to return to the largest metropolis in Northern Nigeria—Kano. Historically, this thousand-year-old community had served as a trading center and distribution point for trans-Saharan caravans and traders from all four directions. As far back as 1824, it was referred to by Captain Hugh Clapperton (supposedly the first Euro-

Kano marketplace

pean to enter Kano) as "the mercantile center of the whole country
. . . and at least as important as Timbuktu."[1] Heinrich Barth in 1851
called Kano "this African London, Birmingham, or Manchester,"
and described "its clay houses, huts, sheds, green, open . . . pasture
for oxen, horses, camels, donkeys and goats . . . deep hollows containing ponds overgrown with the water plant . . . or pits freshly dug
up to form material for some new buildings. . . . The people in all
varieties of costume, from the naked slave up to the most gaudily
dressed Arab."[2]

If one entered the heart of Kano today, this might very well be
what he saw. There have been changes, of course. The officially
estimated population in 1933 was about 100,000 within the city
walls, 320,000 within fifteen miles of the city, and over a million
within thirty miles of the city. The year 1958 saw the addition of a
modern airport; industries have flourished; hospitals and schools
have slowly appeared. But back in 1950, as one approached the
city walls one still saw the carefully tilled lands, farmed with guinea
corn, millet, ground nuts, and occasionally cassava, onions, or rice.

The thirteen gates that pierced the eleven miles of the broken
down wall encircling the inner city were still standing, though some
had already been widened to permit cars to pass through. Residence
in the old town, within these city walls, was still segregated and
restricted to local Hausa-Fulanis. The few Europeans and Asians
(360), and Africans from outside Hausaland (6,600) living outside
the walls in 1933, had multiplied slightly in number by 1950. Railroad yards and tracks (built in 1911), police barracks, together with
some sturdy stores and offices, were tied together by reasonably
good roads. The heart of the city had (and still has) closely packed
houses of mud, separated only by narrow alleys serving as footpaths,
open sewers, and drainage ditches—wide enough to permit a horse,
donkey or camel to pass, but not a car. Hundreds of stagnant borrow
pits, large and small, dotted the landscape then as now.

In addition, the emir and his subordinate pyramid of district,
village, and hamlet heads, all chosen by him from hereditary aristocracy, have been unchanged over the century and a half of Fulani
rule, notwithstanding the arrival of the British at the turn of the
twentieth century. As has been pointed out in a previous chapter,
the resort of the British to a "sole Native Authority" tended to

A corner of Kano City

Sewer—and children at play

centralize the legislative, executive, and religious powers of the emir and his deputies to an even greater extent than had existed previously. If anyone came in conflict with the law or the administrators, he was tried before the alkalis appointed by the emir. When the British arrived, though they eventually lost out, there were among them some who felt that their authority should not be shared with the emir through Indirect Rule. H. R. Palmer one of the strongest proponents of this thinking said "After all, the only friends we really have are the talakawa (common people) . . . The Fulani are only sojourners like ourselves. Why should they take the meat off the bone we have taken from them?"—and Aminu Kano wanted to give the entire carcass back to the talakawa where he felt it came from in the first place. Dr. John Paden in the conclusion to a paper presented at the University of Ife in 1968 said "In summary, the powers of the Emir of Kano probably increased overall during the colonial period . . . [though]—there was always the potential threat of deposition [by the colonial structure]."[3]

It was this city of Kano—with its cosmopolitanism, ethnic complexion, and Moslem sects—that produced Aminu Kano. It was this mammoth Goliath Aminu now proposed to tackle. In addition, he was taking on the approximately thirty other emirates that constituted the Northern Region. Even more, he had to deal with the establishment's desperate struggle to keep itself intact, to remain in power. It is difficult for a Westerner to realize how deeply the traditional society had penetrated into the total fabric, the very pores of every individual in it, but an understanding of this fact is essential if one wants to delve into the extent of Aminu Kano's challenge.[4]*

Sarauta, or the inherited status of the aristocratic few, represented the core of the system, for control was imposed in this way: The emir appointed his judicial representatives (alkalis), his executive and administrative assistants from among particular clans, and a select few of these in turn chose the emir's successor, thus making for self-perpetuation. But there was flexibility, too, for a rigid and unbending society that made no allowance for change

---

*M. G. Smith points out that in Zaria, one of every four compounds had an employee of the Native Authority Government.

would not be likely to weather the many crises it undoubted faced over the years.[5]* The "Native Autocracy," as Aminu referred to it, hadn't waited for the '50's and Aminu Kano to prove its flexibility. In its past, it had permitted social movement for the ambitious within the prescribed classes, clans, and trades, at the same time ensuring that upward mobility was achieved more through clientage and personal relationships than through ability. An intricate system of patronage for both competence *and* loyalty provided the only way for a worthy man to advance—until modern politics entered the scene. Even non-aristocratic prosperous traders (*attajirai*) did not assume the expected stance of a bourgeoisie, so long as concessions were made to keep them on the side of traditional relationships. Most of them stayed within the limits of the predetermined class structure. The growth of marketing boards and their political control by the traditional authority fostered an interdependence, unlike Western development.

As the traditional government in Northern Nigeria adapted itself to modernity, it became clear that a changeover to the democratic forms advocated by Aminu would be literally revolutionary, since in order to do so, power would have to be wrested from one class by another. He conceived that this revolution would take place by changing the old feudal, static society to a full-fledged modern state—and if this meant a deliberate mobilization toward rebellion, he was ready for it. He had the firm support of George Padmore, one of the really influential leaders of pan-Africanism and anticolonialism, first in England, then in Ghana. At one point Padmore quarreled with Kwame Nkrumah, his disciple and ultimate champion and protector, saying that NEPU was better organized for class struggle than Nkrumah's own party, the CPP. Therefore, he argued, the struggle for African independence should be based in Nigeria and that all funds for that struggle should go to the NEPU. This he

---

*Professor C. S. Whitaker in a lengthy doctoral thesis deals with the interplay between the old and the new in Northern Nigerian politics, showing clearly how the system has adjusted itself so as to maintain power when under external pressure to change. He observed that "Those originally possessing political power might make 'creative adjustments'. . . in a way that would also conserve important traditional patterns. . . . We can now see, in the case of Northern Nigeria, how each of these possibilities was . . . manifested. . . ."

confirmed after visiting Kano in 1956 and 1957 and after correspondence with Aminu. He felt that the Nigerian modernists were closer to the people and that, contrary to Nkrumah's approach, they attacked the chieftancy system directly.

Aminu knew how difficult it would be to achieve his goals, for he never deceived himself as to the state of the North at that time. As he said later, "If by some miracle we were able to achieve a full-fledged democracy overnight, we would undoubtedly have to resort to the same class for administrative roles. They are the only ones sufficiently educated to take over the reins of government."[6]

This realistic assessment was what kept him close to the people, in spite of his militant revolutionary ideals. Although he assumed that capitalist reformism could not produce the desired results and his struggle therefore included socialism, he, and subsequently the party he led, talked with the people directly about specific issues, rather than trying to impose revolutionary, utopian, and inconceivable goals upon them. The talakawa were not ready to receive an advanced ideology. Objective observers have all reported (whether favorably or unfavorably) that NEPU was most effective on local issues. And in many cases, though the leaders were unable to wrest consistent political control away from the vested interests, they did force concession after concession in the interests of the talakawa.

Aminu's ideas about how best to accomplish this revolution underwent some change over the years, but in the 1950's they were fervent, clear, militant, and idealistic. On many occasions, he was accused of being too militant, but he never seemed to lose the masses by being too far ahead of them. Rather it was fear of, and loyalty to the traditional rulers that were his consistent enemies. His efforts at that time were directed first and foremost against the family-compact rule (perpetuation of royal and aristocratic dynasties), whereby a small group could continue its hold on the people, and secondarily against the British for retaining this archaic system.

Aminu's own attitudes toward tradition accounted to a great extent for what success he was able to achieve in his approach to the tradition-ridden masses. While recognizing that it was basically harmful and against progress, he knew that it could not be swept away entirely. He and NEPU tried to make use of certain conventional attitudes rather than fight them, approaching each group within a community on whatever level they found them, in this way establishing rapport quickly and effectively. As Aminu said, "A bowl rotates faster at the top than at the bottom."[7] Their strategy depended on which portion of the bowl they were working.

During Aminu's political years, when he knew he would face a hostile crowd in a conservative area where he might have been painted as a Christian, or a friend of Christians, he would begin his speech with the words of their own imams and mallams. Often when he used this approach he could see their initial hostility soften as they warmed to the ideas he expressed. Aminu put it, "One must scratch that part of the body or mind that itches." Whenever the people wished to group according to vocation, Aminu and his supporters helped them to form trade organizations, such as the NEPU Blacksmiths' Association and the NEPU Butchers' Association, in the traditional patterns. Although he recognized this as a compromise, he considered it a necessary compromise, with a purpose. He faced up to the enormity of his challenge with equanimity and decisiveness as though there were no other choice.

Although Aminu entered the political arena with a reputation that reached almost messianic proportions, and although many observers consider the years 1950-1959 the most important period of his life, one cannot help feeling that the roadwork, the arduous day-by-day activities, were what made it important, rather than high-level decision-making, and the conscious implementing of a predetermined plan. The preparatory years were behind him, he had made his big decision to become a professional politician, and he now assumed his role as a mass leader, with the form and shape of his future clearly in focus. That is not to say that this period beginning with the organization of NEPU, and ending with Aminu's election to the Federal Parliament in 1959, did not abound in excitement, decisions, and crises.

When Aminu arrived in Kano from Maru, he immediately set about his political tasks, reaching out in a dozen directions. His diary notes that he arrived on November 6, 1950. Within one week he had discussed the possible initiation of a Moslem Congress with a half dozen leading people; planned the organization of a new type of school; and chaired a meeting of NEPU. Before the month was out, he had attended a dance in his honor; lectured on indirect rule;

received and accepted an offer of a full-time organizing job for the Northern Teachers' Association (of which he was general secretary) at the munificent salary of eight pounds per month; and launched the inaugural meeting of the Moslem Congress. He was a veritable windmill of activity, ending up a month and a half later, with the memorable December convention of the Northern Peoples' Congress (NPC) in Jos.

That meeting was the scene of Northern Nigeria's first open confrontation between the forces of conservatism and radicalism. The majority of the Kano contingent, led by Aminu (finally free of the restraints of government service), advocated politicizing the NPC, either by declaring itself a political organization, or by accepting the newly organized NEPU as its political and/or youth arm. The conservatives were determined to purge the organization of its radical element (namely, Aminu Kano, Sa'adu Zungur, and their followers). They used the nonpolitical nature of the organization and the large number of civil-servant members (legally forbidden to participate in political activity) as their rationalization, even though there is ample evidence to show that they too had begun to think in terms of reorganizing it as a political party. They advanced two alternatives; either the NEPU should disband or its members resign or be expelled.

Before this question reached the floor, however, the agenda called for nominations for new officers. The radicals chose Aminu as their nominee for the office of secretary. Pandemonium broke out. The chairman lost control of the meeting and adjourned it until the following day. At a caucus far into that night, the radicals decided to withdraw from the Congress because the opposing group favored the emirs and wanted to protect the Native Authority—and incidentally because it became clear to them that they would lose all votes. Those who remained reaffirmed their desire to accomplish change without upsetting the applecarts of the emirs. All the members of the radical caucus returned home at that point, to await further directions from Aminu.

Aminu had been busy on many fronts. When he returned to Kano, one of his points of concentration was the so-called *Islamiyya* schools. He knew that so long as obscurantism and mysticism surrounded the religion of the area, it would be very difficult to introduce modern government and modern institutions. Up to that time, the extent of his reformist religious efforts had been to sift through the Koran and its commentaries, hunting for those verses and sections that upheld man's search for knowledge, in order to show that the Islamic religion was not merely a dogma, static and conservative, but a guide to modernity. He pored through the Commentaries written throughout the ages all over the world, including those of Abdullahi, brother of Dan Fodio. He used his own liberal interpretations in his lectures and writings, but not until he resigned from government service did he have the time to pursue a more basic and longer range policy regarding religion, geared to the youth and the schools.

He first tried to convince the leading mallams of Kano to update the teaching in the thousand or more Koranic schools in Kano Emirate alone, by introducing Roman letters and broadening their subject matter. When unsuccessful on this level, he suggested forming a Northern Nigerian Moslem Congress for the same purpose—which would be achieved principally through the organization of new schools independent of the Native Authorities. As always with Aminu, discussion led to action. He persuaded men like Inuwa Wada (though this gentleman quickly fell away when "I lost interest because of the political leanings of the volunteer teachers"),[8] and anyone of influence he could find, to visit the mallams and gain their support, however reluctant. But he himself did not wait. He proceeded to set up the first such school, starting with about thirty (increasing to sixty) children of sympathetic parents. Among them was Hauwa, a five-year-old girl who was "given" to Aminu and Hasia by her admiring mother when they left Maru. They set out to prove that any five-year-old child educated by modern methods could in one year recite the Koran better and learn more Arabic than a similar child in an old-style school could in five years. In the second year, the three R's would be introduced alongside of Koranic teachings, making it unnecessary to transfer the child to the elementary school for that purpose. Aminu felt that a child so trained could read, write, and even interpret the Koran as he himself had done in his childhood. Each of the two or three teachers was paid only a pittance, but they were devoted and the results were obvious. Hauwa and many of her classmates learned their lessons even faster than children in the government schools, because of the additional attention and greater degree of commitment in a private school environment. The education officer who was invited to visit the school was so impressed that he integrated it into the education system. Within a year, about ten such schools were established in Kano, Kaduna, Jos, and other places. The founding group, mostly NEPU supporters, hoped to establish a Department of Reformed Islamic Education that would stand for "refining" rather than "defiling" Islamic education. Lawan Dambazau, a follower of Aminu and an able Arabic scholar, was made director of education.

In the next few years, the establishment came to recognize the obvious political overtones of the schools and to accept their existence as a challenge. The broad mallam support that had been achieved was intimidated and fell away, and many school buildings were wrecked by anti-NEPU hoodlums. During and after the 1951 elections, they beat up some of the teachers, broke their signs, and browbeat the landlord of one of the buildings—with the active support of the emir and the passive support of the British. But the pioneering educational efforts continued. Even though only about two or three of the original schools remain today, there were from fifty to sixty throughout the North, and some were actually taken over by the government or the Native Authorities. By 1958, they had lost most of their political quality and Islamiyya-type schools, offering mixed religious and secular training, became an accepted form of elementary education. Many of the old-style schools adopted modern techniques—blackboards, tables, desks, and the teaching of the English language—and the higher Arabic schools now require a knowledge of the three R's for admission.

Religion was so deeply interwoven into the fabric of Hausa-Fulani society that Aminu had to adapt his politics to it at all times. In order to mobilize a cadre of followers for his political cause, he had to call upon a force within each individual, to supersede personal interest, for when opportunism was the dominant motive, the Native Authority path would undoubtedly yield them greater fruits. He analyzed Gandhi's success in lifting millions of Indians to a high level of dedication, and endeavored to adapt Gandhi's nonviolent techniques to Northern Nigeria. Miss E. P. Miller, a well-known long-time Christian missionary of the Church Missionary Society, living in Kano, observed Aminu in the course of applying these techniques and in his developing relationships with the masses. She concluded that, devout Moslem though he was, Aminu was the bearer of the cross of Jesus Christ, and referred to him as the "Gandhi of Nigeria." The two of them had warm feelings toward each other. Aminu visited her when she was alone, isolated, and going blind. She, in turn, worried about him in times of crisis. Even when taken ill in London, she continued to communicate with Aminu until her death.

Though there were similarities, there was one basic difference between the approach of Gandhi and that of Aminu. When Gandhi spoke of *satyagraha,* or nonviolent resistance, (literally translated as "soul force"), he was thinking of its beneficial effect not only on the individual who employed this technique but on his opponent as well. He wanted people to make the world a better place to live in through the exaltation and uplifting of the self. Not so with Aminu. He also called upon people's better instincts, but at all times emphasized the *group.* He seemed to see asceticism as helping to achieve a political goal, but never really felt impelled to cleanse himself internally. Self-sacrifice was for the collective good, subordinating one's life to raising the economic and educational level of one's people. Security, even one's personal life, marriage, and children all had to be fitted into this guiding principle, and he did not hesitate to ask the same dedication of his followers.

Satyagraha, as conceived by Gandhi, implied trust in the human nature of friend or enemy. "A *satyagrahi* is never afraid to trust the opponent. Even if the opponent plays him false twenty times, the satyagrahi is ready to trust him the twenty-first time, for an implicit trust in human nature is the very essence of his creed."9 Aminu did not have such implicit faith in individuals. He would be quite ready to forgive a man the twenty-first time, but far from ready to trust him. Yet he never harbored a grudge, for he tried to combat ideas, not people. When he took no action against political rivals, or breaches of ethics within his own party, it was because he always accepted the best in those about him. He kept hoping that eventually the best in them would become the dominant quality. Until then, so long as they supported the proper position, he would accept them again and again. If they never arrived, at least he would have had temporary traveling companions.

Although it is said that Gandhi did not believe in self-denial or tormenting the flesh for its own sake, his life style seemed to indicate otherwise. He felt that the needs of the body were simple and that devoting time and emotional energies to rich living wasted the human spirit, in this way distracting the self from realizing its full potential. Aminu, on the other hand, arrived at self-denial by minimizing the self and maximizing the group. Since group achievement was the ultimate aim, pleasures of the flesh and self-indulgence became unimportant. To achieve political power was the goal. If that meant ignoring the body's needs, what did it matter?

During the first years of NEPU organization, Aminu truly believed that nonviolent techniques were the most effective means of gaining adherents to its humanist cause. But he was never really a satyagrahi in the sense that Gandhi meant it. He was too much of a realist to trust implicitly the human nature of his friend or his enemy—or even himself. When he fasted, he was steeling himself for action, not improving himself by a denial of the flesh.

After the NEPU office was opened, a group of young dedicated northerners gave up their jobs to run the affairs of the party. They had no salaries or any regular source of income, so they would pool the small one- or two-pound contributions. At lunchtime, they would go to any *sabon gari* (strangers' quarters) restaurant for a "four-two" meal—laughingly referring to the fourpence they spent for yam stew and the twopence for meat. Four-two became the name of their daily food allowance even after it reached the heights of seven shillings for married workers and five shillings for singles. One of these young men, Yahaya Sabo, reports that it was two years before he could manage to bring his wife to live with him in Kano. Thus they denied themselves not for the uplifting of their spirit, but simply because they had to.

Aminu soon discovered that the NEPU rank and file admired nonviolence and self-sacrifice in its leaders, although they them-selves did not adopt these concepts quite so readily. Many of the lesser lights in and around the party proudly tell of Aminu's patience with the talakawa, of how he would give alms to impoverished, dirty people, urge them to bathe and to launder their clothes—saving his anger only for occasions when the talakawa were victimized. One admirer related that when "A District Head in Gashua molested beat and even threw some NEPU supporters to the bottom of a well, Aminu suggested that when NEPU came to power, only good not evil be done to him, for if we do evil we are the same as they."

Yet another recalled a similar incident in which NEPU supporters in Jos set upon some NPC people in retaliation for severe repressions against NEPU. Many people were hurt in the fracas. Ten days later, Aminu, passing through Jos, berated his sympathizers instead of praising them. Even if they had been victimized, he said, they should still leave such matters to the courts—and to the ultimate judge, God. Because their cause was just, they would ultimately triumph, without the need to take vengeance.

Many more anecdotes of this type could be cited to illustrate this nonviolent approach that characterized the early phase of Aminu's NEPU activity, but when the violence, jailings and killings during the political battles of the 1950's raised the struggle to an unprecedented peak, Aminu openly told his followers to strike back. "The road to freedom is full of thorns and fire, yet happy is he who follows it!" And by 1961 Aminu said that "he who allows himself to be arrested for a crime he did not commit will be expelled from the party, but if he resists and comes to us on a stretcher, he is a hero."[10]

It is his political soul and the flexibility within Aminu that derived from it, that made him different from Gandhi, though they employed similar techniques. Integrity and humility were qualities they shared, with Gandhi's essential concentration on the development of the individual in the process of approaching the end, through abstinence, religion and nonviolence. To Aminu the crux was the goals; modernization, education—and national liberation—and the most effective way to achieve them was through the morality inherent in religion, abstinence and non-violence. This approach gave him latitude to change the means to "selective resistance" if this method proved more efficacious in reaching his goals without compromising them.

Aminu started his life using Dan Fodio as a model; was influenced to a great extent by Gandhi in the early political '50's and then through pragmatism and deep understanding of his people, he was able to flex enough to survive the pre-independence and the First Republic period, to emerge as an effective force for the future without having made any basic compromises. The ties to his traditions and the Koran merged with his Gandhian self denial and his ability to apply modern techniques to the drive for power to yield the man that is Aminu today. As a youth, Aminu considered himself foreordained to lead his people out of the wilderness. He couldn't seethe inwardly or erupt erratically and emotionally in the presence of injustice, for his outlet was in the doing. He was Moses, the man of action. Though he wanted and revered power in order to accomplish his destiny, he would not have it at a sacrifice of basic principle.

We know the wind, not because we see it but because of its effect on us and the objects around us. We feel it on our faces, we see boughs gently bending, leaves fluttering, and we know the wind. So with a leader of men. What effect has he on those around him? Who is being blown? Who is being bent? When the wind that was Aminu Kano was beginning to be felt, some were just brushed; others will testify that a tempest blew in their direction. It is not his family and immediate circle of friends and associates of whom one speaks, but of those who at first knew him not, yet knew of him.

Yahaya Sabo was a senior sanitary inspector in Lafia who had heard of Aminu through his friends in Bauchi. They had written and spoken excitedly of a teacher who spent most of his time with the students, as though he were one of them, and intimately discussed their future and that of their country.

When Aminu came to the town of Lafia in 1949, to help organize a branch of the Northern Teachers' Association and of the Northern People's Congress while the latter was still a cultural organization, Yahaya insisted that he stay in his home. The visit and subsequent ones were short, only a few days at a time—just long enough for the bedazzled young men of Lafia to gather open-mouthed around Aminu while he explained the political process to them before moving on to the next town. When the first meeting of NEPU was held in the old El Duniya Cinema in Kano, Yahaya was present, as he was at the next in Kaduna, representing the Lafia branch. But his employer, the Lafia Native Authority, had refused him permission to take the necessary time off, and upon his return asked him for a signed statement explaining his absence. Whereupon he resigned to join the aforementioned "four-two" club in the NEPU office in Kano, becoming one of the core of young men who abandoned what they were doing to devote themselves to The Cause.

Timothy Monu, born in Jos of Ibo origin, grew up among Hausas, played with them, and spoke their language. After achieving Standard VI at the age of thirteen, he went to work for two years in the tin mines near Jos. He had a strong antipathy to the many injustices he saw all about him—the lack of education for all but a minute percentage of the children; the bowing and scraping of the peasants before their social superiors; or a farmer carrying millet for 36 miles to give the emir his "share".

When he heard Aminu being attacked by the authorities for his militant stand against these injustices, he realized that one did not have to accept his fate but could influence it. Timothy still retained a feeling of kinship for the downtrodden among the northerners even after he moved to Lagos in 1953 to work in the Ministry of Information as a copy typist. It was through some friendly Hausa traders in Lagos that he started to attend NEPU meetings each Sunday. He rose quickly in the local branch, but did not meet his idol until he joined a large group of party faithful who gathered to greet Aminu when he was passing through the city. He too left government service for full-time politics, but didn't come to the party leader's attention until he organized a mass rally in Lagos as assistant secretary general of the Western Region of NEPU. The police and all concerned feared they would be unable to control the large numbers of people, but Timothy assured them that his verbal appeals would do the trick. When he proved to be right, Aminu congratulated him as a true leader and fine nationalist.

Tim also told how ecstatically Aminu was greeted at a NEPU convention in Jos, when the farmers and traders took a day off to greet him in a long procession to the house where he was staying—just to shake his hand, look at him, or touch him. After a time,

Aminu asked him to function as a sort of personal secretary, which he continued to do for several years with a deep mutual trust growing up between them. At the time of the disturbances in Kano in 1966, Tim functioned in no man's land, saving lives of Ibos and Hausas, for he was accepted in both camps. But tensions remained high enough to force him to leave immediately thereafter, not to return for a year or two. He lives in Kano now and remains a staunch supporter of the democratization of the North—and of Aminu.

One other young man whose life was profoundly influenced by contact with Aminu was Uba Adamu in Kano. His personal testimony went as follows:[11]

"I was first posted as a teacher while still a student in Form I, for the need was great. I met Naibi Wali, who introduced me to Aminu Kano because he thought we shared common views. Aminu's educational discussions were of such a nature that he became a god to me. He insisted on regarding me as a friend, and refused all manifestations of the respect due him as a mallam, such as prostration or the removal of shoes in his presence. I would rush to carry his belongings, or open the door, but he always rejected any submissiveness to him.

"My admiration for him was necessarily a secret; for my father would never accept the relationship, nor would the people of Mandawari District, where I lived since I was an N.A. teacher. I didn't dare see him often, and then only at night, disguising myself with a blanket over my head and wearing shorts and singlet. . . . I remember that once he discussed how lightning was made, insisting that it was not the movement of angels lashing the clouds with their whips, as so many of us had thought, but the movement of air currents creating electricity and thunder. We listened to the radio, and he explained world affairs to us. One night he had returned from the emir's palace, where extended discussions took place regarding the badges marked *Sawaba* (Freedom), worn by the NEPU youth. He told us that the old mallams who were present had said it was un-Islamic to wear badges made by non-Moslems. But, Aminu had asked, what about the Jew Yusuf, a prophet in Islam, who was given medals to wear by the pagan pharaoh? And what about the emirs who wore the medal of the British Order of St. George, and others? He laughed, and said the learned discussion ended when the leading

mallam clenched his teeth and muttered his parting words to Aminu:
'I hate you!' "

In Aminu's more detailed version of this event, he told of being
challenged in an emotional fulmination by Mallam Nasiru and members of the emir's council, as a *bagyawa*—the Hausa-Muslim version of a heretic—for encouraging the wearing of the Sawaba
buttons and for cooperating with Christians, in alliance against the
traditional religious leaders. This was as serious a charge as a Christian heresy in the Middle Ages, and Aminu treated it as such. On the
morning when he was summoned before the powerful emir's council
to answer these charges, he performed the ablutions of a man facing
impending death (last rites), as did the two lieutenants, Danladi
and Lawan Dambazau, who were permitted to accompany him.
Passions were running high and common sense dictated that they
not go, but they did. Ignorance and lack of enlightenment were profound in these circles—and frightening.

The palace was filled as they entered the inquisition chamber,
dry-mouthed and apprehensive. Those assembled fell into a dead
silence until the hearing began. The head of civil administration repeated Mallam Nasiru's charges. Before substantive argument began,
Aminu pointed out that the charge was frivolous and that in any
case the Emir's Council was not a debating society. The discussions,
he suggested, should properly be held separately and the results
reported back to the emir. All agreed, and a date was set for the
argument.

The large group in attendance at this second meeting included,
among others, the civil administrator, the police chief, the madaki,
the defendant Aminu, and his two advisers. No one was surprised
when Mallam Nasiru arrived accompanied by two people, their heads
and hands loaded down with all his reference books with place
markers in the appropriate pages. But they were taken aback when
Aminu disregarded Mallam Nasiru's books, choosing to defend himself in the common knowledge. Everyone knew, he said, about the
defense alliance Mohammed had made with the Jews around Medina.
Wasn't this the same as the NEPU's alliance with the NCNC? When
the current emir wanted to build the largest mosque in the North and
called upon Ibo technicians to do it, was that not an alliance? He
had obviously won the argument even before Mallam Nasiru had

a chance to present his evidence. Only after a compromise restricting the wearing of NEPU badges to mass rallies, rather than flaunting them in their residential quarters—in order to avoid provocation— did the frustrated Mallam Nasiru hiss his parting words at Aminu.

Uba Adamu continued: "Aminu understood my enthusiasm for learning and greatly encouraged me to continue my studies, permitting me to use his precious library. I am of the Sulibawa clan, which, as you know, is royal. But my grandfather, who was a junior brother to the current emir's grandfather, fell into disfavor and was deposed as a district head. Now, with the decentralization, I am one of the three district officers (appointed by the governor, but to be elected after the Military Government leaves). Each of us is responsible for over a million people—and the son of the man who replaced my grandfather as district head is serving under me! . . .

"Aminu is believed more readily than are other educated men, for he speaks to the people in their own language. And what cleanliness we have in Northern Nigeria can all be traced to Aminu Kano."

Aminu, when queried as to why he tolerates gross inefficiency and ineptitude in a steward or driver, shrugged and said, "Here people must be trained if they are incompetent, not dismissed." It was through the propagation of these attitudes that Aminu and NEPU imparted enough self-esteem to the talakawa for them to refuse to do the free work for the emir which they had been doing through the ages.

Political alignments and the violent struggles they created may have tended to blur Aminu's influence on his countrymen, but many are the allies and foes, students and teachers, royalty and talakawa who reflect deeply, in some shape or form, the indelible mark their contact with Aminu left upon them. Nor do they hesitate to speak of it freely. The wind blew strong and far.

When Aminu the politician visited a town, Aminu the Islamic scholar was called forth. His reformism was both religious and political, attracting, among others, young students of the more progressive Koranic teachers. The party stalwarts felt that his scholarship could be well utilized in direct contact with the people through the Tafsir. This is the traditional process of translating the Koran from Arabic into the Hausa vernacular, with accompanying explanation and interpretation, and is usually done in front of a

mallam's house at the time of Ramadan (the Moslem month of high
holiday and diurnal fasting). Though Aminu originally undertook
the Tafsir to offset the preachings of Mallam Nasiru, who taught
that support of NEPU was a religious heresy, in Aminu's hands, the
Tafsir readings were rapidly extended to other towns he visited.
Large crowds would gather to hear him, and he and his local adherents would reap the accompanying political by-products. In his
interpretations, he would choose such quotations from the Koran and
the prophets that illustrated the concepts of morality that he and his
party stood for. But it was people's knowledge of him through
hearsay and his personal performance that put them in awe of him
and caused them to greet him with ecstatic shouts of "Ame--ee--een!"
—and reach out fanatically to touch him or a garment of his. At
times it seemed more a crusade that he led than a political campaign.
"We taught the peasants to suffer for a cause," explained Aminu.
"Before this, people would suffer unjustly, merely in the conflicts of
private gain. We believed that if they were going to suffer, they
should have a guiding purpose to see them through it." The old
mallams had a different explanation for this phenomenon of self-
sacrifice. They simply said that the NEPUites must have swallowed
some potion. Why else would they neglect their work for an ideal,
when for hundreds of years, it had never been that way?

Lawan Dambazau once said in NEPU, "We are a party of
those whose slogan is 'We don't agree.' " The statement of the Emir
of Zaria—that the damage done by Aminu was that he taught the
talakawa they could say no—had its literal application on one
occasion. When addressing a Katsina audience, telling them to resist
the injustices of the Native Authority, Aminu was asked, "If they
want to know who authorized it, what shall we say?" He responded,
"Tell them that Aminu said so!" Another time, the town criers in
the Kano streets started an announcement with, "The Emir of Kano
salutes you. . . ." But before they could go any further, the children
interrupted with, "Aminu Kano said we shouldn't accept!"

Aminu's songs, and those of others in and around NEPU, ex-
tolled the virtues of self-sacrifice and condemned intemperance and
high living, "People of Nigeria, I call you to have done with . . .
greed, gambling, and drinking. . . . Follow NEPU; it is its aim to
stop us from living a life of pleasure, or relying on . . . a particular

tribe. . . . Here is a (man) without covering; his evening meal is a mouthful of cassava. . . . He does nothing but shiver."[12]

The young girls sang their own song. Where they got it no one knew. "I was born to a sawaba, trained by NEPU, and am married to Aminu Kano. . . ."

Maitama Sule said: "Aminu is the hero of the oppressed and the talakawa, and the youths adored him, many secretly. He never used his position for riches, always for people. He is made that way."[13] The crowds of people who waited to catch a glimpse of him, or the many who jammed into his living room nightly to catch a few words of enlightenment, were living testimony to the adulation that hordes of people had for him—and Aminu the realist used this to try to build a people's political power through NEPU.

The decade of the 1950's produced two warring parties in the North, the Northern People's Congress (NPC) and the NEPU. The organizers of both originated in the same small group of educated northerners; yet at the start neither of these groups represented the power structure. The Native Authorities, resisting all modern politics and wanting to maintain the status quo, saw no reason for any political organization. Only after the changing political format, with its challenge to the establishment, became evident to the N.A.'s did they realize that they could not retain their power without making some adaptations to modern politics. It was the formation of NEPU, followed by its immediate surge of strength in the North's first elections in 1951, that provided the impetus for its counterpart, a conservative political party. The electorate was to select the new government, and if the emir and his entourage were to retain power, they had to control the vote in some way.

Constitutional reform had begun in Nigeria with the Richards Constitution in 1946, but this first move did little more than create a regional set up and the administrative forms to carry this out. In the process, the British, in order to win over the Sole Native Authorities to a parliamentary structure which the constitution set above them, had to guarantee the emirs control of the administrative apparatus. Obviously, a direct approach to the electorate could not be permitted, for the nationalists would very likely be able to gain control and wipe out the old autocratic forms. The only feasible approach, therefore, would be to accommodate the educated elite outside the N.A.'s by permitting them to advance to higher levels of government—but only indirectly, through the local government apparatus. Nigerian members of the Northern Regional Assembly would simply be appointed by the traditional leaders.

In this way, the same lack of significant alternatives to the clientage system which had dominated Hausa society in the past would continue. This typically British approach to the introduction of indigenous self-government in the North was responsible to a considerable degree for the indirect but subservient role played by most of the North's educated non-aristocrats in the NPC.

The hue and cry against this and other onerous provisions set up by the Richards Constitution led to a scrupulous reappraisal by the new governor, Sir John MacPherson. Consultations took place at every level throughout the nation, lasting two years and ending with the previously mentioned elections of 1951, held in a few urban areas in the North. Until then, the Northern House of Assembly, at that time only an advisory body, was made up of men like the Sardauna of Sokoto, Abubakar Tafawa Balewa, Makaman Bida, and a host of other representatives of royalty and aristocracy, all appointed by the local emirs.

Thus, the emirs and their appointees still held the real power, disdaining both NPC and NEPU and not wanting to soil their hands in any relations with the young upstarts, cultural, political, or otherwise. Imagine their shock in September 1951, therefore, when NEPU and its ally, NCNC, swept to victory in seventeen out of the the twenty-six seats contested in Kano, and won similar victories in Zaria, Jos, Kaduna, and every other area opened to the electoral process. Of course the British had guarded against the possibility of defeat for the traditional authorities. They had made the election a three-tier indirect process that permitted the emir's appointees to out-number the elected delegates at the last tier, in this way completely excluding all opposition from the House of Assembly, victorious or otherwise. This obviously unfair state of affairs was duplicated at a lower level for a long time thereafter, even after local reforms had begun; for when segments of local councils were elected, they were permitted to function only in a limited fashion. The district heads continued to act with or without the sanction of these councils, and development funds were made available to them only at the N.A.'s discretion, depending on the traditional status and personal standing of the particular district head.

This power dominance had a profound effect on the political fate of the North and the country as a whole. Despite the tremendous popularity of the anti-establishment approach of Aminu and NEPU, it gave the traditional rulers a chance to adapt themselves to approaching self-rule. "The red light is showing. May its warning be heeded before it is too late," said the "nonpartisan" *Nigerian Citizen* on October 25, 1951.

Without bothering about any of the formalities, the powerful Sardauna Ahmadu Bello and by this time his chief lieutenant, Tafawa Balewa, hastily joined with the pliable leadership of NPC to declare the organization a political party overnight. On September 30, 1951, almost immediately after the election, the British Chief Secretary of Government in Kaduna (a Mr. Gobel) came to the home of Isa Wali, then the assistant secretary general of NPC, and demanded that he turn over all the records.[14] When Isa protested that he could not do this unless it were so voted at a meeting, he was told that he was no longer eligible for membership in this political organization because he was a government employee. Yet not until an NPC meeting was held one year later was this decision formalized and the Sardauna installed as vice-president—and this a short nine months after the NPC had rejected the NEPU adherents for demanding the very same thing.

Aminu posted an indignant letter to the senior resident of Kano pointing out that "A mass rally of over 15,000 souls [taxpayers] . . . adopted some very strong resolutions, . . . [declaring] the last stage of the election null and void and earnestly wishes you to make an . . . immediate review." He and NEPU promptly attempted to show, through mock elections conducted in an orderly fashion, that direct elections could work even if adopted immediately. NEPU and its friends collected enough money to send Aminu and an accompanying lawyer to England to plead their case before the British Parliament and the general public. Through the intervention of Thomas Hodgkin, a scholar and teacher, and John Collins, a minister in St. Paul's Cathedral, they were able to have tea with sympathetic members of the House of Lords, meet Fabian MPs, and generally create enough of a stir to be noticed and finally heard at a meeting with the British Secretary of State.

It was this issue of direct elections that set the stage for the political battles of the 1950's, for here began the really severe repressive measures against NEPU. New rules sprang into being immediately. A gathering of more than ten people was an "assembly," regardless of its purpose, and required a special permit, frequently denied. N.A. police instituted wholesale arrests for any who attended NEPU meetings, since these rules were applied only to the political opposition. The NPC became an open arm of the law, and the law an extension of the political party. "The NPC would work hand-in-hand with the Department of Adult Education of Gusua to avoid duplication."[15] Hundreds of NEPU sympathizers were jailed for "disrespect" or for calling their political opponents abusive names. Many were imprisoned for wearing party badges or shouting party slogans. Children were arrested for singing NEPU songs or writing the letters NEPU on their garments or on the walls of their homes. Hoodlums roved in the dark, beating up NEPU sympathizers. Gambo Sawaba, a NEPU women's leader, was beaten by six men and left lying in the bush for two days before NEPU protests led to her discovery by the police.

The alkali courts were free of any restraint, imposing prison sentences and/or strokes with a cane with impunity, since no audience or members of the press were permitted to observe the legal proceedings. All that was needed to prove guilt under Moslem law was to produce two witnesses with acceptable testimony, and no appeal to higher courts was permissible in most cases.[16]

When these repressive measures were coupled with the pressures of the traditional clientage system permitting a person to advance through loyalty and patronage on one hand, and the denial of jobs and basic rights to the disloyal on the other, the results were effective, as might have been expected. Usman Bida, whose friendship with Aminu extended back to 1937-1942, when they were classmates and friends in Kaduna College, told Aminu that he could no longer see him when he came to Bida, because of Usman's relations with the emir. Haruna Dan Birni felt close to Aminu and

NEPU, yet under intense pressure he resigned from NEPU to become president of the Kaduna NPC chapter—though he continued to maintain discreet contacts with NEPU people.

It was almost a religion for Aminu and his cohorts to sacrifice for the party in those years. Large groups of people were learning how to break down walls and the process was full of the pleasure of adventure for the participants. Yet the people who turned to NEPU in 1951, and were victorious, found themselves still completely excluded from the power structure by the full force of the deeply entrenched Native Authorities. In large part, the NEPUites responded to this tyranny bravely. Although Aminu tried to inculcate the principles of nonviolent civil disobedience in his followers, he succeeded to only a limited degree. Many of them listened to his sage advice not to resist the overwhelming state power—and many did not. Political street battles were not uncommon, and in some instances the resistance was active and aggressive. The repression included the aforementioned Islamiyya schools and involved women and children as well as men, but the struggle continued.

A group of hooligans supporting the NPC organized the "Yam Mahaukata" (Sons of Madmen), with semiofficial sanction, to fight against "southern dominance." They subsequently extended their terrorism to a group of NEPU adherents who taunted and disparaged members of the traditional hierarchy when they left Kano airport for the 1953 Constitutional Conference in London. NEPU retaliated with a "Positive Action Wing" (PAW), to defend themselves against the hard-hats of their day. (The Yam Mahaukata wore wooden, or "akushi" hats; the PAW, calabash helmets.) According to NEPU sources, wood signifies death and calabash life.[17] When one member of the Shehu of Bornu's household was killed in an interparty street fight, the next day six members of the opposition party were killed in retribution.

Aminu told his followers one of his father's parables to strengthen their capacity to forbear. It was of the tyranny of King Solomon's time, when the city of Tadmur was being built by jinns. When they complained that twelve hours of labor per day were too taxing, their chief reassured them that they still had twelve hours for rest. After their workday was increased to twenty-four hours, he pointed out that when they carried stones to the site they returned empty handed. But after Solomon required that they return the unused stones to the original site, the chief finally said that it was time for God to intervene. Within a year Solomon died, the building of Tadmur was abandoned, and the jinns had permanent relief.

In the struggle to outmaneuver the opposition, security information became important. Aminu had extensive contacts within the camp of the traditionalists. Many aristocratic relatives and friends secretly supported him, willingly conveying information, but were unable to openly break their ties with the hierarchy. One royal young woman within the palace walls, referred to as "Otomi," after an Indian counterpart during the Spanish occupation of Mexico, was greatly dissatisfied with the marital arrangements made for her. She gladly bore information of value to the NEPU people, until, after a series of misadventures, including a flight and imprisonment, the emir finally canceled the arranged marriage and permitted her to marry her loved one. International recognition of the intensity of the repression in his homeland came when Aminu projected it while in England at every opportunity he could. Fenner Brockway, a Labour MP, said in Parliament on November 4, 1953: "At the London Conference, Mr. Aminu Kano was one of the most helpful participants; yet he had gone back [to] find members of his party being imprisoned . . . beaten up by gangsters. . . . I ask . . . the Colonial Office . . . [to] secure that minority parties in that country, and particularly in the Northern Region, shall be guaranteed political and civil rights." This international presence created by Aminu through letters, his protest visit in 1952, and his attendance at all the constitutional conferences, served only as a slight restraint on the Native Authorities who wanted their excesses to be kept under cover.

The violence that characterized the period erupted in yet another form in 1953. The MacPherson Constitution that had set up the indirect electoral system in the North in 1951 also established a central House of Representatives in Lagos. Its members were similarly chosen, i.e. indirectly, by the Northern, Eastern, and Western Houses in the ratio of 2:1:1—as the North was at least as populous as the two southern regions combined. Anthony Enahoro, a leader of the Western Region's dominant party, the Action Group, moved a resolution urging self-government for Nigeria by 1956. The northern NPC parliamentarians, led by Sir Ahmadu Bello, Sardauna of Sokoto already the acknowledged traditional leader of the region, felt that the backward north would be overwhelmed by the south if self-government came too soon. They amended the resolution to read "self-government for Nigeria as soon as practicable." This created an impasse, a walkout of the NCNC and Action Group legislators, and an atmosphere of interregional antagonism. The northern members were stoned in the streets and generally subjected to abuse by the Lagos crowds as well as by the southern press. They responded with an eight-point program that, if attained, would have been tantamount to the secession of the Northern Region. The southern leaders, attempting to muster support for their "self-government now" proposals, undertook to send delegations throughout the North.

In the midst of all this tension, one such delegation, led by Chief Akintola of the Action Group, scheduled a meeting in Kano, the northern metropolis. Kano's NPC leaders and the local authorities regarded this move as provocative. Inuwa Wada, at that time N.A. information officer, set a xenophobic tone the day before the scheduled meeting by saying, "Having abused us in the south, these very southerners have decided to come to the north to abuse us . . . We have therefore organized about one thousand men . . . to meet force with force; those men will [be] singing and shouting that . . . no lecture or meeting will be delivered by the southerners."[18]

With such an inflammatory response it was not surprising that riots broke out in the streets of Kano, ending only after thirty-six persons had died (fifteen northerners and twenty-one southerners) and 241 were wounded.[19]

Curiously, though, Aminu and the NEPU stalwarts who had actively and openly supported the shorter route to self-government proposed by the southerners were not subjected to attack. Nor were the Yoruba (Western Nigerian) residents of Kano City who supported the Action Group and Akintola, the leader of the southern delegation. The brunt of the Hausa ire was directed against the more numerous and more vulnerable Ibos (centered in the sabon gari, or strangers' town). This eruption of ethnic intertribal rivalries, and the uneven social and educational development that accompanied it, led ultimately to a regionalized compromise for the nation:

dropping the federal "self-government now" demands in order to achieve unity.

The relative influence of political differences and of intertribal or cultural antagonisms on this Kano upheaval has never been accurately determined. There is little doubt, however, that the retention of old autocratic and arrogant forms of government lent itself readily to such violence, since the Native Authority itself invoked the same methods against its primary challengers, the NEPU and its local allies.

Historians will no doubt find it fascinating to compare these disorders with those of 1966 preceding the civil war, but that for the future. Suffice it to note that the Yam Mahaukata, organized about that time, proved very useful against their local antagonists. Officially sanctioned violence in suppressing opposition was characteristic of the decade of the 1950's. Of course it might have resulted in such turbulence and disorder that the regime would have toppled, but the more likely concomitant was to so weaken the opposition as to render it almost totally ineffective. And if at the same time the establishment had welcomed back into its folds of patronage and clientage any defectors from the rival camp, its tactics would have been that much more likely to succeed. This dual approach finally did erode the cadres of the opposition, frightening the rank and file into sullen submission and at least temporary acceptance. Built into this process, however, was the very factor that brought about the eventual downfall of the regime: the polarization of monocentric regions, with area of origin, rather than ideology, creating the differences in parties.

Throughout this travail, Aminu succeeded in maintaining an almost unbelievable balance on a very sensitive scale. Relationships had to continue with allies who could be trusted only to a limited degree; with antagonists whose differences had to be exploited; with friends and enemies whose position could change like shifting sands, depending on the attraction of the bait dangled in front of them. If any individual was ready to offer his hand, no matter how sinister his prior role, Aminu was ready to accept it. Though he carefully concealed key information from new allies, he cooperated with anyone who would accept the NEPU program. This approach had its drawbacks, such as the loss of five of the eight NEPU Federal

MPs elected in 1959, when they crossed the carpet; and constantly shifting relationships, alliances, and sectional leadership. But it also preserved some continuity of internal leadership in the party, and in relationships with the more progressive wing in the NPC, the opposition party, and the NCNC, NEPU's southern ally.

Each of the southern parties became dominant in its own region, with a hierarchy of leadership fairly well established. Nnamdi Azikiwe ("Zik") led the NCNC in the East, and Obafemi Awolowo ("Awo") led the Action Group in the West. With Awolowo, Aminu's relationship was for the most part rather distant and formal. They did spend time together on board ship on the way to the London Constitutional Conference, and Aminu on one occasion slept in Awo's home while en route to Lagos, but their contacts were mainly political. Since they never really saw eye to eye in this respect, they remained somewhat aloof, with no personal antagonisms ever flaring up. On the one hand, Awo thought NEPU too radical and that it should be eliminated; on the other, he and his group made a constant effort to woo NEPU away from its alliance with NCNC by offers of massive financial or political support. (At one point NEPU's intelligence staff found that the Action Group was trying to get rid of Aminu.) From Aminu's point of view, their attempts to win NEPU away from its NCNC alliance were based not on ideological grounds but on their greater affluence, and if successful, they would have denied NEPU's independence of action. This personal non-relationship between Aminu and Awo continued into the military era where for a period of time they served as fellow cabinet members. The channels remain open but relatively unused.

With Azikiwe it was quite different. The two first met in Bauchi in 1946 when Zik was touring the North for the NCNC. Aminu's friend and political associate, Sa'adu Zungur, introduced them. Zik was well known as leader of the nationalist forces of that day, and he in turn knew of Aminu's growing reputation and his vitriolic pen. They met again in London in 1946 and 1947 and on other occasions, and developed a liking for one another through Aminu's youthful exuberance, and their common ideas. In 1954, when an alliance was formed between NEPU and NCNC, they saw each other at executive committee meetings. Although it too was essentially political, their contact was closer. Aminu knew Zik's writings through his chain of newspapers and respected them. Their stated goals were essentially the same, with Aminu defending Zik when he was under attack for financial irregularities in intraparty factional struggles or otherwise. He felt that those who opposed Zik had no legitimate ideological differences with him but did so only as part of a power play. However, after self-government was finally achieved, and Zik took over as President of Nigeria, Aminu felt that the softening up process had deepened sufficiently to be irreversible. Zik had run out of steam.

By the time the first coup took place, in 1966, Zik had been compromised beyond the point of effectuality. For him the presidency of the nation became a sort of semi-retirement from nationalist activity. The active reins of party administration and decision-making were taken over by Michael Okpara and his company of diehard, crude, pragmatic politicians, lacking ideological direction. The opportunist trends which crept into party affairs, thereafter, greatly affected the NEPU-NCNC alliance, with Aminu's initial reservations strengthened. He retained an independence of movement that permitted him to support one faction or another on the basis of the controversial issue involved, without committing himself to the faction itself. For instance, his support of the Western leaders Adelabo and then Adisa in their intraparty struggles never committed him totally to either of them. Thus he stuck to his support of the NCNC alliance despite misgivings, but never submitted to its dictates.

His special concern for the development of the North, and realization that this was not the orientation of the NCNC led him to act independently whenever he felt that the integrity of the North was threatened—as in the Cameroons plebiscite in 1959 when a segment of the North chose to continue within Northern Nigerian bounds or in a 1958-1959 dispute over whether Ilorin should be included in the Northern or the Western Region. Aminu's influence in support of northern unity served to good advantage in both these instances, even though the NCNC supported the West's jurisdictional claim to hegemony in the Ilorin case.

In spite of this orientation, however, Aminu became something of a hero in the East, the bastion of NCNC; for his consistently incorruptible stance was universally recognized by idealists and radical youth throughout the nation. As leader of their northern allies' struggle to displace the bastion of reaction in the North, they adored him, and admired his unquestioned oratorical powers. Nevertheless his party's constituency was Northern and his influence in the Eastern and Western Regions had to be manifested through alliances and/or pressure at the top.

This deep-seated concern of Aminu for northern development was recognized by all who encountered him in the course of the political wars, whether on his side or no, from the Sardauna on down. Even when they intermittently found themselves in opposite camps, men like Joseph Tarka, Tiv leader of a non-Hausa minority in the Northern Region's Middle Belt area, never questioned Aminu's devotion to the cause of democracy. After the parties eventually closed ranks under the banner of the Northern Progressive Front (NPF) in 1964, and subsequently in the Military Government, Aminu's ideological consistency emerged inviolate in the form of a united opposition party in the North. As Tarka put it, "Though reaction is still strong in the North today, Aminuism is beginning to triumph."[20]

Sa'adu Zungur, his closest political confrere of the 1940's, had left the problems of the North in Aminu's hands and from 1948 to 1951, ventured out as federal secretary of the NCNC, in search of a national solution. But he became disillusioned with the NCNC when the scholarships it had pledged to northerners (Aminu among them) never materialized, and when its role in building an opposition party in the North was ineffective. He continued to work in the NPC for a short time after NEPU came into being, but his friendship and respect for Aminu soon brought him into the NEPU camp. There he functioned mostly in a passive, advisory role, leaving organizational matters to Aminu. His health deteriorated rapidly, until he finally died in the arms of his first, traditional wife, who had been chosen by his parents. Aminu is currently trying to stimulate interest in the building of a memorial library to Sa'adu's memory.

Aminu never cut off any channels of communication regardless of who was in the sending or receiving station. This permitted a strange kind of ongoing relationship between him and the traditional rulers, either on the regional or the emirate level. If he had a proposal that he felt would aid his people, and that had even a remote chance of being accepted by the administration, he would not hesitate to write or visit the appropriate party. This approach would disarm the individual authorities involved, and force them to respond in kind. Tradition in this respect was maintained, even in in the face of great antagonisms. Anthony Enahoro, Mid-Western leader who is now a fellow commissioner of Aminu's, recalls his impressions of Aminu in that earlier period: "He seemed to be very much a northerner, principally concerned with liberalizing the Islamic influence and eliminating the more conservative interpretations of Koranic life. . . . Although opposed to the NPC, he was in the coalition government with them at the center, and a Whip. We who were in opposition found it difficult to understand his reconciliation of these conflicting positions, but it strengthened our impression that he was concerned primarily with reformation of northern society."21

This juxtaposition of consistent opposition to "the more conservative interpretations of Koranic life" with rejection of the personal antagonisms that would normally accompany such a struggle puzzled many southerners, and even northerners. In the early political years, during a visit to the Sardauna, Aminu asked him for a much-needed typewriter. "But am I to supply you with a typewriter with which you will attack me?" asked Sardauna. Aminu replied simply, "Yes. You have the wherewithal, I haven't." The Sardauna acquiesced, to the perplexity and distress of many of his more traditional followers, as well as many of Aminu's.

Since most northern political leaders were graduates of Kaduna College (or its predecessor, Katsina College) and were drawn from a select group of the highborn, there must have been an element of loyalty among them, akin to that of fraternity brothers. During his student days, Aminu was the one among them who had always dared; the others stood back and secretly cheered him on—and were still doing it.

In a general way, the NPC divided itself into two groups—with Aminu to a certain extent as the dividing line. Those who remained friendly with Aminu were polarized around Federal Prime Minister Abubakar Tafawa Balewa; the others gathered around the Premier of the North, Sardauna Ahmadu Bello. The former group was more enlightened and more ready to accept reforms and change; the latter agreed to such change only under extreme duress and with the express permission of the Sardauna. Of course, when the Sardauna cracked the whip, most all of them fell into line, but the divergence was ever present and occasionally took more overt forms.

The progressives for the most part shared Aminu's goals, but hoped to achieve them through gradual and socially acceptable means—or, in some instances, admittedly in such a way that their personal comfort would not be upset. There were men like Sarkin Bai, who in Aminu's eyes would perhaps have been as radical as he, if he had been able to shed the influences of the family and clan dependency on him; and there was Waziri Alhaji, who, after a rapid rise to an executive post in the private world of United Africa Company, felt he could no longer mix with his NEPU colleagues and could better accomplish his lofty goals in the NPC. Aminu warned him he was going into the mouth of the tiger and would be swallowed, but he ignored the advice, went into the NPC, became an MP and a minister, and appeared little different from the others within his party. Nuhu Bamali, eventually Nigeria's Foreign Minister, was an early friend and associate of Aminu's, dating back to the 1940's. He chose the NPC way from the start but remained on close, cordial terms with Aminu, much as did Maitama Sule, the former Minister of Mines and Power, and the Prime Minister himself. Ideologically, Maitama Sule was considered close to Tafawa Balewa's thinking in the Federal Government, and was therefore persona non grata in the Sardauna's camp. When he could, he tried to be a kind of moderator between the two camps, frequently in a jesting way. But at one point, when Sardauna opened old wounds a bit by indirectly referring to him as a slave, Maitama responded in kind. When Sir Ahmadu visited Adamawa, his mother's home province, Maitama called to mind the Sardauna's maternal slave lineage by gathering together twenty unkempt, bare-breasted women to present them to the exalted one as his NPC admirers. The implication was clear.

Men like Inuwa Wada, former Minister of Works (incidentally a relative of Aminu), and Bello Dandago, MP, his former teacher in Kano and later chief government parliamentary whip, didn't hesitate to come to Aminu for advice or consultation. Inuwa Wada had found himself in the Prime Minister's corner by dint of the Sardauna's traditional running rivalry with the Emir of Kano, for Inuwa's primary loyalty was to Ciroma (Crown Prince) Sanusi. When the Ciroma

became Emir of Kano in 1953, he actively feared that Aminu was
out to depose him. Inuwa, who had remained friendly with his cousin,
by some inexplicable coincidence was excluded from the Northern
House of Assembly. After this rather forceful reminder of his
clientage position, he found it necessary to cut off all social inter-
course with Aminu for a decade. In 1963 when the Northern Regional Government, led by its premier, the Sardauna of Sokoto,
succeeded in having Emir Sanusi deposed, Inuwa beat a path back
to Aminu's door posthaste, apologized for his years of self-imposed
social indiscretion, and vowed never again to close his door on his
worthy relative. Since then, things have gone relatively smoothly
between them. Although some of the people around Aminu do not
agree, he seems to think that if Inuwa could be separated from his
associates he would perform better.

During the 1950's, Aminu was concentrating on what he considered the just grievances of not only the talakawa but the educated
non-royal elite (a sort of petty bourgeoisie) that would benefit from
breaking out of the feudalistic confines of monarch, palace, and the
accompanying royal intrigues. These people were mainly traders or
lower ranking civil servants. They wanted to "do their own thing,"
intrigues or otherwise. Some few of them did break the pattern completely, but they were few and became part of the middle rung of
NEPU leadership. The remainder clung to the NPC, hoping to do
what they could from that safe vantage point. Publicly they attacked
Aminu's party and tactics, but privately they remained on cordial
terms. In this way they provided him with a link to the party which
served as the chief governmental barrier to the achievement of the
radical political power he sought throughout his adult lifetime.

Aminu's relationship with Sir Abubakar, the Prime Minister,
and Sardauna Ahmadu Bello, the Premier of the Northern Region,
until their deaths in 1966 was even more complex than their fellow
NPC leaders. In a symbolic way, the following story sums it up:

During the Independence celebrations, Aminu entered the Sardauna's house to pay his respects. The waiting room was filled with
MPs and Ministers of State, all seated on the floor, awaiting the
arrival of the exalted one. When the regal Sir Ahmadu finally
arrived, he surveyed the room and saw Aminu, the only one seated
in a chair. He pulled up a little hassock near Aminu, sat down, and

commented with a smile, "You know, Aminu, we're not all progressive like you." Aminu replied, "But you obviously are the more progressive, for you are able to accommodate yourself to everyone, even me."

A few minutes later, Prime Minister Abubakar arrived, removed his slippers, and sat down on the floor! Not wanting to embarrass the Prime Minister or to show him disrespect, Aminu felt impelled to leave at that point. Sardauna Ahmadu sent one of his household servants upstairs for the usual parting gift, shook his hand, and bade him goodbye.

In his classic study of this three-way relationship,[22] C. S. Whitaker analyzes the class origin of each man, how it affected his position on the political spectrum and his attitude toward the role tradition should play in it. The Sardauna was royal; Abubakar was of slave origin, making him part of the monarchical clientage system and consequently beholden to it; and Aminu was independently aristocratic, outside the power structure. Therefore the first man defended the traditional status quo, the second tried for slow, moderate reform, and the third for radical reform. Although this key observation establishes a framework within which each man functioned, it still does not completely explain the intricacies of their relationship. There are many persons of Northern Nigerian origin who do not fall into this pattern. Even though it may be said with validity that personal development is affected by class origins, obviously individual personality played an important role as well.

As we recall, Aminu's path crossed the Sardauna's as far back as 1944 when Ahmadu was under attack by his cousin, the Sultan of Sokoto, for embezzling the jangali (cattle tax) entrusted to him. In their second major contact, during Aminu's stay at Maru in 1949-1950, so long as the Sardauna was locked in struggle with their common foe, the Sultan, their alliance continued. However, class differences crept in shortly thereafter. The Sardauna decided to fight his battle on traditional lines, vying for dominance within the emirate structure—here parting company with his erstwhile ally, Aminu. Thereafter the Sardauna rose to the pinnacle of power in the North, adapting the old autocratic emirates to new forms only when he was assured of the safety and continuity of the royal heritage.

Fremont Besmer, a young ethno-musicologist doing research for his doctoral thesis among the musicians in the emir's court in Kano, reports a brief song-poem that he uncovered in his studies, reflecting the on-going relationship between Aminu and the Sardauna.

> Go and tell the lizard [Aminu]
> To get up on the wall,
> As I see over there
> A cat [Sardauna] looking for him.

Aminu points out that he never objected to the Sardauna's strong hand, only to how he used it. The fear people had of him, his personality and his prestige, all could have been used for liberation, education, and development—and were not. Although both manifested strength, each used it differently—Aminu's toward changing the class structure, Ahmadu's toward maintaining it.

With the growth of the two opposing parties in the North and these two heading them, the contacts between them became more and more sporadic. Aminu would usually initiate them, either to complain of some repression or injustice wreaked upon his supporters, or merely to pay a courtesy call on Sallah or some other appropriate traditional occasion. They met on state occasions and at various constitutional or governmental conferences, but the one-to-one meetings between them were minimal. The Sardauna had developed a growing fear that the southerners were out to assassinate him, and Aminu was suspect because of his southern connections. Even when the Sardauna wanted to speak to Aminu about his struggle to depose the Emir of Kano, he received him in a room with six ministers present. If he had private words to utter, he would pull Aminu into a corner out of earshot of his disciples.

As the years went by, the Sardauna retreated more and more into religion, using his power to solidify his own traditional position and that of the system he represented. When Aminu accused him of political motivation in 1965, during Sardauna's proselytizing tour of the North, he was hurt and angry, for he evidently was making a genuine bid for religious glory. At times he openly hinted that he thought of achieving an even higher position than he held—for him, the highest position in the land, that of Sultan of Sokoto.

As Northern Premier, he conducted himself in a grandiose fashion, bestowing lavish gifts on all around him, even Cadillac automobiles when the occasion called for it. By the 1960's, he was frequently referred to as "Sarkin Arewa," or "Emir of the North,"[23] and his dress and whole demeanor bespoke this status. He thought of himself as the modern-day Usman Dan Fodio and said, "I too will divide the country between my two trustworthy lieutenants when [my jihad,] the current political battle, is over." This was uttered in Bauchi, the home of Prime Minister Balewa, as he bestowed an alkyabba (traditional cloak of authority) upon the Prime Minister with the words, "To my lieutenant in the south."[24]

Thus he looked upon Abubakar, with Aminu assuming the role of a persistent monkey on his back. He himself was the personification of the old regime with all its trimmings; someone whom Abubakar had to skirt around to accomplish anything progressive. The fact that he and Abubakar were of different schools of thought, as well as different castes, was well known to all. To get anything done either Abubakar had to have the cards so stacked that the Sardauna was outmaneuvered; or he had to convince him that a move was necessary and would not upset the essential traditional relationships; or else he had to comply with the Sardauna's wishes. Since Abubakar had the highest official position in the land and was ostensibly running the Federal Government of Nigeria, jealousies and inconsistencies developed, with the more progressive-minded administrators and politicians grouping around the Prime Minister. All, however, were subject to the same traditional restraints, and deferred to the political "boss" when a direct conflict arose.

At times, Abubakar was able to take action contrary to the desires of the traditional authorities, particularly when the British supported him. His first such courageous act was back in 1950 in the Northern House of Assembly, when he made his famous speech urging reforms in the North. The speech itself expressed essentially the British position and was far from radical, although it evoked angry remarks from the traditional authorities about his lowly ancestors. He assumed the stance he was to keep throughout his political career: "I do not wish to destroy, I call for reform."[25] Aminu and the group around him applauded the action, since legislative spokesmen for progress were few in those days.

Throughout the difficult, repressive years of the 1950's Aminu continued the warm friendship with Abubakar that had begun during their teaching days in Bauchi. At no time did they approach political agreement, nor did they even try to persuade one another, for they instinctively recognized a difference in basic orientation; but they shared a mutual respect and trust at all times. They avoided discussing national or international affairs even after Aminu took on a role at the U.N. and other international conferences. Abubakar felt that at any level, in any post, Aminu would always function in the interests of the nation and the North. Apparently he never permitted himself to believe that severe repression was going on in the North, so that when this fact would seep through to him, he was sorely distressed. Once he was moved to intervene in behalf of an important member of the Bauchi royal family when he discovered that the gentleman had been jailed by the Emir of Gombe. This he did even in the face of open abuse and identification as a NEPU sympathizer by his own supporters.

Abubakar's confidence in British solutions to Nigerian problems continued unabated from the days of the Bauchi Discussion Group on through Independence. Aminu laughingly tells of stopping in Lagos to bid Abubakar goodbye when he was en route to Tunis to the All-African Peoples' Conference held there in 1960. Abubakar insisted that the conference was canceled, for he had been so informed by Interpol and Scotland Yard. This even though Aminu informed him of a conversation with Diallo Telli just prior to his departure—that all was going as originally planned. Aminu took the trouble to cable the Prime Minister from Tunis, "Having a wonderful time. Wish you were here."

Abubakar, although the highest official in the land, never truly felt comfortable with his political bedfellows, for most of them were of aristocratic or royal birth and did not hide the fact. That may be one reason why he remained on such good terms with Aminu, continuing in a quiet way to heed his words, at times even modifying his conduct accordingly. It was felt that at least some of the jealousy and friction which existed between the two top NPC leaders stemmed from the Prime Minister's continuing dialogue with Aminu.

Since Aminu was a Member of Parliament and the ruling coalition government from 1959-1964, and a leader of his party, it could have been assumed that he would eventually get a ministerial post. The fact that he did not was generally attributed to the Sardauna's veto. Abubakar's ambivalent position, however, led him to explain lamely that if he appointed Aminu to a high post he would be accused of buying off the opposition in the North.

One of the most ironic and tragic aspects of this complex relationship developed in 1966, two weeks before the first military coup when Aminu, in private audience, warned Abubakar that he must remove Akintola, Premier of the Western Region, because he no longer had the confidence of his people in a very explosive situation. The whole nation would blow up if Akintola were allowed to stay. Although it is generally thought that Abubakar, in his hesitant way, wanted to move, evidently he was restrained by the Sardauna. Both Abubakar and the Sardauna were killed in the coup.

Sule Katagum, Chairman of the Federal Civil Service, estimates that "Inwardly, Abubakar was delighted that Aminu could come out openly for more advanced ideas, serving as a spokesman for the less outspoken adherents of the same ideas—even though he himself could never openly support them."[26] This was part of Aminu's charisma. Many junior and senior civil servants felt the same way as Abubakar, but could do nothing about observed injustices except tell Aminu about them and hope he would raise the issues.

Once Timothy Monu told Aminu that he had seen the Sardauna bang his head while entering a car, because he did not bend low enough. Thereupon Aminu made another one of his noted prophecies. He said that a man as haughty as the Sardauna, if he remained Premier, would be dead within a few years. . . .And so it came to pass, though it must also be said, that Aminu did not predict the same fate for the mild-mannered Prime Minister, ever compromising or being compromised.

Abubakar, Ahmadu, and Aminu—the three A's. They represented the three ideological angles of the triangle that was Nigeria; One looked toward autocracy, where leadership was inborn; one to meritocracy, the rule of the educated worthy; and the last to democracy, where leaders were chosen by the led . . . an echo of the American colonial heroes Adams, Jefferson, and Tom Paine.[27] Though Aminu is the sole survivor of the three, Nigeria's fate remains far from being decided.

Then there were the few intimates of Aminu. Since most of his associates in the NEPU came from an educational and sociological background markedly different from his, it was not surprising that only one of his three close personal friends was active in the party. Aminu has been accused of being too secretive, a loner in decision making, but to the extent that there was consultation, he of course turned to his political associates. For relaxation, however, and perhaps a degree of personal confidences, he turned to one of these three who seemed to give it best: Ahmadu Trader in Kano, Sule Katagum in Lagos, and Aliyu Abubakar wherever and whenever they met. Ahmadu Trader played a protective role in Aminu's household. He looked after all the mundane affairs, and assumed responsibility in Aminu's absence. He saw that the automobile was serviced, the driver cared for, and the bills paid. If permission was needed for Aminu's wife to move from the compound, if party chores needed doing or if mail had to be posted or picked up, Ahmadu was ever present. Nevertheless, his relationship with Aminu was far from servile. Not only were his reliability and devotion deeply appreciated by Aminu, but they spent many an hour together, planning, preparing, or just chatting. To a degree, Ahmadu had risen from a simple but prosperous trader to a sophisticated politico and man of the world through great personal effort and ability. He gave generously to the NEPU cause, even as his business fell off because of his personal associations and beliefs. He suffered much abuse and was jailed two or three times, but somehow seemed to take it all in stride. Of late, they seem to have drifted apart somewhat, stemming from what Aminu considered a partisan approach on Ahmadu's part toward members of his household, but they remain on cordial terms, nonetheless.

Sule Katagum, Chairman of the Federal Civil Service Commission, represented something quite different to Aminu over the years. Sule had been one of Aminu's prize pupils at Bauchi Middle School, and had led the highly successful student strike there. The two had remained as friendly as logistics and careers would permit. Sule chose the path of civil service and Aminu politics. Aminu would stay in Sule's home when he came to Lagos (until he became an MP and had his own house), but much of the time they functioned hundreds of miles apart and saw each other sporadically. Whenever they managed to get together, though their ideas were undoubtedly on the same wavelength, Sule—tall, handsomely dignified and imposing looking, must have done the listening, since political participation was denied the civil servant—at least that is all that either of them admit to. Later, the period of military government brought them even closer together, for at that point, politics was denied to all, and Lagos became a city of residence for both.

The third intimate, Aliyu Abubakar, played more the role of an old chum who for decades was in and out of Aminu's life. When they saw each other, they swapped stories of what had happened since their last meeting, and reminisced about the time when Aliyu unearthed a report by a British officer that Aminu was revolutionary, a deliberate instrument to topple the Imperial Government, and about the old days generally. Aliyu, a professor at Ahmadu Bello University in the North, has been a student or teacher most of his life, accumulating a roster of degrees probably unsurpassed by any Nigerian. Aminu had always urged him to continue his studies, and it was largely through his influence that Aliyu took a daughter of Abubakar Tafawa Balewa as his bride. They were always able to joke and laugh together, and let their hair down.

But the persons with whom Aminu came into contact most often were his fellow NEPUites. "A man is a bundle of relations, a knot of roots," said Emerson. Assumedly, some of Aminu's associations are through the branches and leaves of his life as well, but the ties with his open supporters were undoubtedly of the deep-rooted variety. In discussing Aminu's inner party relationships, Maitama Sule commented as follows: "Aminu is of eminently superior intelligence, and rigidly demanded the kind of concentration and devotion he himself gave to the cause . . . perhaps causing him to look down on people somewhat. When this was coupled with a reluctance to bare his mind freely, it might have separated him from his lieutenants and made him somewhat suspect."[28] In part, it may also explain why so few lieutenants of top stature were developed during those political years. Many observers have been puzzled by Aminu's inability to develop a qualified cadre of leaders. Consider, however, that Aminu was the only university-trained leader in the National Executive Committee; that over the years there were never more than two men in that body who had completed secondary school; and even more surprising that, as the party developed over the last half of its existence (1958-1965), from 65 to 75 percent of its top leaders were illiterate.[29] What is startling, then, is that the NEPU leadership functioned as well as it did. Indeed, its paucity of leadership showed up some years later, when the Gowon Military Government sought out former NEPUites for local state leadership, and so few were found who were actually qualified and available.

Though the party started in the early 1950's with a number of mallams, students, schoolteachers, and even minor N.A. officials, they were rapidly frightened or bought off by the highly ascriptive, rigidly controlled society of the emirs. Mallams associated with NEPU lost their pupils; farmers or their families were hit by selectively high assessments and taxes on their land; N.A. officials were sacked; all explaining why so many members of the NPC, the party of the emirs, were secretly sympathetic with NEPU. Again Aminu was daring, while others secretly cheered him on.

Those who remained in the party were an isolated, dedicated band of self-sacrificing but untrained leaders. As the slow and arduous process of training picked up momentum, the leadership dominated by Aminu, frequently had to face the problems of defection, inadequate methods of administration, and frank misappropriation of funds. This led to the curious phenomenon wherein leading NEPU members would be placed on trial, found guilty, and yet would be back on the job shortly thereafter. The dearth of leadership merely emphasized Aminu's earlier philosophy: dereliction requires further training, not dismissal. Open the corral gate to the sheep who has strayed, if he wishes to return to the fold. In some instances, misappropriated funds were returned, but more often the incident was simply closed.

In the attempt to keep NEPU's ideology as the unifying force, Aminu encouraged the young and competent to educate themselves and work their way up from the ranks. If such men emerged, the entrenched leaders felt threatened and had to be placated. Factional struggles emerged from time to time, accompanied by personal jealousies and bitterness.

At no time was Aminu's dominant role at the head of his party seriously challenged, though some may have eyed his position enviously. Rather, there was a jockeying for position below this pinnacle and a vying for his favor.

In 1954, at the national convention in Lafia, a segment of the leadership attempted to change NEPU's alliance with NCNC to the Action Group. Aminu pleaded with his members that there were no ideological reasons for the change. If they allowed themselves to be seduced for a mess of pottage, would they not do so again, when enticed by other more alluring bait? At Aminu's insistence, a secret ballot was held guaranteeing free choice to the entire national executive, regardless of any bribes previously accepted. The vote was 74 to 11 in favor of retaining the NCNC ties. The eleven members who lost, left the fold after unsuccessfully attempting to take a significant segment of the rank and file with them. Some went over to NPC, putting great strain on Aminu and NEPU's inadequate cadre pool. This drain on the sorely tried leadership continued when more tangible electoral victories were not forthcoming over the years. It was even further accelerated when Aminu became a Member of Parliament, a position that frequently removed him from the scene of active day-to-day party leadership. The family needed the strong hand of the father to prevent squabbling.

Abubakar Zukogi was an early adherent of the NEPU. In fact, his agitation for popular reform actually predated the party, for he was one of the founding members of NEPA (Northern Elements Progressive Association), precursor of the NEPU. Though of royal rank, he remained consistently opposed to the autocracy of the North—this in the face of intense pressure from the state, including four years' imprisonment (1954-1958). He was generally considered, and considered himself, the number-two man in the party. His highly personal approach to his position of leadership made him somewhat difficult to work with, especially when the more promising younger men being educated and trained for leadership came upon the scene. Two among those with the greatest prospects, Tanko Yakasai and Yahaya Abdullahi, clashed with Zukogi and each other at various times, but all eventually remained loyal.

These internecine struggles were not ideological, with the one exception of Tanko Yakasai's unsuccessful attempt to inject a militant pro-Chinese influence into the party, after a visit to that country. "When a person like Tanko showed his ability to rise above his lack of education, to learn English and administration, or when someone like Yahaya Abdullahi appeared with both competence and education, the loyal older and more entrenched but possibly less capable members naturally felt threatened," explained Aminu. He continued, "Yahaya (and others like him in the party) sacrificed by giving up his government position to join us, with nothing else to fall back on but his ideals. His indiscretions were those of inexperience. Tanko was indefatigible and worked day and night without pay or reward. If we encourage young people like these to stand up and fight, we must stick with them. Zukogi and Tanko are now commissioners on a state level, and Yahaya Abdullahi is making his way up in the External Affairs office. Where would they be today if we had rejected them?"

Aminu was always ready to conciliate the party's internal financial irregularities, unlike his insistence on publicly expelling Isiaku Gwamma, a NEPU leader, when he publicly proposed a bill in the Northern House of Assembly that would finance the purchase of automobiles for all its members. Outside party ranks, consistently rigid discipline was necessary though conciliation after censure was permissible. Despite these personnel difficulties, there were other NEPU leaders, like Yerima Balla and Yahaya Sabo, who did manage to avoid factional differences and maintain sober voices in the inner party councils in Aminu's absence.

Aminu tried to stay above the in-fighting, stepping in only when the question of ideological purity arose, or when an irreconcilable internal problem demanded judgment from a court of last resort. The esteem in which he was held, whether because of his educational status, his patrician background, his competence and integrity or as is probable, a combination of all of them, was sufficient to permit him to sustain this lofty position. Perhaps the gap between him and the NEPU members, leadership or rank and file, might explain the seeming paradox of a man, universally accepted as a lifetime devotee of democratic procedures both inside and outside his party, who found himself chosen as a lifetime President-General.

Aminu's associations with the southern and northern Nigerian leaders and the rank and file; his friends and antagonists, intimate and peripheral; his political affinities and divergences have all been discussed to some degree in this chapter. One group, however, has not yet been mentioned—the British officialdom. In the 1940's, they considered Aminu to be a promising, if somewhat rash and impulsive, lad whose abilities might be steered into "constructive" channels. To them, this meant getting him to function within the emirate system and concomitantly, to slow him down. With the organization of NEPU, and the discarding of all vocational restraints by resigning his teaching post, Aminu became the leading ogre of the North, to be watched carefully and isolated to the extent possible. The British continued to hide their own activities behind the long, flowing robes of their local cat's-paws, the emirs, but when Aminu bypassed his local targets, the native autocrats, and struck directly at the puppeteers, they responded accordingly.

In 1954, in a speech to a mass rally reported in the *Daily Comet* (a friendly newspaper and the only one published in Kano), he attacked an agreement signed in 1886 by the Queen's representatives of that day, the United Africa Company, and the Sultan of Sokoto. According to this document, United Africa evidently was to receive royalties in perpetuity. But Aminu reasoned that since it was written in English, it was fraudulent, for no Englishman at the time spoke Hausa and certainly no one in the Sultan's entourage spoke English. There must have been intent to deceive, he maintained—an imperialist maneuver to take away the rights of the Hausa-Fulani people. The police deemed this attack seditious and arrested Aminu and the editor of the *Comet*.

When Aminu was taken to the magistrate to be arraigned, the procedure was simply to read the charges, fix bail and accept payment; then to release him on his own cognizance. As he was leaving the preliminary hearing, looking forward to his impending courtroom adventure, an N.A. policeman seized him and took him to the local Chief Alkali's Court, to slap on a second charge; behavior likely to cause a breach of peace; namely, flying a party flag on his car, a privilege heretofore reserved for the emir and the British Resident.

The scene in the alkali court was breathtaking in its day. There was Aminu, standing upright, fully shod, while all others present had removed their shoes and were prostrated on the floor in front of the alkali. The three witnesses had apparently been very hastily briefed for when Aminu insisted that they remain within the courtroom until the hearing was completed, to avert consultation, they were unable to identify him. They had never actully seen him before. Nevertheless, the alkali left to confer with the Senior Political Officer, and returned with a verdict of guilty. But he also reported that he had been advised to restrict Aminu's sentence to three days! Aminu was whisked away quickly, leaving the hooligans gathered outside the courtroom little time for anything but hooting and hissing.

In the jail, the short-term convict lived on tea boiled by a friendly prisoner rather than try to eat the abominable food placed before him. The chief jailer, embarrassed, offered to smuggle him out at midnight and feed him at his own house. But Aminu turned him down, saying the emir would be furious if he found out. The period of incarceration was brief, but the caged bird found time to sing out . . . "The smell of the prison house is a perfume to me . . . [It is a hallway] through which one has to pass before achieving victory against imperialism. They may laugh at us now, but their laughter is only for a time. Forces . . . are working fast to overthrow them. . . . [We must] never falter, meander or submit, but go straight ahead on the road to freedom."[30]

By tradition, a released prisoner was supposed to go directly before the emir to pay his respects, but Aminu informed his captors that as of that day this convention was broken. Whereupon the chief jailer drove him through a hostile crowd to the safety of his own Sudawa quarter. Years later, when musing about this incident, Aminu felt that the punishment would have been much more severe had it come a decade later, during the federal elections of 1964, for by then the fear and antagonisms of the northern leaders were much more intense.

The second trial, in the British Magistrate's Court, lasted ten days. Policemen came from all over to guard the surrounding area. There were eleven defense attorneys, nine from Lagos and two from Kano. Within the month that elapsed between the arrest and the trial, the case had become a national issue, resulting in a show trial of gigantic proportions, unprecedented in the North, with tumultuous crowds milling about in the streets outside the courtroom. About sixty of the police, including women wardens, had entered Aminu's compound, forbidding those within it to move, and removed all his papers.

In the courtroom, the witnesses merely had to state that in their opinion the effect of the newspaper article was seditious. The weaknesses and paucity of the evidence angered the magistrate, but after two days of deliberation, he returned a verdict of guilty. The sentence—four months or fifty pounds—was intentionally limited, to permit Aminu to participate in the elections later that year. He chose to pay the fine.

Following the federal elections and less than six months after the first two trials, came yet another trial. This time a ten-line Hausa song poking fun at the NPC ministers and MPs was once again adjudged seditious. Aminu was accused of writing the poem and he and the man who had printed it were tried. When his battery of lawyers pointed out that there was no evidence that Aminu had even written the poem, and that it had actually been written by one Abba Maikwaru, he was acquitted.

Throughout the social and political explosion that developed in the early 1950's, and Aminu's leading role in it, it was not surprising that his personal life took second place, and suffered thereby. The first and most meaningful thing in his life, the upgrading of the talakawa and the masses of the North from their ancestral yoke, was a man's job and he figured he was the man. Even though one of his particular goals was the liberation of women, with the accompanying extension of the vote to them, achieving it was essentially a man's task. If perchance one woman managed to escape the state of total subjugation in which Hausa-Fulani women found themselves, she could hardly be very effective against the centuries-old concepts of respect, deference, modesty, and their "proper" place. So, Aminu and NEPU busied themselves at the bottom of the political ladder up which both men and women had to climb: granting women the right to move freely about, outside their compounds; extending the vote to them, as had been done in southern Nigeria; and giving them the all-important right to education.

One woman leader, Mallama Gambo Sawaba, was trained in NEPU's School for Propaganda to head up a women's wing, formed in 1953 in Kano. But the restrictive social milieu with which she had to deal was clear when she was arrested, along with about two hundred other women—the first of several arrests. The severe limitations which women themselves placed upon their own activities reflected their lack of political sophistication. For example, at a conference of the women's wing in 1958, their demands for the vote were coupled with a resolution asking for a "law prohibiting women from smoking in public."[31] Aminu's thorough knowledge of the North told him that if they ventured beyond a minimal platform, they ran the risk of alienating large numbers of potential allies among the tradition-steeped northerners, male or female.

When comparing his own public position on the role of women with that of his cousin and close friend, Isa Wali, Aminu is quick to point out the difference in their respective roles. Isa, a civil servant who breached the social barriers, was answerable only to those in the civil service and perhaps the emir. Aminu's constituency was vast, including large segments of the poor, superstitious, and uninformed who had to be approached, not in direct, shocking confrontation, but through a gradual educational process. They would perhaps more readily understand and accept an advocacy of a more advanced social role for themselves, he explained, if it came from one of their own, a Western or locally educated woman.

The loose Hausa-Fulani family ties, permitting children to leave the household in their early years, coupled with the accepted marital pattern of polygamy and easy, frequent marriage and divorce, enabled northern traders to leave home for extended periods without unduly upsetting their households. In his political activities Aminu followed the same pattern. Although he encouraged more equitable relations between husband and wife among those around him, he evidently had neither the time nor the inclination to devote any significant part of his life to altering it. Creature comforts and satisfying family relations were sacrificed on the altar of his greater social and political drive. His time had to be devoted to broader causes than his own interpersonal affairs.

Apparently, his relations with Hasia suffered such a fate. He felt the conditions which any wife or wives of his faced were quite clear from the start. If these conditions were unacceptable, his wife was free to go elsewhere. This did not mean grievances could not be aired, since he felt that discussions of this sort would be uplifting, and give the wife the dignity she otherwise lacked in Hausaland.

Within these limits, Aminu tried to make marriage as comfortable and productive as he could for his wife. When his primary pursuit was teaching, in Bauchi and then in Maru, he had more time for Hasia and a personal life. But when he gave up teaching for politics, he went the whole hog. Hasia was settled in his old family compound in Sudawa and almost immediately began to register dissatisfaction. Aminu became quite unavailable to her, either in Kano or on the

road, but this was further compounded by a mother-in-law problem
—certainly not made easier in a polygamous society. Though
Aminu's father was monogamous, Tasidi, his wife at the time Hasia
moved into Aminu's household, was anxious to establish herself as
uwar gida ("wife in charge of the house")—Hasia, bright and by this
time educated beyond most women of her day, was stealing the center of the stage, teaching the women (and men) the three R's, and
was unwilling to delegate her household independence or responsibility or to be dominated by this jealous mother-in-law. Tasidi fixed
upon Hasia's childless state to give vent to her venom, caring little
how loudly she shouted or how many neighbors were within earshot.
If Hasia couldn't produce a child, she declared, Aminu should get
a number-two wife. If he refused, let him divorce Hasia. Aminu
could keep away from the shrew, but Hasia could not. Thus she went
to her own mother's household and refused to return, resisting the
entreaties of her mother, Aminu, and assorted friends.

Hasia had actually come closer to sharing her husband's life
than did most Hausa-Fulani women, but now Aminu's soaring interest permitted him little time for participating in family squabbles
or even for arbitrating them. Their culture permitted separation with
little upheaval. His concern for her welfare, however, continued even
after she left the household. Hasia herself testifies that when he had
insisted on getting her a job to utilize her education and secure her
future, he was only displaying the compassion that was an innate
part of his character, and wasn't especially reserved for her.

They both remarried shortly thereafter, but within a month or
two after Aminu's third wife joined his household, she was stricken
with smallpox and died. A year later, he was married once again, this
time to his current wife Shatu, but through it all he never lost touch
with Hasia. She attended a subsequent wedding celebration of
Aminu's in 1969, and as recently as 1970 Aminu sent her on a pilgrimage to Mecca. She stayed a few days in Kano to thank Aminu
and spend time with her successor, Shatu.

Shatu, at the age of eighteen when she and Aminu became
husband and wife, had already been married once before for several
years. Her uncle and *waliyi* (guardian or foster parent), Shehu Tela
with whom she had lived from age ten to fourteen (up to the time of
her first marriage) was a vigorous, active NEPU supporter who had

been jailed in the struggle four times. Shatu had been to Koranic school, but did not really start learning Arabic and English until she joined Aminu's household, where those who had learned from Hasia were able to help.

Aminu was still too busy for the formalities of the wedding ceremony, but his relatives and legates carried out a good part of the traditional and religious chores—reading Koranic verses at the proper time and delivering kola nuts, clothes, and of course the sadaki, or bride price, to the bride's kin.

This marriage rapidly fell into the same pattern as its predecessor. Aminu fulfilled such household responsibilities as dispatching frequent letters while away and returning with gifts for his wife and children, but he never let them interfere with the intensity of his national leadership role to the slightest degree.

Shatu eagerly grasped every opportunity to broaden herself, traveling abroad to England, Mecca, and the United Arab Republic and learning English in the process. Accompanying this freedom to travel was a greater freedom at home as well. With Aminu's permission she could move about Kano relatively freely—shopping by car, for instance—without causing too much of a stir. Aminu encouraged her to fill in the long separations that were the norm of his household with self-education; to utilize the social work and first-aid training she had received in England, even to do needlework.

As was common among prominent families, various children were "given" to the Aminu Kano household. By 1969 they numbered five—from Mohammed, aged thirteen, on down—most of them related on Aminu's or Shatu's side.

Although Aminu admits to loneliness at times, he says that his energy is absorbed by the frenetic pace at which he races most of the time, and by the distractions of the many people who surround him —and he has strongly urged his wife to find equivalent diversions. In any case, he does not propose to change his life style or to become a homebody in the future. He remains political from head to toe, and revels in his role.

Aminu's position vis-a-vis the constitutional reforms introduced over the period starting with the Richards Constitution in 1946 and ending with Nigerian Independence in 1960, was a multifaceted one. Tactically, his major concerns varied over the years. It is fairly evident that Aminu's "pie in the sky" was ultimate elimination of the power of the old, entrenched feudal establishment in the North. To varying degrees from year to year he also opposed ignorance and filth, British colonialism, and southern encroachment and domination. These he regarded as his political goals. As long as the British presence was still the dominant force, Aminu realized that the emirate system would continue to be maintained. He therefore zeroed in on the achievement of independence from the British. When it became apparent that this would be just a matter of time, he worked to establish conditions for independence that would most closely approximate his own long-range goals. Through all these efforts ran one connecting thread, the need for education. Without it, no goals could be attained. The educational discrepancy between north and south was fraught with the danger of regional domination—in his eyes a condition only slightly better than the imperialist hegemony prevailing at the time. To avert this danger and to avoid losing sight of his basic goal, Aminu established a political base independent of the northern hierarchy, the NEPU. As we have seen, he refused to permit himself or NEPU to be absorbed into a southern party, or to become an appendage of one.

His first constitutional involvement on a governmental level occurred in 1950 when he went, as a representative from Maru, to the Sokoto provincial conference on constitutional change. After that, he attended every major national constitutional conference right on up to Independence in 1960. In addition, he went to England on several missions to protest the constitutional lag that distorted the electoral process. Testimony from many participants, friendly or unfriendly, Nigerian or British, indicates that his role was active at all of them.

At the 1953 London conference stemming from the "self-government now" struggles and the Kano riots which followed, Aminu and Abubakar Zukogi comprised the NEPU delegation. There were nine other Nigerians, from the NPC, the NCNC, the Action Group, and the National Independence Party. The NPC delegates advanced their eight-point program asking for virtual separation of the three regions, but withdrew it after about a week, probably at the prodding of the British. Although Aminu opposed this NPC proposal and was actively engaged in all other issues of the conference, he concentrated his efforts on the inclusion of constitutional guarantees of human rights for Nigerian citizens. The ostensibly radical southern parties concerned themselves with more parochial interests, leaving Aminu and his colleague, Zukogi, to fight for the human rights clause. The British argued that there had been no such clause prior to or during British occuption, so why include it? Aminu countered by pointing out that Ceylon, India, and Burma had all won this concession, so why not Nigeria? His continued persistence on this issue finally produced British agreement in 1958, the Northern traditionalists notwithstanding.

At the 1954 Lagos conference, Aminu was able to promote discussion of reform of the Northern regional courts, in addition to strong support for a One Nigeria. By 1957, the question of Independence overshadowed all else. Probably as a delaying tactic, the British said that they could not grant independence until the human rights issue, raised by NEPU and the political minorities, was settled. A commission on human rights was set up at that stage, toured Nigeria for one year, at the conclusion of which they submitted their recommendation in favor of the NEPU proposals.

With this fight won, Aminu turned to the specifics of political freedom: women's rights, direct elections, and democratization of the Native Authorities. Here he and his allies achieved only partial success, for in the North, women's right to vote has not been granted to this day. He chalked up this defeat as a compromise necessary to the achievement of independence, but never once ceased the struggle to achieve this political goal on the local front. Still the Sardauna (and his henchmen) would not compromise. Indeed, the Sardauna vowed privately that a woman's role was to make babies and that as long as he was running things there would be no votes for women in the North.

The Nigerian students in England at the time of the conferences represented Aminu's staunchest supporters (students still do), whenever possible making their voices heard. Even though the British Labour party never gave him any official support, individual left-wing Labour M.P.'s and their friends pushed for what they considered the progressive road to Nigerian independence, projecting NEPU's role in the proccess.

Each time Aminu returned to Northern Nigeria, he was greeted by gigantic rallies of his supporters. There he would report his interpretation of what had transpired at the conference, raising funds in the process. The always low NEPU treasury was replenished simultaneously by the sale of badges during these periods of enthusiasm. On one occasion as many as 20,000 badges were sold at two shillings apiece.

As the nation moved toward independence, Aminu immersed himself to full depth in the murky political waters, utilizing every electoral opportunity to challenge opponents with his person and party. With the active aid of the British, the entrenched bureaucracy continued, by fair means and foul, to hold fast to its course and maintain its grip on the power structure. After some electoral defeats and some victories that turned into defeats, in 1959 Aminu finally won a seat in the Federal Parliament from his home constituency in Kano East. With this elevation to the status of a national representative, he found himself in a changing role requiring the transfer of a good part of his activities to Lagos and the federal level. Though for him there was no accompanying shift of power, this could still be broadly considered as a partial changeover from politician to diplomat. He welcomed the shift as a new challenge, even though the national problems soon caught up with him, and deeply embroiled him in the web of coalition politics and the accompanying ideological decisions which were inevitably forced upon him.

10. STATESMAN-PARLIAMENTARIAN

When Aminu the parliamentarian found much of his time occupied with national affairs, the contradictions in his political life were accentuated. His primary goal had consistently been the democratization of the North as part of a united Nigeria. Yet within the brief span of the year following the 1959 elections, his country was to become politically independent of its previous colonial master, with hardly more than a vague approach to genuine liberty or democracy. Notations in Aminu's diary indicate the repressive atmosphere that prevailed prior to and at the time of the federal election:

August 23, 1959	Back in Kano; trouble; fearful parents calling sons to leave NEPU
September 8	Disturbances in Kudu—100 arrests and injuries.
October 1	Hope political leaders will reach decision on maintaining peace.
November 3	Entire delegation to Sardauna re Kano repression all jailed! Weren't even seen!

In the acrimonious atmosphere that followed the elections, a national reconciliation of some kind had to be forged to run the country, since no one party had achieved a majority. What was eventually worked out was a coalition between the NCNC based in the East and the NPC of the North, with the Action Group of the West serving as opposition. This left Aminu's party, the NEPU, in the contradictory position of emerging as chief victim of the bitter campaign, at the very time that its alliance partner, the NCNC, was sharing government responsibilities with its arch rivals: a violent opposition on a regional level—partnership on a national level.

Aminu's consistently maintained dialogue with his opponents stood him in good stead in the face of this contradiction. He reasoned,

186

correctly or otherwise, that from any augmented position of influence he would be much more effective in achieving his goals. But with more than 2,000 of his followers still in jail, he felt that it would have been unseemly, at the very least, for him to accept a ministerial post with prestige and no power, coalition government notwithstanding. Unless it was a ministry such as Internal Affairs, in which he could do something about the repression, an appointment of this sort would have been pointless. In any case neither the powerful Emir of Kano nor the Sardauna of Sokoto would be likely to permit it. Curiously, the Prime Minister even passed Aminu over in May 1962 for an appointment as Resident Commissioner of Economic Development—a sort of roving ambassador in the Ministry of Economic Development, to be based in Washington, D.C. It was generally felt that the heavy hand of the Sardauna was the decisive factor in both these cases. Nevertheless, Aminu did agree to accept a post as Deputy Chief Government Whip, where he continued to play what he considered to be an independent role, accepting or rejecting resolutions on the basis of their validity, not party loyalties.

Up to this point, the attempts of NEPU's ally, the NCNC, to embrace political groups in other sections of the country had led to a loose alliance, permitting great autonomy on the part of their parliamentarians without the imposition of strict central control. This arrangement fitted in well with Aminu's insistence upon keeping his options open. It enabled him to place his relations with individual NCNC MPs in much the same category as with his friends in NPC. That is, he accepted their proposals when in agreement with them, and rejected them when he disapproved. For example, Ekotie-Eboh, an NCNC party boss and Minister of the Treasury (subsequently killed in 1966, during the first coup) was the man to whom one went when something needed doing. Whether or not he could be considered straightforward, Aminu had to approach him as though he were, meeting with him on parliamentary or party business only when necessary. Otherwise, they were in two different worlds. As a vice-president of NCNC, Aminu met with Michael Okpara, Fred McEwen,* and others at party meetings regarding the financing of

---

*Michael Okpara, Chairman NCNC, Premier of Eastern Region; Fred McEwen, Organizational Secretary, NCNC.

NEPU's electoral expenses by NCNC, for this became the nub of the relationship between the two parties.

Aminu's speeches in Parliament immediately and clearly indicated his freedom of action. He supported any parliamentary attempts to expand women's rights and human rights; and to wipe out corruption and all vestiges of colonialism even after Independence.[1] Aminu didn't feel too conflicted, for as always, he tried to vote on the issue, and to avoid factional friction.

His cordial relations with Abubakar Tafawa Balewa, chosen again as Prime Minister in 1959, and with all those NPC'ers who naturally fell into Balewa's camp, permitted him to accept posts of national responsibility, even as their respect for him enabled them to accept him in such roles, regardless of local antagonisms.

Thus he was a logical choice as a delegate to the U.N. in New York City when the long-awaited Independence finally arrived in 1960. To his NPC antagonists the appointment was a mixed blessing. On the one hand, the gadfly could do less damage on distant shores than at home; on the other hand, the prestige carried by the position tended to build Aminu up as a national leader. Nevertheless, the Prime Minister, knowing Aminu's competence and interest in foreign affairs, felt the country could benefit from his talents. Recognizing these same contradictions, Aminu accepted the appointment gladly. From his point of view, in addition to its advantages, it would give him a much-needed respite from the political wars—an opportunity to shore up his energies and replenish his arsenal.

During the federal elections of 1964, neither Aminu nor any of the other politicians came to the U.N., for they were busy contesting their seats back home. Since regional assembly elections were held in the first few months of an election year, Aminu was able to remain on the local electoral battlefront without seriously interrupting his U.N. duties. His assignment on the U.N.'s Second Committee (Economic) taught him much, carrying him to trade conferences in Geneva and elsewhere and developing his expertise in economic affairs.

Overall foreign policy for Nigeria was determined by the Foreign Ministry, so that if the need for a significant shift in position arose in the U.N., permission had to be obtained from Lagos. But unlike some of the larger countries, Nigeria afforded opportunities for the use of individual initiatives. As leader of a party out of power, Aminu had a great deal more leeway to take far-out positions than he would have had as a leader of government; yet surprisingly enough, he approached decision-making on the international front quite soberly. His radicalism was applicable principally to the local scene. At this time he was a "relative" revolutionary when dealing with the emirate system; for his goals were modernity, radical administrative change, education, enlightenment, and economic improvement. In a feudal society, a staunch democrat is a revolutionary, whereas in a democratic context he becomes just another liberal.

Thus Aminu's influence, in the U.N. and wherever an international position was called for, was toward progressivism and vigilant neutralism. He was a militant pan-Africanist and opposed to multilateral pacts, with their accompanying intracontinental rivalries. Unlike the Nkrumah brand of pan-Africanism he did not rule out more realistic halfway points, such as regional unification as part of an over-all, stronger version of the Organization of African Unity (OAU) on whatever basis it could be achieved.[2] Judging from Aminu's prior political history, one might have expected an anti-Western slant, but it never emerged. He could have been considered more "Eastern" oriented than his NPC colleagues only if his willingness to accept economic aid for his country from whatever source it came, or his militant championing of non-bloc diplomacy (exclusive of the African bloc) could be categorized as such. "We seem to keep our door open at all times to the West, simultaneously maintaining a closed door policy to the East . . . unnecessary conditions are placed in the way of Nigerians who wish to go to the Eastern countries; . . . the double-faced policy our government often adopts toward some of the countries of the Eastern Bloc leaves much to be desired in our foreign policy."[3]

Aminu's independence, so characteristic of the political wars of the 1950's, carried over into his international stance as well. Illustrative of this was his position vis-à-vis pan-Islamism, Israel, and the Middle East. On the one hand, he was accused of emulating Nasser and the United Arab Republic in his attempts to upgrade the judicial system in Northern Nigeria by abolishing the Moslem

courts and his sympathetic identification with Nasser's attempts
to modernize Egypt. On the other hand, even though he felt that
pan-Islamism was never a serious force in Nigeria, Aminu scored
the Sadauna for trying to lead the North out of the Federation of
Nigeria and into the Arab world through his overt religious sym-
pathies and prejudices.

Aminu met Golda Meir at Ghana's Independence celebration
in 1957, and eventually visited Israel as an official guest of the
Israeli government. When he addressed himself to Nigerian Moslems, his concern was less for their possible anti-Jewish feeling than
for any anti-Christian feeling. They had relatively little experience
with Jews or Israelis, but anti-Christian laws had not been uncommon in the past, and Christian missionaries had been stoned at
times. Consequently, he felt free to encourage technological contact
with Israel for what it was worth to Nigerians, and to oppose the
anti-Israel position urged by some of his fellow countrymen.[4]
Though his commitment to Islam was deep, he associated himself
with the moderns of the Moslem world in his attempts to introduce
a nonfundamentalist approach to the religion locally.

His independent attitude applied equally to the Western world,
to China, and to the Soviet Union. Thus he was free to make personal
decisions on the basis of issues rather than loyalties and international patronage, and to remain on cordial working terms with most
parties to international disputes. The maturing of his human, personal relationships made him invaluable to Nigeria's U.N. delegation and the committees he served, while teaching him a great deal
at the same time. He found he could frequently pave the way for
successful consideration of his resolutions through the simple de-
vice of clearing them with the key countries and blocs before he
even presented them.

Now instead of working in the restricted milieu of Northern
Nigerian and party politics, criticizing the local authorities or the
Action Group, Aminu had to defend the interests of his country in
relation to the world—temporarily swallowing some of his own in-
tramural complaints in the process. He began to mellow, to gain
new perspectives and tolerance as he observed delegates from the
Eastern and Western orbits at work. The job was a national duty

to him, a school and an opportunity to rub shoulders with the world; and he thoroughly enjoyed the broadening process which accompanied the assignment. Concurrently he managed to befriend many foreigners both within the U.N. among the diplomats of the world and without, among the native New Yorkers. The parochial leader of his countrymen was being graduated into the world of statesmanship. When he had the chance to invite two international guests to the Independence celebration in 1960, he chose two Americans: Dr. Mercer Cook and Miss Maida Springer (who had been instrumental in inviting him to make a trip to the U.S. in 1959 under the auspices of the American Society for African Culture [AMSAC])

It was at one of those informal social gatherings mentioned in Chapter 1 that someone asked about his mode of dress in the various countries he visited. "What determined whether he dressed Nigerian or Western style?" His laughing response indicated that, even as in his relations with his family and those around him, so his sartorial habits were determined by their political effect. In Nigeria, he most frequently wore the long, straight, simple robe known as a caftan, avoiding the royal turban and the flowing large-pocketed gown worn by Hausa-Fulani aristocracy yet staying within acceptable limits as far as the talakawa were concerned. In Lagos and the south, he would wear the traditional northern garb, the *riga*, specifically establishing himself as a northerner.

When abroad, his mode of dress varied with the circumstances. In 1951-1952, at a gathering in London during one of the constitutional conferences, Aminu was the only one to appear in Western dress, to the chagrin of the tradition-minded British officers present. When one of them expressed disappointment, asking "But where is your native dress, Aminu?" he evoked in response, "Aren't you Scottish?" After an affirmative reply, Aminu returned with, "Then where is your kilt?"

Aminu explained his dress in the U.S.A. in these terms, "At the U.N., we had to establish our self-esteem and integrity, to inform the world that we existed as a national entity, so I wore national dress." Now since it is no longer necessary, I wear Western clothes. In London, too, I resort to Western dress, for there the prevailing attitude toward someone in African attire is still to look down upon the wearer as a colonial, whereas in France, where an exotically dressed African is an 'intellectual,' I often return to caftan or riga."

The only time on record that he ventured to become a stylesetter was in 1967 at a mass rally in Kano welcoming the formation of a separate Kano State. Aminu arrived dressed in a simple, unadorned cotton overblouse extending a bit below the waist, with no collar and a row of buttons down the front, and trousers to match. He urged all he could to adopt this practical garb for work and play, since he considered the flowing traditional robe inefficient and impractical. This style, now known as the "Kano State Suit," has since become extremely popular.

Aminu's graduation from the political arena of the Northern Region to the national and international scene required that he raise his sights accordingly. When he considered the relative merits of radical vs. gradual change, he could no longer think solely of how fast the Northern Region's autocracy could be altered to conform to the theoretically more advanced state of the other regions—or, for that matter, even of raising the national level a mite higher. He had to think of Nigeria in relation to other nations, capitalistic or socialistic. To what degree should other nations be emulated? Was one master plan better than another? How could the gap between developed and underdeveloped nations be closed? And so on.

Characteristically, he refused to accept any one country as a prototype; rather, he drew from its ideals. Democracy was not what existed in the U.S. or Great Britain, but that "system which permits the people . . . to determine their rulers . . . and to effect their succession without violence according to a rule of law." Socialism or communism was not the U.S.S.R. or the People's Republic of China, or Marx amended by Lenin or Mao, but "an ethic of selfless devotion, of militant partisanship, of rigid adherence to principle . . . practical opportunism, of exaltation of one . . . supreme principle."[5]

He also questioned and fought against the concept that because coercive circumstances existed in other countries when they went through their industrial revolutions, Africa must inevitably follow the same cycle. He still felt strongly that Nigeria could skip the horse, bicycle, and automobile stages and go right to the aeroplane; intermediate steps could well be leapfrogged.[6] His grasp of these problems was quick and penetrating, but he seemed to understand the problems better than the possible solutions. His integrity and independence made it easier to see more than one side to a question; consequently, it also made solution systems difficult to arrive at. Thus his international responsibilities tended to make for less polarization in his thinking, and perhaps less certainty as to where he was going and how he was to arrive there. The pragmatist in him, his ability to make a realistic appraisal, together with an ability to act— all tended to modify his national stance, making him less of a radical and more of a practical politician, more in the Kennedy image than a Tom Paine. Though this made him a more effective public servant, his image back home among the intelligentsia, students, and youth became somewhat blurred. There were some who attributed the change to his acceptance of a role in a coalition government that included the NPC—the devil incarnate, the hub of his verbal diatribes, the group responsible for the deaths, jailings, and persecution of his followers. A segment of the political savants began to think of him as an intellectual capitulator, as having gone the way of all flesh like so many Nigerians before him.

Intense discussions during this period found him troubled about these apparent contradictions himself; for he saw them as well as, or better than, the many who observed from afar. He could always answer to himself for an action or decision, but his constituency would not necessarily see it in the same light. The numbers of followers who gathered in his living room in Lagos or Kano or when he was touring had not diminished. To those who were close to him, Aminu had not collapsed or even faltered. But among those who were further removed—at the University of Ibadan, in local administrations, and elsewhere—there were doubters. The venue for the stage was changing but still Aminu had to remain at one with his audience. To become a local warrior once again would require a different orientation. He had to move forward, while simultaneously calculating how to put this movement into context on the home front. That task, it turned out, was not easy.

NEPU, Aminu's political base and alter ego, was in difficulty. At its core, the party had been built and maintained on a diet of ideological devotion and self-sacrifice: on the "return of all confiscated lands . . . to the peasants; taxation with proper representation; and the abolition of privileges."[7] Yet the succession of elections, each bringing its share of repression and torment to the individual victims, was taking its toll. "NEPU's task was to create among the peasantry a conception of an attainable alternative social and political order. . . . The obstacles were indeed formidable . . . [rendering] . . . futile election victories short of [success] at the regional level. The net result was . . . [to deny them] . . . visible examples of the prospective fruits of change."[8]

All around them, sycophancy and self-serving seemed to be on the ascendant. Instead of being punished for their evil deeds, those who had succumbed were being rewarded for their opportunism. Those who had remained steadfast were not only losing the elections, but were suffering doubly after the fact, when the northern clientage system began to move in on them inexorably. "Simply by identifying itself with a viable organization of society, the NPC could offer blandishments that were real and immediate."[9] On one hand, these blandishments were dangled in front of the victim's eyes. On the other, they denied traders access to their goods, and farmers faced an intensification of the same unjust tax system that had driven them into opposition. The very ones who had sacrificed most, who had remained loyal through jailings, beatings, and the travail visited upon them, in despair were beginning to look around for a feathered nest of their own. Just as they had become radicalized in the struggle, so they were being prostituted by the climate of opportunism that permeated the nation. Their cause, exterminating evil, was getting no place. The moral fiber of the country was slowly crumbling.

In the south, whatever ideological base the NCNC had had began to disappear. Zik had accepted its loose, independent relationship and alliance with NEPU, avoiding conflict in this way; but now the NCNC leaders were ferreting about for favor, for jobs, for work and trade contracts with government. They were looking with disfavor upon the more ideologically consistent NEPU, their northern ally, thus acting in a fashion very similar to the NPC, their northern opposition. Everyone in the country seemed to be grabbing for a larger share of the pot. Michael Okpara, leader of the NCNC after Zik became Governor and then President of Nigeria, proclaimed in a convention speech that a party that does not win elections will, like a flower, wither and die. Power was becoming the glory.

In February 1961, without prior inquiries or consultation, Joseph Tarka, Tiv leader of the United Middle Belt Congress (UMBC) sent a telegram to a NEPU convention urging a united front. Since NEPU was in agreement on the granting of a separate Middle Belt state, Aminu felt the idea was good. However, he felt that with the UMBC's affiliation to Action Group, the telegram could only be interpreted as an open invitation for NEPU to leave its NCNC connections. He concluded that if any such major move were contemplated, it should have been discussed in advance, to avoid the obvious implication that Tarka was buying NEPU for the Action Group. He believed, also, that any such move should bring with it an improvement in status, not merely a nominal change in alliance. Therefore he opposed it.

Six months later, in August, the tangential approach of the UMBC was followed by a more overt move on the part of a group of NEPU leaders who chose to challenge (from within the party this time) Aminu's adamant insistence on continuing the party's ties with NCNC for lack of a viable alternative. NEPU should become a "free and independent" party, they said, cut its ties to NCNC, and refuse to participate in the federal coalition. Though they made no mention of any negotiations with Action Group's leadership, it was an open secret that alluring financial bait had been offered them to switch their allegiance. When it came to a showdown, the Executive Committee rejected the dissidents resoundingly and gave Aminu's leadership an enthusiastic vote of confidence. Although the opposition made claims of taking several thousand NEPUites with it,[10] their faction was badly beaten. During the following year, some of the disaffected went over to the NPC, and a few of the leaders slowly aligned themselves openly with Action Group, but most found their way back into NEPU. The party had retained its integrity, but suffered a further shattering of its already hard-to-come-by trained cadres.

For the first time, Aminu's unquestioned ideological dominance was subjected to criticism from others in the NEPU leadership. None of them ever seriously questioned his strategy or integrity, only his tactics. Some of the more militant among the cadres had made a trip to China in 1960-1961[11] and returned, eager to push the party further to the left. The decision to participate in the ruling government NPC-NCNC coalition had stirred the fires of internecine conflict, opening up the otherwise subsurface sores. Aminu had no exciting victories to fall back upon to soothe his followers, nor did his position permit them the analgesic effect of licking their opened wounds in self-solace, or even the satisfaction of defiantly sticking their tongues out at their tormentors.

The tenor of the times began to affect his own party. NEPU was becoming more isolated. To further complicate matters, financial irregularities were discovered, leading to several expulsions and continued erosion of the party leadership.

These organizational struggles tended to lower Aminu's tolerance level. As an individual, his ties with the people of the North were still ironclad. He was revered by millions as their leader. They stampeded to see him, to hear him, to touch him. But the organizational pyramid which was built around him, ostensibly at least, as the means for the common man to gain power was teetering. He was distracted by his national governmental functions, and those whom he left behind were bickering and taunting one another.

In the midst of all this internal mayhem, and the usual external repressive pressures came the 1961 elections to the Northern House of Assembly—and NEPU succeeded in winning only one seat. Each preceding election campaign had brought the wrath of the authorities down on the heads of their challengers, but Aminu had consistently exerted a moderating influence where he could, pleading with his followers to avoid open conflict. In this 1961 campaign, he pulled out all stops and urged them to hit back. If attacked unjustly, resist. Desperation and frustration had mounted to a fever pitch, so they did not need much urging—but the measurable results were dismal indeed. Obviously some revisions were in order.

If rebuilding was to be done, the best place to start was in the land of his origin, Kano. This was Aminu's original constituency and still represented his well of strength. But the serpent who guarded the well had to be slain before the people could start drawing water from its depths, as had Bayajidda in Daura a millennium before. Even though Aminu was now an MP from a Kano constituency and definite inroads had already been made into the previously unchallenged authority of the emir, Kano's king was still the major force with which Aminu and the local NEPU had to reckon.

Traditionally Kano had always been the strongest challenge and threat to the hegemony of Sokoto. The Sardauna, in a sense an extension of the old traditional Fulani empire, functioning now in Kaduna instead of Sokoto, was by this time known unofficially as Sarkin Arewa (King of the North) instead of Sarkin Musulmi (King of the Muslims and Sultan of Sokoto), indicating the adapted revised form of the traditional hierarchy. Emir Sanusi of Kano the most powerful emir in the Fulani empire haughtily considered himself an independent sovereign beholden to no one. Thus when Ahmadu Bello, Sardauna of Sokoto and Premier of the Northern Region, came to Kano, the emir would send the Madaki, his own prime minister, to receive him; on the same diplomatic level as Sir Ahmadu, according to his tradition-soaked way of thinking. The Sardauna, powerful and pompous with his own sense of status and tradition, did not take kindly to treatment of this sort and invoked his updated power over the emir whenever possible. This created a three-way battlefront. Aminu, with NEPU behind him, attacked the emir on the emirate level and the Sardauna on the regional level, and they in turn used NPC to attack him, their common enemy, as well as each other.

However, the traditional rivalry between Kano and Sokoto was too strong to submerge, even in the face of a common threat. The enmity of decades surfaced as far back as 1959, at the official celebrations for the granting of Northern self-government. The Emir of Kano had been doubly offended—first, by not being seated with the important dignitaries, and then again when he was rebuked for trying to seat himself, uninvited. The irritation was further aggravated by delicate conflicts of protocol in 1961, when the Emir was chosen as temporary Acting Governor of the North in the absence of Sir Westray Bell, the British Governor.[12] Their rivalry continued with each piece of legislation introduced in the Northern legislature that tended to pare the power of the emir's local authority. Emir Sanusi challenged, either overtly or covertly, any bill that superimposed civil authority over his head. For his part, the Sardauna used his civil power to demean the traditional status of the emir by such measures as appointing a member of a Sokoto royal slave lineage to a position of authority over him.

The personal conflict spilled readily over into political conflict within the NPC and eventually led to the appointment of a Commission of Enquiry into the Deteriorating Financial Situation in Kano Emirate, followed by a Governmental Statement on Kano Native Authority Affairs. Finally, in April 1963, Sanusi abdicated the throne, to retire in exile.

As ciroma,* or heir apparent, Mohammadu Sanusi had spared no effort to insure his own succession to the throne. He had tried every conceivable way to make himself the obvious choice of the kingmakers and had succeeded. But he was highly personal and almost paranoid about NEPU, as if it had been organized solely to keep him from the emirship. When Emir Abdullahi, his father, passed away and he was immediately chosen as successor, Aminu and about ten of the NEPU leaders paid him a courtesy call to extend condolences and wish him luck. As they left, they ran a gauntlet of jeers and taunts from the palace servants and found all their bicycle tires deflated when they emerged from the palace.

This guarded suspicion and distrust between the emir and Aminu continued in spite of the facade of politeness with which they treated each other. In 1957, both went by boat to London to attend a constitutional conference. On the thirteen-day trip, Emir Sanusi was chosen as imam to lead the prayer, but depended on Aminu to tell him which direction was east and Mecca. Their civility toward one another was maintained during their stay in London. Aminu, wanting to present a picture of unity in the face of the British, paid his respects daily at the Emir's hotel, as did the NPC delegates.

Back home in Kano, when the Emir reported that Aminu had accepted his traditional leadership by prostrating himself, Aminu angrily denied it, pointing out that this had been merely a courtesy call in the interest of unity and compared the Emir to "a lion who grew a mane to frighten the other animals and hide his cowardice. He jails and flails because he's afraid to face his own people with ideas."[13]

Until their falling out, the Sardauna referred to Emir Sanusi as the "hero of the North" for making it next to impossible for the opposition to function in Kano. In a single year, more than one thousand NEPU sympathizers in Kano alone were jailed on one

---

*A ciroma is not guaranteed to be successor to an emir, though he usually stands the best chance.

pretext or another, for political activity. During this period, the Sardauna urged the emir on, regarding him as paramount, above all other emirs.

And then came the fall. Sanusi had challenged the supremacy of the Northern Regional Government, the modern form used to perpetuate traditional hierarchal rule, by dominating the choice of Kano's parliamentarians and attempting to manipulate them to his own ends. At the same time he continued to rule over the traditional centers of power in the emirate, refusing to accept the dominance of the larger political system. The Sardauna, in a combination of modern and traditional techniques, using the power of the regional government and the cooperation of individual alienated courtiers of Kano's inner circle, succeeded in dethroning an Emir of Kano, attempted several times in the past by Sokoto's traditional leadership, but never so successfully.[14] Nevertheless, subsequent events showed that this maneuver carried great political risks.

The aging and ailing Inuwa, uncle of Mohammadu Sanusi, was chosen as a sort of interim emir to establish the legitimacy of the change, since it could be maintained that Inuwa, brother of Abdullahi Bayero, Emir of Kano until 1953, should have been chosen in the first place.

Aminu recognized this controversy for what it was—a knockdown, drag-out struggle of personalities in the style of past palace convulsions, just as the Sardauna himself had experienced in his conflict with the Sultan of Sokoto back in the mid-forties. While the confrontation was rapidly moving toward its climax, he did what he could to stir it up, knowing that no matter which man would be forced to go, the North and movement for reform would benefit. NEPU printed a pamphlet pointing up the historical parallels of Kano dynastic resistance to Sokoto dominance. When it came to possible advantages to be derived therefrom, Aminu was ever ready to play down the tyranny of past political relationships.

Interestingly enough, back in 1961, at a mass rally, Aminu once again ventured a prediction. Emir Sanusi was pushing his power to its furthest limits, antagonizing many people in the process. An incident occurred wherein property was seized from the two widows of a deceased man and, contrary to established law, given to the Emir's wife to use for rental income. Aminu was infuriated when he heard of it. He searched out a relative of the deceased to lay claim to the house, and shouted to the world that if an Emir stooped so low as to unjustly deny an unborn child (one widow was pregnant at the time) a roof over its head, the time would come when he would be deposed and find no place in Kano. The case was brought to the high court, where the judge advised Kaduna to get the Emir to give way, since it had become a *cause célèbre* by this time, with the entire country looking through the window. The Emir finally had to retreat, but attempted to cover his tracks by having his hirelings break the windows of the house and permit animals to wander in and out, so that he could maintain that it had been abandoned. NEPU raised the money necessary to restore the house to full use.

The world of Northern Nigeria was shaken to its roots by the clash between the two giants of tradition. No one had dreamed that so powerful an emir could or would have been deposed by legal means, with nary a display of force. A new era had been ushered in. Never again would an emir move as an independent sovereign. If he wanted a place in the new world, he had to fit himself into the new national context. Inuwa Wada, who had refused to deal with Aminu for the decade of Sanusi's reign, came to him and said, "Sanusi feared your election would topple him, but it was his friends who deposed him, and you who defended him (Aminu had directed his political associates not to testify before the Moffett Committee of Enquiry or take sides since Sanusi was not being charged with political malfeasance, and he apparently anticipated the conclusion). I will never separate from you again. My house is your house."[15]

Sanusi's friends re-formed their ranks. During the interregnum under the ailing Emir Inuwa, a new party, the Kano People's Party, emerged, dedicated to the return of ex-Emir Sanusi or his son, Ado Sanusi. One of the goals in their manifesto, "to free the country from one-man rule,"[16] made their orientation quite clear. Within several months, the leaders asked for an alliance with NEPU. The request was granted on the basis of the NEPU program, without any NEPU commitment to the restoration of Sanusi.

Toward the end of 1963, the NPC leadership, in a move to stem the dwindling of its support in Kano, called on its people to come to the palace to greet the failing Emir Inuwa. When they provocatively threw stones at NEPU supporters en route, instead of returning fire, the NEPUites decided to try the same tactic. On the following night they paid a courtesy visit of their own. A tremendous crowd, estimated at over 35,000, turned out. A delegation of sixteen was chosen to approach the Emir, physically pushing away the Madaki and other courtiers in the process. They told Emir Inuwa to get rid of these court men, for they were no friends of his, and "The city belongs to us!" The emir thanked them and asked them to pray for him. No one molested them as they returned to their homes, but the Emir died that very night.

The secret police reported these happenings to the Sardauna, who realized that the next Emir had to be a popular one, or there would be trouble. The name of Ado Bayero was on NEPU lips for he had been a relatively progressive man. Sardauna wanted another, but he agreed and Ado was recalled from Senegal, where he had been serving as Nigeria's ambassador.

Although Aminu had steadfastly opposed the emirate system, he had always followed the traditional custom of treating emirs with the civility and respect expected of a northener. Gifts were exchanged, usually initiated from rich to poor, an aristocrat to a client, or elderly to the young. When Aminu paid his respects to the Sardauna, even in the bitterest of times, he would be given an expensive gown, or a cash gift. The gowns Aminu would pass on to his father or a mallam. (The mallam in turn would send Aminu a bag of grain or a shank of cloth.)

Emir Ado Bayero observed this pattern of exchange, except that, because of his more advanced educational status and progressive orientation, the gifts were on a higher level. Whenever Aminu returned from Europe or the U.S., he might, for example, present the Emir with a book he thought would interest him. He had been on reasonably good terms with Ado in his pre-emir days, and had teased him at times about his royal heritage. When Ado worked as a bank clerk and rode a bicycle, Aminu had banteringly suggested that a motorbike would be more suited to his status, for some day he would be emir. As chief of police, Ado was reputed to have been relatively fair, sometimes even to the point of disagreement with his brother, the Emir. When he was chosen Emir of Kano, Aminu cabled from New York congratulating him on the fulfillment of his prophecy. On the political scene however, not much changed, for the electoral repressions continued and even intensified.

The schism which developed in Kano when the emir was deposed gave new life locally to NEPU's waning political challenge, but at a heavy emotional price. Sanusi's out-of-favor supporters were now willing enough allies, but these were the same people who had been among NEPU's worst persecutors. What did they have in common with their former opponents as a basis for cooperation? Certainly not the restoration of Sanusi; on the other hand, all were against one-man rule, the major principle of the KPP. As the months went by, the "people" from the Kano Peoples' Party officially came over into NEPU, and a movement for an independent Kano State burgeoned forth, though it did not take shape as an effective, unified, full blown force until after the 1964 elections.

The tugs and strains within Northern Nigeria's traditional structure increased during the 1950's as modernism and Independence approached, contributing greatly to the instability of the region. The conflicts brought on by the long-existing rivalry between Kano and Sokoto Emirates; and the class conflict between the masses (talakawa) and their rulers (sarakuna), with its overlapping Habe vs. Fulani dissensions all continued apace. To these was now added the new challenge of the young, educated elements, who opened up a new area of conflict between the regional and emirate centers of authority.

The simmering political pot was agitated by yet another unsettling factor: the religious brotherhoods. These religious fraternities involved a complicated system of loyalties to specific Moslem leaders of the past, who at one time or another had set themselves up as authentic interpreters of the true Islamic faith. As each generation passed, disciples of the founders of these two groups (Sheik Khadir and Sheik Tijjani) managed to convince the followers in each of these two groups that they were the legitimate inheritors of the mantle of interpretive authority. Each, in turn, had their representatives (muquaddams) throughout Northern Nigeria and West Africa, in the major centers of their influence.[17] The originator of the Fulani empire in Northern Nigeria, Usman Dan Fodio, was a member of Khadiriyya. All the Emirs of Kano, starting with Emir Abbas (1903-1919), were followers of Tijjaniyya, thus abetting the rivalry between the royal houses. Kano became the Hausa-Fulani center for Tijjaniyya, Sokoto for Khadiriyya. Naturally, warring political groups tried to influence and win the support of these religious fraternities. The Tijjaniyya movement took strong hold among the talakawa right across Hausaland. This being the case, when Tijjaniyya strength grew up in areas such as Eastern Sokoto, the British understandably regarded it as a factor leading to instability. When Aminu was in Maru Teachers' Training School in Sokoto Emirate and raised the simple question of an imam's improper performance of religious ritual it was earth shaking because of the fear that it might be stirring up the Khadiriyya-Tijjaniyya rivalry.

Aminu's early assessment of the relationship between religion and his political goals led him to avoid involvement in religious controversy. Although his family was generally under Tijjaniyya influence, he was never initiated into the order. Nevertheless, as Prof. C. S. Whitaker points out, "A natural alliance existed between the *turug* (Tijjaniyya) and NEPU in certain parts of the Upper North—where membership in the two organizations was usually reciprocal."[18] But Aminu was engaged in spreading social and political ideas which would attract educated and progressive-minded young men, not one religious order or another. The youth of both Khadiriyya and Tijjaniyya tended to be NEPU sympathizers, while the government and the conservative mallams openly preached against such allegiance and tried to influence them through their respective orders. Mallam Nasiru, Khadiriyya leader of Kano, who was close to the palace and an official in the Emir's court, preached against NEPU to the old and young of his order, as did Sheik Tijjani, current Tijjaniyya leader. In spite of these pressures, most of the younger men remained loyal to NEPU. Extracts from a sad and wistful letter to Aminu in 1964 indicate the pull still exerted by religious and traditional beliefs; the level and type of pressure the society put on the young NEPU supporters; and the growing gap between the two generations. The author, a school teacher, and NEPU nominee for Sumaila in the federal parliamentary elections, had been jailed for alleged incitement to violence.[19]

Dec. 20, 1964

To the President-General of NEPU, Chairman N.P.F.

Dear Sir:

My withdrawal [of candidature in the federal elections] is depressing to me. . . . I was forced to withdraw due to paternal influence. [Now] . . . Inuwa Wada will be returned unopposed due to the pressure of my father. . . .

I was pleased with my arrest, thinking my father would be annoyed with my treatment, but the old man wouldn't give way. Immediately my father heard of my nomination . . . he came to Kano. . . . I had already been under detention for seventy-five days. . . .

I was asked to come to the prison interrogation room. . . . To my dismay my father was seated [there]. . . . I fell to my knees and greeted him. . . . The first thing out of his mouth was, "Choose between the two: your candidature or me, your father!" He threatened to disown me for life and for death, unless I withdrew. . . . It was this statement that moved me, for I never know what would be my fate . . . on the religious side. [Instead] I offend you, my second father. . . .

The Magajin did not use any direct threats or personal influence on me, but I would not deny that his influence was used indirectly through my father. . . . Whether he was threatened I do not know. . . .

My withdrawal has nothing to do with money or threats, but solely a father's earnest desire which I am forced to entertain. . . . I still support you and your party. [I will come back] into active politics when and if my father happens to die before me. . . . In deep mourning I have composed the poem below, [entitled] "Disappointment."

> How much do I value the blessings of a father,
>   for to me they are precious and dear.
> As the winds of change draw so near,
> I leave my desires for his sake for the world to hear,
> My father's annoyance is what I really fear.

In permanent devotion and eternal allegiance to you and your party.

Yours obediently,

MUSA SAID ABUBAKAR (Disappointed)

The most revered interpreter of Tijjaniyya today is one Sheik Ibrahim Niass, of Wolof descent, resident of Kaolack in Senegal. He has gradually established his authority over the years through study and learning, divine inspiration, and acceptance by a significant segment of mallams, particularly in and around Kano Emirate. He is widely considered as being of the highest of fourteen orders of saints (*Gauth*) and the one and only Reformer of the century (*Mujiddad*).

Dating back to the time he met Emir Abdullahi Bayero of Kano in Mecca, years ago, the sheik slowly gained acceptance as spiritual leader in the emirate. His relationship with the Emir had political as well as religious connotations for Islam holds that only through a system of Moslem government can the conditions be set for the purification of Islam. While the French pushed Ibrahim as a Moslem leader for all of North Africa, the British tried to establish the Emir of Kano as a British counterpart. Suleiman inadvertently foiled these colonial machinations by introducing the two, ultimately leading to their joining forces.

The Emir of Kano strongly needed an outside spiritual authority to counteract that of the Sultan of Sokoto, as temporal and religious matters in the region were deeply interwoven. The spread of Reformed Tijjaniyya throughout Hausaland, creating the first genuine trans-ethnic Moslem group in Nigeria, greatly strengthened his hand.[20] When Emir Sanusi permitted himself to be initiated into Tijjaniyya he knew it would tend to neutralize much of the class protest movement of the 1950's. When he became a religious deputy of Sheik Ibrahim, he could come on stronger by representing the masses on a religious front. This position in the hierarchy, however, was not necessarily restricted and exclusive; if they so chose, other religious leaders could each reach Sheik Ibrahim independently.

Since Ibrahim had such a revered status, Aminu could not afford to ignore the political ramifications. The students of the more enlightened Reformed Tijjaniyya mallams served as a source of support for NEPU. On the other hand, the orthodox mallams close to Emir Sanusi attacked Aminu and his followers as sacrilegious and ungodly. In 1962, when Sheik Ibrahim Niass came to Kano, he sent Aminu a secret message to meet him in Kaduna. Aminu reports that the meeting elicited the following advice from the Sheik, who knew full well the effect NEPU was having on the Tijjaniyya youths:

"Don't let the British or anyone divide you from the non-Moslems. Work with everyone; use each other to come to power. Don't let them divide you, as the French try to do in my country." Sheik Tijjani, one of the conservative Tijjaniyya leaders of Kano who was present at the meeting, tried to report that Ibrahim had condemned the NEPU, but Aminu called a mass rally to tell his version of what really had transpired. He proposed that both he and Sheik Tijjani send sworn affidavits to Sheik Ibrahim for his corroboration. In 1963, when Emir Sanusi was deposed, Ibrahim cleverly appointed him Caliph (his representative) of all West Africa, in this way retaining Sanusi's followers for Tijjaniyya.

During the 1964 federal election campaign, Aminu found it judicious to visit the great Shehu Ibrahim at his home in Kaolack, to identify himself with this very large group of religious devotees. Ahmadu Trader and Salihu Garba, followers of both Ibrahim and Aminu, accompanied him and took photos of all the significant symbolic acts of endorsement: Ibrahim clasping Aminu's head in his hands, putting food in Aminu's mouth, and embracing him. A calendar with these photos was used in the election campaign to eliminate any doubts that Aminu continued to enjoy the Shehu's good graces. The orthodox leaders of Khadiriyya and Tijjaniyya may have been clashing among themselves on ritual or political grounds, but the young NEPU followers of both seemed to be united within the fold.

Religious brotherhood politics entered into Aminu's tactical thinking principally as a defensive measure, since the thrust of his ideology was away from any mysticism that tended to enshroud religion, and toward the separation of temporal and religious authority. If one segment of religious thinkers fell in as natural allies to achieve this goal, they were welcomed; and if one segment attacked this liberating approach, he would defend against it—and counterattack.

While these efforts at repair and rebuilding of political alignments were going on in Kano, a region-wide effort was progressing simultaneously. In the southernmost sections of the North, known as the Middle Belt, the move toward an independent state had progressed even further than in Kano—to the point where the disaffection wtih the dominating NPC superstructure had precipitated rioting among the Tivs in 1960 and again in 1964. The United Middle Belt Congress, the principal opposition group in that area, led by

Joseph Tarka, had been associated with the Western-led Action Group, but by late 1962 had broken with it. Their appeal to a NEPU convention in 1961 for unity in the North was rejected by Aminu and the NEPU leaders, but it did indicate long-standing community of interest. Thus when affiliation with Action Group was no longer a factor, a series of conferences took place between Aminu and Tarka. These led eventually to a formal alliance, known as the Northern Progressive Front (NPF), in October 1963.[21] Over the years, NEPU had supported the breakup of the monolithic Northern Region, to give adequate voice to the larger minority groups. The NPF was the logical outcome. The Kano People's Party, several smaller groups, and even some NPC dissidents were included in it.

Shortly thereafter, the leaders of the southern regional parties, the NCNC and the Action Group, consolidated their position by forming their own coalition. When the northern and southern groupings joined forces in the United Progressive Grand Alliance (UPGA), the polarization of Nigerian political forces was pretty much completed. The NPC succeeded in getting only the National Nigerian Democratic Party (NNDP) in the West and one or two small groups as allies. (The NNDP was the party that broke away from the Action Group in a factional split in 1962, in order to remain in power in the Western Region when Awolowo, Enahoro, and company were jailed, ostensibly for treasonous activity.)

Aminu had long sought such a polarization, looking toward a division on ideological grounds, but until then opportunism, local tribal loyalties, and corruption—with the attendant carpet-crossing —had been rife in all parties. The grouping into two major alliances lent some ideological substance to the oncoming federal election contest, for the Nigerian National Alliance, (NNA) the NPC-led group, was generally status-quo oriented and UPGA was geared toward liberalism, socialism, reform, and change. But obviously nepotism and self-seeking did not disappear with the formation of the two alliances. The UPGA people never really had a chance to hold power and consequently to be tested in action, and, as pointed out earlier in this chapter, motivations other than altruism had penetrated rather deeply into NCNC, Action Group, and even into NEPU.

In the North, the uniting of all opposition parties into one group revived Aminu's hopes of making a major impact. The Northern Progressive Front was a key to victory, for in the 1959 elections the

Action Group and NEPU had split the anti-NPC vote in the North. If their unity produced even slight improvements in their position in the North, the Grand Alliance could become the majority party nationally and be called upon to organize the government. They even thought of possible organic unity, going from a Grand Alliance to Nigeria's first truly national party. What had been started in despair and demoralization had rapidly developed into a real possibility for significant progress. Moreover, there were strong indications that Aminu—because of the strategic importance of the northern opposition as well as the universal respect in which he was held—was a likely choice for Prime Minister in the case of an UPGA victory.

None of this, of course, had an effect on Aminu's and NEPU's major stumbling block, the power of the Local Authorities and the emirs of the north. Alliance and unity notwithstanding, they still had to face the continuing repression and intimidating presence of authoritarian police and civilian administration. The NPC recognized this in considering the oncoming election battle. With the effective regional state apparatus at their disposal, its leaders were not too worried about the North, but the West was crucial. So long as their ally, the NNDP, retained control of government in the West, as did the NPC in the North, together they could continue to dominate the country. However, the unpopularity of the NNDP in the West was fairly apparent, and draconian measures were indicated.

As the elections drew nigh, charges were levelled by UPGA leaders that the governments of the Western and Northern Regions were forcibly preventing UPGA candidates from even filing their nominating petitions and posting their bonds; that meetings and campaigning were flagrantly prohibited. Political thugs attacked and fought back openly in the streets. In a letter to the Provincial Commissioner on December 3, 1964, Aminu charged, "Aminu Abdullahi was said to have been beaten up . . . and thrown like a dog into the police cell . . . and died in the night [several hours later]."

At the NEPU headquarters in Kano, confused and disoriented political refugees appeared, homeless after their farms had been burned to the ground. The NEPU officials gave each of them a few shillings per day and a spot on the ground to lay their heads. Their numbers grew as the election approached, building up to over a thousand people with their entire families. Together with the fees for the lawyers hired to defend the party's victims, they represented a severe drain on NEPU's election coffers. In the same letter mentioned above, Aminu stated that "Thousands . . . all of them [UPGA] by inclination . . . have been victims of tyranny by illegal arrests and lockup, by summary trials. . . . Awful stinking police cells have no more space for newcomers." Fred McEwen, in a personal interview in August 1969, recalled that "In 1964 in the North there was much violence—and beatings and imprisonment. I was in Kano in September for two days when we conducted an around-the-clock investigation to prepare evidence on injustices, a huge endeavor. Aminu was 100 per cent with us and knew everything. He was frustrated at times, of course, but remained constant. Everyone came to him for their needs. The pressure was tremendous. A lesser man would have broken down."

The NEPU President-General met with Ibrahim Musa Gashash, NPC party leader in Kano, to try to avoid bloodshed by arriving at some procedural agreement on the conduct of the elections. Gashash agreed to try to persuade his party leaders to avoid bloody clashes, but all to no avail. By the end of September, events had reached fever pitch. Daily entries in Aminu's diary read:

September 28, 1964   Kano arrests increase. See electoral committees re booths and protection of boxes.

October 1   Kano situation still hot.
October 5   Waves of cold-blooded arrests of NPF members.
October 15   More arrests of leaders and supporters.
October 16   More and more refugees in NEPU offices.
October 22   NPC-NNDP determined to win by any means. Letter from Sardauna to me.

During the last few weeks of the campaign, the violence rose to a crescendo. Pitched battles continued. Opposition supporters were stoned, homes and cars burned to the ground. Two months before the election, Prime Minister Balewa called the leaders of all the parties to a conference and succeeded in getting everyone's agreement to a sixteen-point program for a peaceful and fair election— which everyone promptly ignored. President Azikiwe warned that the nation was approaching the breaking point and would split asunder if it continued its downward path toward national cataclysm.

"As . . . the period . . . for the official nomination of candidates closed and the large number of unopposed candidates in the North [and West] became known to the UPGA leaders, they began to call for a postponement of the elections on the grounds that serious obstacles had been placed in the way of UPGA candidates attempting to secure official nomination in the Northern and Western Regions."22

By December 28, two days before the scheduled election, the turbulence, the calls for postponement, the threats of boycott, and even possibilities of secession had reached such a point that President Azikiwe called on Prime Minister Balewa to delay the election six months. He further requested that the U.N. be asked to supervise the election. The Prime Minister refused, maintaining that postponement would be beyond his province, and under the jurisdiction of the courts. Three of the six members of the Federal Electoral Commission resigned on the eve of the election on the grounds that the chairman had announced there would be no postponement, without having secured the concurrence of the commission.

When it became clear that victory would not be possible without being able to run candidates in many areas, with many of the candidates in jail, and with full NPC and NNDP control of the ballot boxes in both the North and the West, UPGA decided upon a last-minute boycott of the election. Communication and discipline in its ranks were not developed to the point where the vote could be cut off completely, but the more aware and disciplined ranks stayed away from the polls. The lopsided results were 200 seats for the NNA to 54 for UPGA, out of the 312 seats available. Aminu's constituency turned in a vote of 1,700 NPC to 690 NEPU, out of a possible total of 40,000 eligible voters. (In 1959, with a far smaller registration role, a vote of approximately 14,000 won the seat for Aminu.) A violent end of the first Federal Republic of Nigeria became an immediate possibility. Presaging events of a year later, the instability and lack of solid democratic roots has come to a head.

After five days of intensive day and night consultations with Aminu, Tarka, and the NCNC and Action Group leaders, President Azikiwe and Prime Minister Balewa accepted a compromise advanced by Chief Justice Ademola of the Federation and Chief Justice Mbanefo of the Eastern Region, which permitted the Prime Minister to form a government of national coalition.

Aminu and most of the rank and file of UPGA, including the militant Zikist Youth Movement in the East, regarded this settlement not as a compromise but as a sellout. Aminu knew that so long as the election was not completely nullified and so long as the aggressive, autocratic Sardauna and his cohorts continued to dominate the government electoral apparatus, no democratic solutions were possible. New elections in the East and a few constituencies in Lagos and the West were possible, but obviously could not be held in the North.

By January 16, Action Group and NCNC, in top-level meetings, concluded that, temporarily at least, they would give the Balewa government a fair trial. In essence, what this did was to preserve the state of self-serving opportunism that had prevailed to that date. The Action Group would have a chance to recover its control in the Western elections coming up that year; the NCNC would dominate the Middle West and the East; and the Northern Progressive Front would be left at the mercy of the Northern Region's apparatus of repression. "When Zik and Abubakar Tafawa Balewa agreed," observed Fred McEwen, "there was too much compromise. As far as the North was concerned, the NEPU would have been destroyed, with no future."[23] All this just as the country was approaching a major climax; just as the opportunity for the full flowering of a national culture and economy was within its grasp; just as it knocked on the gates of an unlimited future.

11.

NADIR

While gamboling through the open fields of his political adolescence and early manhood, Aminu had been certain that Nigeria could not advance if the old emirate system survived. He had rejected the possibility of any blend of traditional and modern innovative government into a viable, progressive form, via constitutional monarchy. The entire traditional structure had to be eradicated—in essence, a revolutionary approach to eliminating the form as well as the power of class dominance.

In the political arena, his ideas were gradually altered. By mid-January 1965, with the electoral and post-electoral crises behind him, he arrived at the reluctant and bitter realization that the talakawa were not strong enough, united enough, courageous enough, or enlightened enough to throw off the ancestral yoke, though they might welcome such an upheaval once it was achieved. The combined total power of the British overseers, the federal authorities, and the local traditional rulers had been and remained just too much for them. Aminu had joined the struggle initially to eliminate the reinforcing power of the British, and was arrested several times in the process, but he hadn't fully sensed that the real value of the British to the traditional rulers was to train their successors in the use of modern techniques of suppression and enforcement of power, before they stepped aside. The elections of 1951 were a new governmental procedure to which the emirs had not yet worked out an adequate response, with the NEPU victories a result. But feudal rulers quickly learned that a combination of modern and traditional forms—clientage, religion, intimidation, jailing, brutalization to the point of murder, preventing opposition candidates from filing, ballot stuffing, and so on—was extremely effective. While the British were on the scene, the more overt forms of suppression were controlled, and the 1959 federal elections had the semblance of fairness. But in 1964, the first post-Independence elections, all stops were removed.

Aminu's nationalistic approach and his alliance with southerners (NCNC) had just not been enough. Either the entire system had to be overthrown or one had to gain control of the top in some way, in order to impose changes and eliminate traditional government on the local level. During the 1964 elections Aminu and his allies attempted to combine forces throughout Nigeria to wrest central control from the entrenched northern traditionalists, and subsequently impose another target goal upon them, i.e. local democratic government. The attempt had failed.

Nevertheless, failure was somehow not an acceptable concept for Aminu. Though he had participated actively in the negotiations immediately following the elections, he felt that the compromise worked out was a return to the old politics, which had yielded such bitter fruit in the past. The UPGA alliance had completely abandoned the North to the power barons. Even the more progressive element in the NPC was silent, afraid that to speak out against terror at that point would be political suicide.

NEPU hastily convened top-level meetings, not only to discuss its future but to try to fend off impending bankruptcy, an aftereffect of the disastrous federal elections. A bad tumble down a flight of stairs, resulting in a broken ankle, did nothing to help Aminu maintain an even keel in those troubled times either. Even Shatu, his wife, contributed to the turbulence by exploding a minor personal feud against some visitors paying courtesy calls.

Although the elections had been boycotted by the Northern Progressive Front, several UMBC candidates, including Aminu's colleague Joseph Tarka, were elected from the non-Moslem areas of the Northern Region. In spite of the existence of a supposedly "broadly based" coalition government, Tarka had not been chosen by NCNC to represent them as a cabinet minister. And to add insult to injury, by February 15, a short month and a half after the elections, Tarka was jailed, again for "use of abusive language against the Sardauna," this time for four months.

The disruption had been so great that no one knew what was left of the NEPU apparatus. Thousands of sympathizers had become refugees, their property destroyed, party records confiscated. No matter how disoriented were the remnants of the political movement, Aminu and the central working committee felt they had to convene another NEPU congress, to determine where to go from there. Radio announcements and word-of-mouth communication notified potential participants, for direct, organized contact had broken down in many cases. A "White Paper on Political Problems Facing Nigeria" was prepared to present to the assembled group, assessing NEPU's role and possible organization changes.

Amazingly, more people showed up than at any previous convention. Hundreds of branches sent delegates and even paid their convention fees (increased to five pounds per branch from the two pounds required at past conventions). It was an inspiring revival of spirit for them and gave them courage to go on, even if in low key. Though there was some internal dissent, what dominated the convention were the suggestions for unifying all the opposition elements in the North, including NEPU, the new Kano State Movement, and the United Middle Belt Congress, into one organic progressive party. Even the possibility of calling on southerners from East and West to join them in an all-encompassing national party was discussed. Aminu's presidential message outlined the basic needs for his country, considering the possibilities of (1) a presidential or parliamentary system; (2) creation of new states; (3) changes in the judicial system; (4) guarantees of law and order; (5) changes in electoral law; (6) improvements in economic and educational development; and (7) alterations in foreign policy.

Today almost all of these reforms have been begun or accomplished, or are being actively considered in the post-military era. Specific demands for separate Kano and Middle Belt States have already been met. Pleas for scholarship aid, even addressed to the impoverished NEPUites, almost immediately yielded a dozen scholarships for Northern students to study in the Eastern Region. Judicial reform is well under way.

Some of the people associated with the Kano People's Party, formed in 1963 and merged with NEPU for the 1964 election, began to feel they were being swallowed up and thought of breaking away to form an independent group. Aminu the tactician came to the fore at that point. He, together with the NEPU leaders, the leaders of the two factions of the KPP, and some dissident NPC members, formed a new non-party group known as the Kano State Movement. On April 14, 1965, a mass meeting to launch the new organization brought out what was reputed to be the largest crowd in Northern Nigerian political history.[1] Ahmadu Trader, Aminu's long-time ally, was chosen its first president and Aminu its political adviser.

At the time, Mallam Aminu's role in this local alliance was questioned by some of his associates, as well as some independent academic observers, for many of the KPP people were supporters of the former Emir Sanusi and perpetrators of the grossest attacks on Aminu and his party. Yet it was part of Aminu's political pattern to work with persons of any ilk who accepted his basic goals, no matter how temporarily—and the KPP people had come into his party, not vice versa.

In this instance, as in many others in the past, when he and his political boat were in danger of being capsized, he managed to weather the severe storms, to stay afloat on the political high seas. He was functioning more out of inertia than out of conviction during this low point in the year 1965, making only what seemed to be the obvious tactical moves. He labored to tie together the disparate elements in Kano that were uniting around the cry for an independent Kano State. He rejected an NCNC offer of 150 pounds a month for personal sustenance because all his associates were completely ignored. He conducted discussions with the UMBC leaders to try for all-Northern unity or an all-Nigerian party. But he lacked conviction. Though his tactics continued at a fast pace, his strategy needed reevaluation—and somehow without strategy to tie his thoughts together, he tended to lose heart. To recognize that the stage was not yet set for the real-life drama he had written did not mean that the play was invalid. If he thought of leaving politics at that point, it was more in terms of a moratorium than a defeat.

The electoral process, at least in Nigeria, was failing him. He could not see through the morass of continuously building up a powerful opposition force, that was crushed periodically with each election attempt, destroyed hundreds, and damaged thousands. The popular appeal of his crusade remained but it was no longer an ever-growing democratic opposition. It was more like a tide past its peak, with each succeeding wave breaking high on the beach but exposing a little more sand as it receded.

A man is a man, is a man, is a man—Aminu was getting tired. There seemed to be only careful retrenchment in the offing. The Western Region election was building up into another major crisis of violence, repression, and conflict. And Aminu needed a break— time to stand off and reassess, time to reflect.

For the first and only time in their long political relationship, Prime Minister Abubakar became suspicious of Aminu's motives. His conviction that Aminu always moved out of suasion, not malice, was shaken when some of his ministers told him that not only was he, the Prime Minister, threatened with bodily harm from an UPGA plot that had been hatching, but that Aminu knew about it and had said nothing—and Abubakar was angry. It took some months of ferreting about for information and subsequent explanations to convince him that these accusations were fabricated out of whole cloth with evil intent. Shortly after Abubakar finally realized and acknowledged his mistake, he asked Aminu to do a short tour of duty at the U.N. in New York City.

The assignment came at just the right moment. The Western Region elections had been held in mid-October 1965, under conditions of virtual civil war and chaos. The ruling NNDP had declared itself victor in the face of overwhelming evidence of majority support for its opposition, the combined Action Group-NCNC. Campaign turmoil degenerated into post-election chaos. It was obvious to Aminu and most political leaders that drastic measures were necessary. But what?

In this unsettled frame of mind, he arrived in New York City and went through the routines of his assignment, but remained meditative, seemingly remote from those around him. Six weeks earlier, he had visited Tanzania and gotten a picture of "African one-party democracy" as practiced there directly from the lips of its high priest, President Julius Nyerere. Perhaps that might work in Nigeria under other circumstances, but surely not in his strife-ridden country at this moment in history. The temptation to go into the NPC and try to win control away from the reactionaries was ever-present, but Aminu knew that all those who had attempted political infiltration in the past had been swallowed up and lost.

All the opposition elements in the North were approaching organic unity. In the South, UPGA, too, had a semblance of unity. But another sellout such as the one following the federal elections of 1964, if repeated in the West, with each sycophant grabbing for a bigger share than the next, would be disastrous. How could he think of returning to electoral politics under these circumstances?

Aminu's political life had followed that of Nigeria very closely, originating in 1942, just as Nigeria was emitting its first peeps of national birth. He was organizer or an integral part of every "first" in Northern Nigeria as the country matured into nationhood: its first regional organization, first trade union, first cultural organization, first political party, and so forth. At Independence, he was emerging as a statesman and an ardent adherent of a rapid forward movement. Now he found himself at his own nadir at the very moment when his country's existence as a nation was at its lowest ebb. Corruption was rampant in East, West, and North. The iron fist was using every means at its disposal to victimize and eliminate opposition. Aminu was despondent. He had no public office, his party was off balance, still trying to recover from the last shock inflicted on it and already bracing itself for another in the near future. The setting up of underground cells was considered, if it became necessary.

Those who had been through years of self-sacrifice were beginning to be convinced that their cause was not going anyplace and now was the time to look after a personal career; there were ample opportunities for capable men who were ready to put up with the status quo. During this depressing year, 1965, Aminu had advised a number of his colleagues to find positions in which they could be self-sustaining over a period of time yet remain available for a more propitious political moment. Aminu himself seemed ready for a quiet retreat in which he could hibernate, to prepare for the political spring which some day would surely come: a seat on the sidelines long enough for the alignment of forces in his country to change sufficiently to bring him back for another try; perhaps an ambassadorial post remote from the turmoil he inevitably faced while in Nigeria.

The annual meeting of the U.N. Conference on Trade and Development (UNCTAD) in preparation just about that time seemed a good start. His position on the U.N.'s Second Committee (Economic Affairs) as one of Nigeria's politico-economic representatives, enabled him to make constructive suggestions to the Ministry of Trade regarding Nigerian's efforts in this area and at the same time to inform Lagos of his own availability as Nigerian delegate to this conference upon completion of his U.N. stint.

His suggestion was well received by both the Prime Minister of Nigeria and the Minister of Trade.[2] A notation in Aminu's diary on January 5, 1966, read: "Saw Prime Minister—settled UNCTAD appointment.") Aminu felt this would give him a satisfactory perch from which he could consider new political initiatives when the moment for action would present itself.

So with the assurance that he would be back in New York in two or three weeks, he returned to Lagos, leaving a portion of his personal effects in the home of friends to be picked up upon his return. It was, in fact, three years before he returned. The January 1966 coup intervened, precipitating the rush of subsequent upheavals that drastically revolutionized Nigeria's basic relationships—and Aminu's along with them.

During Aminu's forty-day absence from Lagos the struggle and killings which followed the Western Region elections had continued unabated. On December 30, the day of his return, he was greeted with the news that several northerners had been killed in the Western Region. In an extended discussion with the Prime Minister[3] Aminu warned his friend Abubakar that Akintola, the declared but shakily installed Premier of the Western Region, had the confidence of no one. He should resign or be removed, and a caretaker government installed under federal auspices. But Abubakar stated his belief that the easterners were plotting all this disruption in the West, and that they would get their comeuppance. He reassured Aminu with, "Don't worry, Molotov, everything will work itself out." The implication was that dissension was being fomented against Okpara in the East, in retribution for his disruptive role in the West—almost a guarantee that things would *not* work themselves out.

On January 6, Aminu left Lagos for Kano, where a Kano Province NEPU conference had been set up to try to work out a modest modus vivendi for continuing as a party. NEPU was moving closer and closer toward unity with the other opposition elements in the North—this in the face of the disarray in the country and in NEPU-NCNC-UPGA party alignments growing out of the Western Region anarchy. Further complicating matters was a rank-and-file crisis of confidence in the NCNC leadership during that year, when the very dubious post-electoral coalition compromise left the leaders and their organization at loggerheads.

Upon his arrival in Kano, Aminu was given a message by Shatu, his wife, that his former teaching associate at Maru, Abubakar Gumi, now Grand Kadi (Chief Justice) of the Northern Region courts, had telephoned and wanted him to return the call immediately. Aminu did so, to learn that Northern Premier Ahmadu Bello had asked the Grand Kadi to arrange an urgent and secret meeting as soon as possible. After the Sardauna's return from Mecca on January 10, a meeting was arranged at the Grand Kadi's home in Kaduna on Sunday, January 16. The rendezvous never took place, for on January 15, the Sardauna was killed by the soldiers who conducted the first military coup.

What the substance of the conference would have been can only be conjectured, but a day or two after the Sardauna's demise, Aminu consulted Abubakar Gumi, the only other person aware of the projected meeting, who thought that the Sardauna was attempting to mend the home fences, in the face of his troubles in the south. It was the Grand Kadi's opinion that the Sardauna might have been having second thoughts about the extent of the northern repression and wanted to work out some sort of electoral agreement for the impending Northern Regional Assembly elections.

The month of January 1966 ushered in a totally new era for both Nigeria and Aminu, one marked by the attempt to impose national unity through military rule and civil war. Ordinarily, leaders of men, when faced with a sudden military takeover, have to fall in line or retreat into involuntary retirement in order to survive. Aminu's creative approach to politics found a third course open to him: subtle resistance and gradual organizational involvement, while remaining on dry shores out of the easily reached marshes of illegality and subversion.

12.

CROSSROAD

The end of 1965 found Aminu Kano at a vital crossroad. He was at a low ebb, his morale wilted, his party beaten and battered, with no representation in either the Northern Regional or Federal Parliament. No matter that it was because of the conscious boycott of the Federal election and open brutalization of NEPU's membership. The party supporters were discouraged too—out of work and discriminated against. Aminu was advising many of the party cadres to go back to the jobs they had left before becoming organizers, so that a core of right-thinking people would be on hand, to be re-awakened and reorganized at a propitious moment. They were all thinking in terms of a holding action, for the country was too disrupted to permit continued political activity.

Then the lid blew off. The military coup blasted onto the confused, strife-ridden political scene. "The immediate event behind the coup," said one researcher, "appears to have been a meeting between the Northern and Western Premiers, during which it was widely believed that the decision had been made to use the army to impose a drastic solution to the disorders precipitated by the Western Regional elections."[1] Whether or not this course was actually projected, evidently the five army majors who planned the coup thought so, and moved swiftly to launch their historic blow. It is quite possible that the Sardauna's desire to meet with Aminu was related to these behind-the-scenes events, but Ahmadu Bello's sudden death made his plans quite unascertainable.

Perhaps the coup plans misfired, as seems to be the case. Nevertheless, the rapidly breaking events started on the night of Friday, January 14, with the assassination of the Sardauna and Akintola, the Northern and Western Regional Premiers, Federal

Prime Minister Abubakar Tafawa Balewa; Ekotie-Eboh, a cabinet member; and a significant number of high- and low-ranking military officers. Major General Aguiyi-Ironsi, the general officer commanding the Nigerian army at the time, intervened to form an interim military government, with the blessings of, and in consultation with, what was left of the federal cabinet. Though Major Chukuma Nzeogwu, the leader of the five majors who initiated the rebellion, successfully took over the Northern Region, within three days he reluctantly agreed to call off the coup and to accept his superior officer's rule over all of Nigeria. He received assurances from Ironsi that none of the officers and men involved in the coup would be punished, and that none of the politicians against whom the coup was executed would be returned to office. He was convinced that the stated objective of the coup—the establishment of a strong and united nation free of corruption, tribalism, and regionalism—would be carried out. By Tuesday, January 18, Major Nzeogwu appeared publicly with Major Hassan Katsina, Ironsi's newly appointed Military Governor in the North, to state that they were working together in the national interest.[2] All this in spite of the fact that his group evidently had no intention of installing Ironsi if the coup had been completely successful nation-wide. In turn, Ironsi showed his lack of good intentions when, after guaranteeing Nzeogwu safe conduct to Lagos, for talks, he promptly had him arrested upon arrival there.

The military takeover was greeted with much enthusiasm by people throughout the country, though understandably the reaction of the old NPC and traditional leaders of the North had an element of "wait and see." The fact that northerners were by far the principal victims and that no Ibos were executed; that Ironsi, his advisers, and all five majors were Ibo, rendered these leaders of the newly formed government suspect in a country that had been brought up to and over the brink, by the violent, ethnically tainted political turmoil of the preceding year. But the less thoughtful, more emotional and impulsive members of NEPU were elated by the January events. They saw their old enemies, the political representatives of the feudal lords, being turned out—and what could be better? As former allies of the southerners, they assumed that they would be given power in the North and that they would be the ones to administer the long-sought-after local reforms, thus eliminating the despised "family compact" rule.

As in the past, however, the majority of the NEPU members looked to Aminu for leadership and guidance. He approached the new situation soberly, advising caution to all whose ear he could reach, telling them not to rush into anything half-cocked. He suggested that the more exuberant democratically minded northerners temper their reactions and observe the further moves of the new military regime. He knew the possible pitfalls—the twin evils of ethnicity and personal opportunism. Transfer of power did not guarantee by any means that the problems of corruption and regional rivalry for control of the center would be solved.

From all corners of the nation, telegrams and statements of support for the new regime poured in. But Aminu waited a bit, eventually sending a cautiously worded telegram on behalf of the NEPU, wishing the government well. He did not swear allegiance, as most others had done, but expressed the hope that the regime would be able to fulfill its national tasks of unification, democratization, and development.

As events unfolded, Aminu's precautions seemed to have had some basis. Whatever Ironsi's capacity as a hard-drinking general officer, or as a field officer in the Congo or Tanzania, when ensconced on the seat of power he proved to be far from an astute political strategist. The obvious move to unify the country upon his assumption of power would have been to look for allies in the four regions. Since Nzeogwu's "mutiny" had decapitated the politically "in," and much of the military leadership of the North, to move quickly to find supporters there was essential. Aminu, leader of the northern opposition for a decade and a half, revered by large segments of the northern population and respected by all its sectors, was the obvious one to whom to turn. Why Ironsi and his advisers did not do so remains an unanswered question. Martin Dent, in a penetrating article, points out that "among the radicals, Ironsi rapidly made enemies where he might have made friends. Within three months of his coming to power, Tarka, Aminu Kano and Maitama Sule were meeting in Kano to consider how to meet what they regarded as a common threat to Nigeria."[3] It was not until April 16, three months later that Ironsi deigned to give Aminu an audience in Lagos. At the meeting, Aminu tried to discuss the problems of the North with the Supreme

Commander and how to meet them, but to no avail. Ironsi, Aminu reports, visibly speaking through an alcoholic haze, spent three-quarters of an hour haranguing him with a jumbled concept of how to unify the country. He never stopped to listen, never gave Aminu an opportunity to suggest an alternate course of action. Thereafter, if Aminu wanted to transmit his ideas to the Supreme Commander, he had to communicate through the Emir of Kano, a somewhat unreliable transmission belt for his radical ideas.

The arrival of the military on the national scene in all likelihood could have changed the picture drastically, had those who succeeded in seizing power chosen to pursue revolutionary goals. But they didn't. It became clear to Aminu that the Ironsi regime had no such plans in mind when they turned for northern support, not to the radical forces he himself represented, or even to the more enlightened leaders of the NPC, but to the very autocrats whose power he was hoping to vitiate. "To the radical element in the North, it did not appear that there had been any significant changes in the North".4 Not until the second coup did these goals come in sight once again. Meanwhile the welcome and elation which greeted the January upheaval were quickly dissipated. Instead of looking to the people, Ironsi was leaning heavily on the entrenched upper level of the civil service and the tradition-encrusted emirs, the chiefs, and their advisers. It was more like an attempted revival of the old indirect rule of the British colonialists. And this antiquated administrative concept was no longer viable.

This was a strange, confusing period in Nigeria's history, and Aminu's role was even more so. Knowing full well that the chiefs and emirs would fight democratization and the updating of political organization, Aminu had hoped to impose these concepts upon the local emirate governments by gaining control of the center. So long as his alliance with southerners kept the door open to the possibility of this achievement he maintained it, despite mounting disillusionment with their role and a steady stream of blatant attacks from the more conservative northerners. And now the southerners who were in control in Lagos showed no signs of concern for the democratization process.

For the past fifteen years, the regional structure had been growing in power. With the events culminating in the abdication of the Emir of Kano, it had firmly and unequivocally established itself as the dominant force in the North. Yet those who had wielded regional power up to that point were also being bypassed. Aminu felt that the rudderless group that remained, particularly those who had quietly supported his goals from within the NPC, could be utilized in the struggle—just as he had attempted to do with the followers of the deposed Emir of Kano in 1963-1964.

But the former NPC leaders who had survived the coup all ran for cover. The less they were seen at that point, the better they liked it, for the corruption and nepotism of the political days had all been laid at their feet. As individuals they wanted dissociation—a moratorium on political activity to permit the country to simmer down and find some order, some direction.

What was left? A vacuum. Someone had to intervene, to defend the North's interests against the encroachment of Ibo tribal domination—or so it seemed to the northerners. In the interim, all political activity was restricted and discouraged, though not officially banned. "Aminu was never a follower, only a leader. . . . The North was like a brood of chicks, old enough to appreciate the need for leadership, but not mature enough to lead."[5] Aminu at this juncture had to make momentous decisons. He had been a federalist, a One Nigeria man all his political life. Now he was faced with what he interpreted as an attack on the integrity of the North, and no one else was in the wings waiting and available to organize its defense. As had been his destiny since his schooldays, he rose from the depths of his political depression, daring once again, with his colleagues still nudging him forward. On the one hand, he undoubtedly could have advanced his own cause by capitulation; on the other, if he moved where his impulses were directing him, he would risk the wrath of the military government. But counterbalancing these negative considerations, and all-important to him—he had to decide what was right for his country and his North. And unless Ironsi declared the North an "education disaster area" in order to raise its level, no proper federation would be possible.

Thus, what on the surface might have seemed to be flip-flopping, could be interpreted as a deft utilization of changing forces to achieve a long-range purpose. Some observers at the time thought that Aminu would have been even more consistent had he tried to weld the common people of the East and the North together at the same time, but as the days went by, the feasibility of such a course evaporated. The conviction grew in Aminu that cooperation and national unity were not in the offing, even though consolidation at the center was. The new word was "unification," but Aminu, attuned to the North and its needs, read this in only one way; domination.

The sands of nebulous political alignments had shifted once again. Aminu's long-smoldering fear of southern domination had finally culminated in what he considered a genuine and serious threat to the development of his first love, Northern Nigeria, and had altered the balance. He felt that, to remain true to his original goals, he now had to look beyond NEPU for alliances with northerners who had been his former enemies, against southerners who had been his former allies. He was searching for a means to emerge with his principles intact, from the bottom of the well where he found himself, his party and his ideals.

In the meantime there was an immediate practical problem. With no politics, and no money, Aminu, as well as his former associates, had to find some means of subsistence. He rather enjoyed the process, and did find work of a nonpolitical nature. Three of his friends in Kano—Sani Darma, Ahmadu Trader, and Yahaya Sabo—included him in a small trading company which they organized, called the Northern Nigerian Food Supply and Transport Service. They rented an office, secured transport, and began by purchasing yams in the Benue area and shipping them northward to Kano.

Aminu, as has been pointed out, never had much of an acquisitive drive, nor any interest in ostentatious accumulation. But somehow if he thought of it at all, he felt that if politics ever failed him there would always be something he could do—be it in teaching, or civil service, or business. He was never bothered by the deep concern of individuals in Western-oriented culture for their welfare in old age, or the need to put aside some small (or large) nestegg on which to retire. Hausa culture has always required that an indigent be provided with food and shelter by a close or distant relative, so that no matter how poor or undeveloped the region, there was a kind of built-in social security system. On a higher economic plane, this cultural pattern could give rise to a serious social problem known as nepotism. But Aminu, with his group orientation, lacked a sense of private property and never seemed to know where his pocket gave out and where his friends' and neighbors' pockets began. When his income from politics was regular, and greater than his fellows', his capital never accumulated either through excessive in-flow or limitation on the out-go. The outward flow, however, would stop sharply when begging in any form was involved, or when it was obvious that the largesse would be dissipated—for example, by an alcoholic. He much preferred to give money for education or economic advancement, helping people to help themselves. Later, when he had to build a new home and tried to gather together the funds to pay for it, he found others around him pitching in too—a rug, cement, furniture, and so on. These items were less an attempt to curry his favor (he was in a far from favored position at that point) and more a recognition that Aminu Kano had denied himself sums when they were available to him, unlike many other politicians.

But the need to provide sustenance could never amount to a full-time occupation for Aminu. He could think only in social and political terms, even in a period when politics was forbidden. Now as always, Aminu's ability to maintain friendly relationships with men of all shades of opinion stood him in good stead. Recall that these relationships included not only men like the Sardauna and Prime Minister Abubakar, but also extended to most of the lesser lights in the NPC and the traditional authorities as well (the Sultan of Sokoto, the Emir and Madaki of Kano, the Waziri of Bornu, etc.). Many of them had been his teachers or pupils, so he could approach them on a personal basis with ease. Though in the past most of the NPC leaders had moved only with the express approval of the Sardauna, their feelings on his death were ambivalent. ("The attitude of the northerner always varied between veneration and dread and still does to some degree. When the ruler disappears, the dread does too, but what of the veneration?")[6] Everyone breathed more freely, but in no sense did they feel unfettered. They gave Aminu their quiet blessings and wished him success. "We all knew that Aminu Kano could never betray the North and that he knew the Ibos better than anyone else because of his associations."[7]

He moved carefully about the country, using his personal friendships as an excuse for his travels, reporting all his movements to the military. He had to pay condolence visits to Abubakar Tafawa Balewa's mother and widow in Bauchi and his cousin in Katsina. He called on the Sultan of Sokoto after the Sardauna's demise. He went to Lagos to see Ironsi. En route, he tried to allay the northerners' fears as much as possible, and to placate and calm the populace while bringing together those who mattered to discuss their common future. When it seemed that the Ironsi regime was turning more and more to the chiefs and emirs, he had to exercise extreme care to avoid being jailed or provoking repressive measures. Everywhere he found former NPC and NEPU leaders in agreement with his ideas, and a readiness to accept him as their spokesman and replacement for the vacated seat of leadership.

But many of Aminu's friends and supporters were unable to think in these terms of new alignments, new allies. They found it difficult to follow the complicated maneuvers and consequently new cleavages opened wide. Men like Lawan Dambazau, a loyal and devoted NEPU associate from the early political years, were finding themselves outside the pale. Lawan had always enjoyed being at the hub of organization. Yet now Aminu and his associates did not include him in their activities. When Aminu started moving around the countryside to try to unite the North, he avoided discussion with Lawan or anyone else not directly involved in the process. When Constitutional Committee hearings were held in Kano, at which NEPU and NPC people testified, Lawan was left out. He assumed that Aminu was responsible and since he was not in a position to analyze the shifting and broadening of the struggle, he was understandably suspicious of Aminu's role. He felt that perhaps the former NEPU president was being groomed for big things and was leaving his old associates in the lurch. But Aminu quietly went his way, close-lipped, communicating only what was pertinent and only when called upon. Certain other former associates who rigidly retained the strategic approach of the 1950's believed he was abandoning them ideologically, so that a strong, swirling undercurrent of confusion and dissatisfaction developed for a time. Aminu, in his effort to be effective and yet circumspect, did little to dispel these doubts. He advised everyone to reserve judgment and not to be too hopeful. It was the subsequent chain of events, not persuasion, that was most effective in eventually winning the recalcitrant ones over to support his position.

Several groups in the North other than the former politicians—notably the students, the Ibos, and the civil servants—had views clearly germane to the situation at hand. Sani Zangon Daura, now a commissioner for the North Central State, summed up what he considered the students' attitudes at that time: "My friends at the University of Lagos and myself (I was a student there) felt the Ironsi regime was attempting to dominate the North. We felt the only leader who could be trusted was Aminu Kano, for he was spotless. He played the role of father of the northerners. All of us northern students—NPC (my party), NEPU, or non-party people—agreed that Aminu should be leader, with no question of politics."[8] Evidently there was no other northerner of stature to whom they could turn during that period.

The Ibo population of the sabon garis of the northern cities, and Kano particularly, had almost unanimously looked to Aminu and the NEPU-NCNC for leadership, up to the time of the first coup, with many of their leaders coming daily to Aminu's house or office, seeking guidance. But on January 15, 1966 the spigot had been opened and out flowed the waters of chauvinism and tribal pride. The parochial northern politicians had dominated up to then, but now it would be the Ibos' turn to call the shots, and the trail of Ibos who visited Aminu began to peter out perceptibly. This apparently was the interpretation of events by the Ibos as well as the Hausas. Ironsi was hailed by the Ibos as a leader and the military as the group that had put an end to the Sardauna. Many northerners reported that indiscreet Ibo traders flagrantly displayed the Sardauna's photo in the marketplace with sneers and taunts: "This is your leader? What happened to him? Take care the same doesn't happen to you." To what extent these provocations actually took place and contributed to the general ill-feeling is and was debated widely, but it is quite clear that the Hausa-Fulani masses believed this attitude of the Ibos was the prevalent one.

The existence of this ethnic rivalry did not prove in any sense that it was the root cause of the political differences or group prejudice, but it most certainly did represent a serious source of conflict. Because of the interlacing of causes and effects, of the manipulators and manipulated, no one aspect of the complex could be eliminated. The fact that self-hatred might have been the root of a group antagonism did not make that anatagonism less real. Thus, if Tiv or Hausa hates and kills an Ibo because he feels that he himself has been denied a place in the sun and sees the industrious Ibo making his way up the ladder ahead of him, the motive still remains group hatred and ethnic prejudice. Coupled with economic deprivation, is this not generally at the root of social prejudice? One group gets ahead of another, sometimes stepping on the less favored on the way. The two groups develop anatagonisms—one with envy, the other with disdain.

The presence of these antagonisms in themselves obviously didn't produce civil war, secessionist or coup attempts. It was only when changing objective conditions produced a combination of factors that such upheaval broke out.

To cite tribal anatagonisms as the cause of the upheavals of 1966 in Nigeria could be considered simplistic, but one can query: Would these 1966 eruptions have occurred if tribal antagonism had not been developed to the point it had? Although it is true that masses can be, and have been, manipulated for opportunistic gain, would this have been possible if the seeds of discontent had not already been sown in people's minds? Regional loyalties had been built on these rivalries, and over the years had been utilized for better or for worse, but mostly the latter. Thereafter the faucet couldn't be turned off at will, resulting in flooding and loss of control. In any case, the northern Ibos went unpunished for instead of taking punitive measures against the verbal excesses of the northern Ibos mentioned above, the local resentments were permitted to build up to the May violence.

The civil servants, on the other hand, were called upon by the Ironsi regime to handle the administration of government, greatly enhancing their role. Aminu's influence among them, particularly the northerners, was more extensive than with any other group. Alpha Wali, in a personal interview, said, "His political opponents think of the civil servants as his disciples, even in some instances when there is no contact." They were not beholden to the politicos and their status was determined, at least to some degree, by standards somewhat removed from the political merry-go-round. In this way they could manage to stay off the ladder of opportunism and clientage, and to communicate their ideas to Aminu. One rather highly placed civil servant, who was in Kaduna at the time, reports that everyone in the North rejoiced when the first coup took place but that on January 22, 1966, when Abubakar Tafawa Balewa's death was announced, he and his colleagues were confused. They delegated him to go to Kano to consult with the Emir and Aminu Kano. He said, "They assigned me to go to Kano for discussions. . . . I was unable to see the Emir because it was Sallah time (a time for celebration in the North), but I spoke to Aminu. He said that though he had been sharply against the Sardauna's politics, he was never against him personally. [Aminu] was always against the idea not the man. . . .

"We all decided that education and schools were the key. Our lack of these permitted the partial coup. . . . Aminu was the only one who stood as a brave man, not hiding his feelings, giving his advice to the military. He was for us a good consultant, including his ideas on education and commerce."[9]

Another influential civil servant, when speaking about local reforms introduced at a later date, commented, "The best educated can usually be found in the civil service, and they tend to distrust traditional administration." Also, he said, "Most local reform was introduced by the civil service, but Aminu Kano's political activities set the stage."[10]

This long-standing interplay between Aminu and the civil servants, particularly the young ones, was of great value to him in attempting to weld together a united northern front. Their evident distrust of traditional administration was also important, for the civil servants felt squeezed by what they came to regard as an Ibo rule from above, in Lagos, and the traditional rulers down below. Aminu, in his emerging new role, could well be their champion.

By the end of February, the Lagos government appointed a committee for consultation and inquiry into constitutional review, headed by Chief Rotimi Williams. Its members circulated throughout the country, ostensibly to solicit the views of persons of note on how the nation should reorganize itself for the future. When they visited the southern areas, the committee consulted with persons at universities, churches, and at any nonpolitical center who might have ideas on the reorganization of the country. But in the North—since, in effect, all political consultation was banned—to ask for suggestions on constitutional change meant total reliance on the testimony of the local traditional authorities. Therefore, in order to present their own ideas, Aminu and his close friends met in the house of the former lawyer of NEPU, to prepare what they called a "yellow paper," opposed to unification and in favor of the creation of new states, women's vote, and democratization. (This paper eventually served as one basis for talks under the later Gowon government.) Aminu then petitioned Hassan, the Military Governor of the North, and the committee itself for the right to present the testimony of this group. In addition he wanted the leaders of thought in the North to get together to exchange views on a regular basis, as had already been done in the south. At the same time he met with other former colleagues and opponents to try to work out united views on the constitution and to pass them on to the Native Authorities or to the committee. Most of these leaders gave Aminu their blessings and hoped a representative conference could take place.

The Committee for Constitutional Review had gone to Kaduna and Zaria before they arrived in Kano. They had heard opinions that evidently ran counter to the central government's preconceived and previously stated notion that a strong unified central control was to be the system of the future.[11] The Emir of Katsina even raised the question of the sincerity of a study group ostensibly looking for national unity, yet which had such gross underrepresentation for the North on the committee itself.

Suspicion and mutual distrust grew rapidly. The times were tense. The committee received the local comments in Kano, including the NEPU memorandum, went on to Katsina, and then was suddenly recalled. Instead of further hearings, the next move from Lagos was Ironsi's ill-advised and now infamous Unification Decree #5, issued on May 24, stating: "The former regions are abolished and Nigeria [is] grouped into a number of territorial areas called provinces.

"The public services of the former federation and regions become unified into one national public service under a National Public Service Commission.

"On March 3, . . . press release . . . calling attention to the fact that political meetings were, in spite of my order, being held . . . leads me to the dissolving [of] all organizations of the type scheduled therein and banning [of] any manifestations of their political purposes."

The Military Governor for the North, Hassan Katsina, summed up the situation simply with: "The egg is broken into a big omelette!" From a northern viewpoint, these harsh measures by the military

in the face of evidence of strong regional disagreement were far from
conciliatory and far from moving in the direction of Ironsi's stated
aims of national unity. Rather, they proved to be the opposite, an
extreme provocation.

A myriad of elements in the North were driven to unite against
the federal government. The masses felt threatened by the more
aggressive and industrious Ibos in their midst. The radicals and
minority groups were incensed by Ironsi's rejection of their goals of
local autonomy and democracy, as well as of them as individuals.
The traditional ruling groups, heavily dependent on their previously
controlled regional governmental structure and no longer capable of
freely manipulating the public will, could not conceive of themselves
as being more than tools under Ironsi rule, for they saw their bases
of power crumbling. And by extending the unification decree to the
civil service, Ironsi alienated the last group of potential supporters,
the civil servants. Obviously, the long-smoldering, multilevel differences between North and South could not simply be legislated away
by decree. Unification meant elimination of any special consideration
to northern civil servants, who generally trailed far behind the Ibos
and other southerners in education and seniority of service. This
group, perhaps the best organized and most articulate in the North,
no longer felt the need to exercise any restraint upon the popular
surge of anger. They openly showed their own opposition to the
decree two days later, in a raucous but reasonably well-disciplined
demonstration. About two hundred Kano students, the civil servants
of the future, took to the streets, gave the Emir a written statement
of their views to present to Hassan, and dispersed. Aminu, caught in
the swirl of the protest, rescued one or two of his Ibo friends and
urged any of them who came to him for advice to leave for the south
immediately. The fever quickly spread to the masses, in all likelihood
inflamed by disgruntled elements among the old NPC bureaucrats
and traditionalists. The rioters, seeking to release their frustrations
against more tangible targets than the government in Lagos, turned
their ire against the Ibo traders in the larger towns of the North. By
noon on the following day, the Ibos were attacked and had begun to
defend themselves. The following day, May 28, the disturbances had
spread to Kaduna and other urban centers, stopping only after

hundreds of people, Hausas as well as Ibos, were killed in anger and in self-defense throughout the North.

Ironsi's and his advisers' inept misreading of the reaction to his Unification Decree had resulted in disaster. Incredibly, despite this tragic eruption, Ironsi continued to push ahead, seemingly without regard for the consequences. After the May riots his response to a memorandum submitted by the Sultan of Sokoto to Hassan, stating the grievances of the North, was this: "The government now recognizes that one of the main reasons for the disturbances . . . has been ignorance of the government's real intentions"![12] Though the Sultan accepted this explanation and commissions of inquiry were set up, still no concessions of any consequence were made. The only action Lagos took was to turn even further toward the past, by convening a conference of emirs and chiefs in Ibadan at the end of July. While the emirs were still in Ibadan, Ironsi's regime was abruptly ended.

After the May disturbances, an investigative tribunal headed by Sir Lionel Brett, an expatriate, and former supreme court judge, was established on June 27, and August 2 set for its first meeting. But the tribunal never met. The homes of a number of former politicians, including Aminu's, were searched, and the vast exodus of Ibos continued. With no mechanism to redress their grievances, many of them left, confused—with Aminu's name on their lips. In the words of Fred McEwen, former national secretary of the NCNC, "The Ibos felt that his role wasn't what it should have been, that he should have done more for them, but I can't see what he could have done."[13]

Complicated as it must have been for him to maintain it, Aminu's circumspect behavior proved wise in the long run; for when the police ransacked his home and the party headquarters, they found nothing of an incriminating nature. But some of the old NEPU stalwarts evidently did not fare quite so well.

A peculiar and beclouded interplay was set up between Aminu and those who, for one reason or another, had not fully accepted his leadership during the previous few months. Rumors flew about that some people were trying to incriminate him in the May disturbances and, on the other hand, that these same people were in fact

involved in stirring up the Hausas against the Ibos. The police reported
that, in the course of searching the homes of these latter suspects,
leaflets and other materials of an incendiary nature were found. The
people involved (Lawan Dambazau and nine others, including one
or two NPC people), were placed under arrest. Upon learning of their
detention, Aminu reports that he immediately went to the police to
demand the reasons. He was told by Ali Abdullah, one of the prisoners who was ill in the hospital, that if Aminu would make a statement
in Ali's behalf, the police would release him. Aminu did so, but
before such action was taken, the prisoners were shipped via police
van to Kaduna, by order of the government and upon the advice of
the then Provincial Secretary in Kano, a Mr. Nelson. When Aminu
insisted that they be tried promptly, the court conducted an investigation and released them. But they were quickly rearrested and de-
tained, on instructions telegraphed from Lagos. They remained in
jail for approximately three months, until after the second coup,
when with Aminu's urging, the security police released most political
prisoners, including the above-mentioned group.

It is difficult to get a reasonably objective picture of what
actually happened between Aminu and these few of his former Kano
associates during this period, for Aminu, in a relatively favored
position today and being the person he is, can afford to be conciliatory. He tries to minimize what he considers an unfortunate
difference during an indisputably difficult period. Similarly, the
antagonists in the controversy, such as it was, are reticent to discuss
those troubled times, since reconciliation has taken place, and there
is now only one camp in any case.

After his release, Lawan slowly began to visit Aminu's home,
and to exchange the customary gifts, although he did so with some
trepidation, for he feared there might be hostility. But Aminu greeted
him cordially, though never quite with the old pre-coup intimacy.
To bridge the gap and to try to find a place for Lawan, Aminu suggested that he undertake to write a history of NEPU—which he did,
in reluctant and leisurely fashion. Lawan has also become involved
in a trading business, since he did not consider writing as a full-time
occupation.

During the two months between the May disturbances and the
second coup, Aminu was sent a questionnaire. Where and when was

he at the time of the riots? What did he think caused them? And so on. But the federal administration did not seem to use the information or to adjust in any way. They continued to think that the Unification Decree would resolve all conflict. In point of fact, the reverse occurred. The conflict ate its way into the military instead.

Rumors again flew back and forth—about impending coups and countercoups. The Ibos were going to kill all remaining northern officers, political leaders, emirs, and chiefs. The northerners were to do much the same to the Ibos. It rapidly became evident that in the unstable situation, the unresolved antagonisms were going to blow up once again.[14]

It did. Ironsi was in Ibadan at the time, busy explaining to the twenty-four emirs and chiefs why the measures he had pushed through were good for Nigeria. The anti-corruption campaign was to be stepped up, he told them. Inefficiency in the civil service would be wiped out, and the military governors of the regions would be rotated. He even suggested that the emirs be posted around Nigeria in similar fashion, an idea so alien to their concept of local loyalties that the Emir of Kano walked out of the meeting.

The second coup was initiated on the night of July 29, but it was no more concluded as originally conceived than was the first coup. Kismet, the ancient Islamic belief that events will unfold in inexorable pathways, returned to the scene. Three Ibo officers were killed by their northern colleagues in Abeokuta Barracks, followed by similar actions throughout the country. "By ignoring the more radical politicians of the North, as well as the Action Group, and the old opposition, Ironsi had lost the chance of winning support from elements which had previously been in alliance with the south and could have made a bridge between opposing regions."[15] Within a scant six-month period, Ironsi had dissipated the tremendous surge of popular united support for him to the point of chaotic regional and ethnic dissension, the overthrow of his regime, and the threatened breakup of a nation.

As Ironsi was being led out to be shot, on the night of the July coup, he thanked the northern officer in charge for his hospitality. The officer in turn saluted and said apologetically that he had his orders. Ironsi allegedly admitted complicity in the first coup under interrogation at this point, but no corroborating evidence has been produced to authenticate this. "In Ibadan—Ikeja—[and elsewhere the soldiers]—refused to let their officers interfere, while they killed their Ibo comrades and officers."[16] Brigadier Ogundipe, the army's most senior officer sent a fighting unit along the Lagos-Ikeja road to try to stem the mutiny, only to have the men of the unit ambushed and routed. He quickly realized that his control had been eroded, and hastily donned civilian clothes to depart for London.

Gowon was put under guard by the mutinous soldiers and told that he was their choice for Commander-in-Chief. He subsequently achieved effective command power gradually over the next few days, as each of the few remaining members of the Supreme Military Council shifted their support to him.

13.   GOWON AND CIVIL WAR

It is not unreasonable to assume that when a corrupt, reactionary regime is overthrown, the rebels will be progressive and/or revolutionary; and when a countercoup takes place, the reactionary regime will be reinstated. Many Nigerians, young and old, conservative and progressive, saw the circumstances of coup and countercoup in just this light. In retrospect, however, most of those conversant with their country's recent history, regardless of their political bent, feel that this was not the case.

Aminu was one who quickly recognized that the rapidly shifting relationships which were developing were more complex than that, and almost immediately he set about to influence and organize accordingly. During the Ironsi period, he had to convince his former supporters not to rejoice prematurely, and the more cautious among the reformers not to run for cover. He even found himself reassuring his lifetime antagonists, the emirs, that traditional forms at least could be retained even if essential reforms took place. When Gowon took over the reins of government, Aminu was already busy circulating through the North, mustering potential allies. He urged the so-called leaders of thought to come forward to help determine the direction of the new government, rather than to sit on the sidelines, watching events unfold. By this time he had gathered together some of the better educated northerners into a self-appointed discussion group in Kaduna, which considered questions of political importance, such as local reforms, one-party government, and so on. Procedurally, discussion papers were presented and the positions advanced were accepted, altered, or rejected by the group. Among these leaders, Aminu was one who aggressively sought a way out of the maze of charges and countercharges, of whispers, factions, and plots; and he

237

seemed to be the only one, in the group or out, who was ready to go beyond discussion. "For the last three months of the Ironsi regime, Aminu was dominant in the North",[1] testified Ali Abdullah, a former NEPU leader.

When Lieutenant Colonel Yakubu Gowon became head of the government, his attempts to secure broad nation-wide support were enlightened enough to include leaders from all segments of political thought. He and the new military government recognized that, to gain the unity they sought, they had to move forward toward the goals of modernization and democratization, unlike the Ironsi group, which had tried to contain the masses in old traditional forms with outmoded techniques. Their turn toward the civilian leaders in all regions for recommendations on reorganization of government evoked a quick response from the Kaduna based discussion group since they were already mulling over the problems at hand and ready with sober, practical ideas to present to the nation. Subsequently, when the official Northern Nigerian "leaders of thought" convocation took place in Kaduna, this group's previously prepared memorandum on new states was presented for discussion and Aminu chosen to head the subcommittee considering the question.

During the Ironsi regime, consultation in the North was almost exclusively limited to the emirs and chiefs. Any others who had ideas had to submit them indirectly through these traditional rulers. At that time, Aminu suggested to Ado Bayero, the Emir of Kano, that he should do more than pray. He should act as a leader by starting to think of changes, for the power to make changes in local government was his and the times demanded it. He agreed and asked Aminu to submit suggestions to him in writing. When Ado eventually presented these to the other leaders, they were accepted with cheers. However, he never did get around to implementing them himself.

Hassan Katsina, the Military Governor of the North, had enjoyed the relative freedom of movement afforded him up to that point by the exclusion of the politicians, and consequently he was understandably reluctant to accept them as advisers. But under the insistent prodding of Aminu and his fellows, he expanded the concept of using chiefs and emirs as counterparts to the leaders of thought, by forming an advisory committee which included over one hundred northern leaders, representing all shades of opinion, from all thirteen northern provinces. This group in turn chose six men (three representatives and three advisers) to go to Lagos to speak for the North in the constitutional conferences. Similarly, after a long, hard argument, Hassan was eventually prevailed upon to enlist the help of the leaders of the three pre-existing northern parties: Makaman Bida, Joseph Tarka, and Aminu Kano. He asked them to make up a list of five people from each of their former parties, along with several representatives from the universities and the trade unions—a total of twenty-one—to form an official continuations committee. This group would meet monthly to explore issues, advise the Governor, explain government policies to the people, and so on. They continued right through to the post-civil war period, though they ended up having to deal with six separate governors instead of one.

Aminu was a moving force in both groups, perhaps the most influential at the time in welding together some kind of united northern approach to the problems confronting the nation. As one of the North's six representatives sent to Lagos for the conferences, he played a significant back-room role in continuing to push for these agreed-upon policies.

Lieutenant Colonel Gowon had instructed the all-Nigerian constitutional conference to consider four alternatives only: a federal system with a strong (1) or a weak (2) central government; confederation (3); or an entirely new arrangement for Nigeria (4). He ruled out two extremes—a complete breakup of the country, or a unitary state. If the initial impetus of the northern army officers to withdraw from Lagos back to the regions had come to fruition, it would have been tantamount to secession of the entire North and break up of the country. However, in spite of the chaotic and totally unstable condition immediately following the coup, a rapid metamorphosis from a position of regional separation into the realization of the need for some form of national existence emerged through Gowon's own inclination as well as that of his fellow soldiers of Middle Belt and Tiv origins. The about-face of the military and the northern delegation gave the minorities throughout the country their first genuine opportunity to be heard, since regional autonomy would have insured dominance of the largest ethnic group in each of the four regions: the Hausa in the North, the Yoruba in the West, and the Ibo in the East as well as the Mid-West. With a sovereign voice at the federal level, minorities could appeal above the heads of the larger tribal groups. This new position was bolstered by internal pressure in that direction from influential senior civil servants led by Sule Katagum and backed up by Hassan Katsina, and external pressure from the British and American ambassadors.

During the first month or two, Aminu actually consulted with the Supreme Commander no more than two or three times—once with a ten-man delegation from the North and a second time during the Ad Hoc Conference of leaders of thought in Lagos. At first, when Aminu heard that the military was unhappy with the position of the Northern delegation favoring a weak central government, he called Kashim Ibrahim, the head of the delegation, and together with several others, as a committee of five, met with Gowon. He, in turn, impressed them with the need for national unity and the fact that "The army was entrusted with keeping the country intact." Hassan Katsina was rung in too, and hastened down to Lagos to join the consultations.[2]

Aminu's initial acceptance of a loose confederation had been a reluctant acceptance of the reality of the strength of the centrifugal micro-national tugs at the Nigerian corporate whole. Thus, when the army showed itself not only in favor of a strong central government but ready to defend its integrity, he welcomed it, for that had been his inclination throughout his political life. Chief Awolowo, leader of the Western delegation, was at first offended by the sudden shift, but came around. The only group who ultimately rejected the idea of retaining central authority was the Eastern delegation, led by Ibos, who were unfortunately still fearful and shaken by the reality of the ethnic tensions and country-wide disruptions.

The key issue was the further breakdown of the regions into additional states. The great size, population, and power of the North remained the source of much apprehension for the three southern regions. When it had been discussed at the leaders-of-thought meetings in Kaduna, this matter of additional states had been approached with less than unanimity, though a majority seemingly was ready to accept the break-up of the Northern monolith as inevitable. Aminu, as chairman of the subcommittee on this question, submitted the group's recommendation for not more than fourteen or less than twelve states for the new Nigerian Republic. This suggestion was

eventually used as the basis for the breakdown of the regions—
except that Aminu's subcommittee called for seven northern states
and five southern, whereas the final choice was an evenly divided
six and six.

The Eastern Region delegation also objected to any proposals
for additional states, reasoning that this approval would be a diversion from the real needs of the country and would only delay a
durable solution. Quite conceivably, they were also reluctant to
consider relinquishing their hold on their own oil-rich minority
areas. Informed observers felt that no solution would have been
acceptable to the Easterners that did not grant their region an independent sovereignty. Some feel today, in retrospect, that it was then
that the Ibos decided on the eventual collision course of secession
and separation. Aminu's diary contains the following notation for
October 4, 1966: "Account of army mutiny most disheartening.
Speed and action required. East on way to secession." At the conference in Lagos his last attempt to hasten the return to civilian
government, was to approach "Awo, Kashim, Tony, and Eni"
(leaders of the four regional delegations) to try to forge some kind
of agreement on an interim government, but his efforts were abruptly
interrupted by the disturbances in the North and the adjournment of
the Ad Hoc Conferences.

In the past, Aminu had had close political affinities with many
of his southern counterparts, but in spite of the continuing turbulent
disorders in the country, at this point he was evidently firmly convinced that the threat to the North under Ironsi had been real enough
to make him shift his priorities. He felt that the forms of government
—how many states, a strong or weak central government, and so on
—were less important than the need for a unified North.

His concept of his role and that of leadership generally, was
actually closer to the "Hero" interpretation of history. The Marxist
Plekhanov's thinking[3] that out of the interplay of the mass forces
at work, emerges a representative of these forces who becomes the
leader, was altered by him to make the individual a force unto himself, and his relationship to the social forces an integral part of the
history-making process as well. Perhaps this accounted for the gap
between him and his lieutenants in the past. Some innate charismatic
inner strength pushed the individual into a position of leadership, not
the careful nurturing of a chain of command, an orderly passing of

the baton of leadership from the group leader to the next in line nor the emergence of a leader from the surging masses when the need arose. This approach, one might suspect, also permitted him to go outside organizational bounds to look for support. In spite of his insistence on a mass political constituency in constant dialog with the leader, and in spite of his lack of opportunistic ambitions, he seemed to look inside the individual for the inner drives toward leadership. He felt that he as a leader was beholden to the masses with whom he chose to identify and didn't necessarily feel restricted to his past intermediate associates. They too could find themselves roles to play serving this greater mass—and meanwhile the mass felt threatened by the Ibo who for some months past had seemed to them to be sitting over them as the oppressor incarnate.

Despite the long-standing antagonism between northerners and southerners, the rank and file of the northerners were socially submissive. Traditionally, the talakawa were sedentary, fearful, and respectful of power. Not until the traditional authority figure appeared to give license to break the law was blood spilled on a large scale. The Ibo in the North never made any bid for power in the region; such antagonisms as existed were generally restricted to the economic sphere. Even the January 1966 coup did not provoke a violent reaction from the talakawa. That came only after Ironsi had antagonized the local leadership by denying them a share of the power at the center, and compounded their antagonism by the Unification Decree. Only then did the northern masses sense that their own leadership tacitly favored their taking matters in their own hands. The struggles that continued in Lagos under the Gowon government had the effect of permitting this lack of legal restraint to continue. A similar process was going on in the Middle Belt Tiv area as well as in the East and West. The rank and file moved only when they knew that the local power to keep order was weakened—through either disruption or sympathy.

This social immobility and acquiescence of the masses could explain the success of the NPC and of the local authorities' intimidation of NEPU over the years and Aminu's attempt to inculcate non-violent techniques to his followers. Cultural intimidation through traditional, hierarchical, and religious stratification over the centuries was still a dominant factor in the North.[4]

The new government's efforts toward national reconciliation through consultation had been making good progress at the Ad Hoc Constitutional Conferences in Lagos and their regional counterparts, the leaders-of-thought meetings. Such rapid and wide-scale participation of civilian leaders from all regions and of all points of view had a profoundly settling effect both on the leaders and their more enlightened followers. On the other hand, this progress was greatly vitiated by the lack of discipline in the army, then the effective seat of power. The soldiers themselves were indulging in pogrom-like activities, and their unruliness in turn unleashed local savagery and hatred. In the North, thugs and other anti-social elements gave vent to their antagonism against what remained of the Ibo population, with accompanying counter-waves throughout the other regions. In retaliation, on September 23 a number of Hausas were killed in the East, in Port Harcourt and the Imo River area.[5] The rumors and exaggerations emanating from news reports of these events triggered the massive, unprecedented killings of Ibos throughout the North in waves of mutual escalation.

It was a sudden outburst of mass passion, seemingly encouraged by disgruntled elements among the civilian traditional leadership and the army. Perhaps those who had hoped to emerge in the driver's seat, and were diverted by the Gowon takeover of the counter-coup, were trying to discredit him in order to complete their initial design. Aminu wrote on October 2, 1966, "Gowon says there is a plan to discredit him," and even considered the possibility of the U.S. Central Intelligence Agency (C.I.A.) involvement. Violent upheavals like that, followed by an offer to help out he reasoned, could be a big power's attempt to increase its influence—and on the face of things his suspicions actually seemed to be borne out when the United States did so offer on October 5. What appears to be common knowledge is that when the civil war did break out the following year, there was a strong difference of opinion between the U.S. ambassador and the C.I.A. The latter evidently felt that the United States interests would best be served by taking the part of the Biafrans,* while the State Department supported the forces for a strong One Nigeria.

---

*The term "Biafran" was non-existent until the attempted secession of the Eastern Region in 1967.

On October 3, the Lagos Ad Hoc Conference was adjourned to consider the revised and reworked proposals and to reconvene on October 24. That meeting never took place, for the September 30 riots had precipitated large scale migrations and mass flight of Ibos back to their regions of origin. The tenuous dialogue had broken down.

By the time the disturbances finally simmered down, all Ibos had fled the North, and Hausas the East. All constitutional progress had been nullified, and the only remaining contact between Gowon and the Eastern leader, Lieutenant Colonel Odumegwu Ojukwu, was by telephone. The attempt to reestablish military government contact between Lagos and Enugu continued until January when in order to get together, the military leaders had to leave the country and go to Aburi in Ghana.

While these attempts to keep the East within the Federation were going on, the North was having its own problems. The Ibos residing in the North had disappeared almost overnight. Many hundreds or possibly thousands had been killed, but all of a million Easterners left their homes for the region of their forefathers. A gigantic gap was left in northern society that created a problem quite independent of the antagonisms that had provoked the disturbances. The Ibos, in their diaspora had served as technicians, clerks, and civil servants and generally filled a middle rung of the economy that now had to be replaced.

The disruption of the railroads had limited the supply of gasoline and thereby curtailed road transport as well. The North's major crop—groundnuts and the oil derived therefrom, had to be moved southward to the sea, but some three-fourths of the trained personnel had left. Six weeks after the mass flight, services were restored to only about 40 per cent of the pre-coup levels. Postal and telecommunications services also suffered, as did other areas of the economy.

Northerners could replace the traders without too much difficulty, but the trains had to run, the mails had to be delivered, and so on. The government set up a national relief program to allocate funds to restore normal operations in all regions, but with the lack of any agreement in Lagos, the uneasiness and distrust continued. In very short order, the polarization was complete, and the economy of the Northern Region almost at a standstill.

Aminu continued to be totally involved with the conferences and discussions and the advisory role in which he had been placed, completely neglecting his private business. In the course of these discussions however, the educational lag of the northern people was consistently pointed to as a major source of their on-going difficulties. Immediately after the May disturbances and the exodus of Ibos, the need for a crash replacement-training program became evident.

Aminu's multi-faceted activity spilled over into the educational field in the form of an initiative in organizing what eventually came to be known as the Kano Community Commercial School (KCCS). He realized that setting up a full-fledged secondary school for training office and clerical personnel would involve peripheral administrative difficulties that could conceivably be avoided by a purely commercial school of secondary grade. Men like Maitama Sule, Sani Gezawa, Aminu Dantata, Inuwa Wada, and Tanko Yakasai were very receptive to the idea. Even the emir agreed to cooperate, and Hassan, the Military Governor, agreed to cut what red tape he could to hasten the project. Maitama Sule offered the use of his house, which, with minor alterations, served as the school's first home. Within two weeks, two classes were organized and seventy students enrolled, including ten girls and many ethnic groupings of northern extraction.

Thus the first secondary school of any size supported by private subscription was officially opened by the emir at an initiating ceremony. His contribution of 250 pounds was followed by other contributions, totaling approximately 4,000 pounds. Today, the student body has over 400 boys and girls enrolled, a building site has been secured, and a permanent building constructed. The project is an accepted part of the Kano educational scene, with Commissioner Aminu Kano serving as chairman of the board.

The universally recognized need for local government reforms in the North led at this point to a revival of the 1956 Hudson Commission* recommendations for some division of administration and powers between the provinces and the local authorities. Aminu participated actively with the 1956 commission but this effort to

---

*Set up by the British in an attempt to analyze the possibilities of allocating some of the powers of the Native Authorities to other administrative units (provinces).

revive its original proposals was soon abandoned in the maelstrom of regional political tugs and strains, to reemerge later in local reforms of a different stripe.

A man of less inner strength and organizational capacity might have crumbled if he tried to divide himself into as many pieces as Aminu did during these autumn months of 1966. His resilience and stamina were even more impressive when one realized that he had been deeply depressed and ready to go into enforced retirement only a few short months previously. His rapid and relatively complete bounce-back clearly displayed his lifelong ability to continue to function effectively under the most adverse or the most favorable circumstances.

The interregional offers, counter-offers and threats that marked the ensuing months of negotiation culminated in the January 1967 meeting of Ojukwu and Gowon in Aburi, in Ghana. Obviously if it was necessary to meet outside the country for both parties to feel secure, the country's deep-seated problems had not yet been resolved. This despite the federal government's five-point program, committees of conciliation, and repeated invitations to the Eastern leaders to meet with the Military Governors, secretaries, and advisers. Even the minimal agreements arrived at in Aburi were disputed immediately upon the participants' return to Nigeria. Although by this time Gowon and the forces he represented had made it clear that they were ready to break the regions down into smaller states and to consider a flexible distribution of powers between the states and the federal government, Ojukwu and others who spoke for the Eastern region were not drawn any closer. Relations with the East continued to get worse until they broke down completely in May 1967.

While this was happening, Aminu, together with Joseph Tarka, Makaman Bida, and Umaru Dikko, was asked to circulate widely throughout the North, to explain the shift in attitudes of the northern leaders of thought regarding state and power at the center, to the emirs, councilmen, and Local Authority people as well as the talakawa and tradesmen. Each member of this quartet was asked to put his persuasive talents to the test in his own area of influence. They went not as representatives of parties but because each had influence with, and commanded the respect of, an important segment of northern thought: Makaman Bida would appeal to the NPC-based conservative establishment; Joseph Tarka, to the large minority groups; Umaru Dikko, to the students and younger elements; and Aminu Kano, to the insurgents, the talakawa, the intellectuals, and the civil servants.

They circulated throughout the provinces, addressing themselves to select audiences of the Local Authorities, from the emirs on down, and then spoke at mass meetings assembled for the purpose. Their job was to convince those resident in the hinterlands that their position at the Ad Hoc Conference was in the interest of a united national front and a firm unity of purpose. When they began their tour, they were greeted with reservations, but the audiences quickly became receptive and friendly; for everyone was tired of the internecine struggles and looking for areas of agreement. The "forgive and forget" theme was Makaman Bida's domain, particularly in former NPC strongholds. Aminu had to convince the people that they must avert impending economic ruin by filling the shoes of the refugees. Tarka pointed out that the need for smaller states was universal rather than solely the province of the Middle Belt and minority peoples. Umaru Dikko assured the youth that the new policy was to make room for all to participate and that the stagnation of the bureaucracy was on its way out. And they all four participated in the general discussions of the issues.

They were surprisingly successful in convincing their audiences that the secession of the North, seriously considered by the military as well as the traditional leaders, could bring only disaster; that the about-face by the military, politicians, and civil servants would produce the rapid political change and movement essential for national progress. Soon great crowds greeted them wherever they went. Of all people, Aminu, despite his personal feuds with the Sultan of Sokoto in the 1950's, was a guest in the palace when he was in the Sokoto area.

Umaru Dikko personally testified to Aminu's effectiveness on the public platform, describing him as an "eloquent Hausa speaker, . . . one who knows how to appeal to the feelings of the masses in simple, persuasive language—or by making them laugh."[6] Aminu's Citroen had a good going-over and was banged up a bit, but most people agreed that the officially sponsored tour was highly effective.

In the midst of Aminu's frenetic political activity came two significant events of a personal nature—and quite coincidentally on the same day. The entry in his diary for February 19, 1967, reads, "Isa Wali dies. Buried in Kano at midnight. Married to Zahra, Shatu pacified." Such simple notations in a way summed up a lifelong pattern, in which Aminu consistently relegated the joys as well as the tragedies of his personal life to a small corner of his psyche. He would conscientiously observe the amenities and responsibilities of maintaining a home, a family, and personal relationships, but no more.

Isa Wali had had great meaning in Aminu's life. Their relationship combined kinship (their families were related both by blood and by marriage); insurgency (Isa, in his way, had defied the archaic traditional limitations of the past, just as had Aminu); friendship; and a parallel political viewpoint. They had sought out each other's company throughout their adult lives, beginning with Aminu's days in Bauchi, when he bedded down with Isa and Sule Katagum every time he passed through Kaduna, and on up to his hasty visit to Accra but one year before Isa's premature death. He had wanted to discuss the first coup and to reassure his close friend and relative, who was serving there at the time, as Nigeria's Ambassador to Ghana. Yet the notation read simply, "Isa Wali dies. . . . Married to Zahra. . . ." Later he would fulfill his obligations by standing in as "waliyi" for Isa's widow, Zainab, when the time came for her to remarry. Together with the Wali family, he would help oversee the disposition of his friend's assets and liabilities, and the schooling of his children. But the following day's entry in his diary read, "Leave for Kaduna with Maitama Sule for call by H. E." It was politics as usual once again.

"Married to Zahra" had its own significance. Aminu was distantly related to Zahra and had been sponsoring her education for several years. But when Gogo Sadiya, Zahra's grandmother, had come to Aminu to tell him that plans were afoot to marry her off, and that unless Aminu did something about it, her education would be at an end, he stepped in and on February 19, married her himself. This enabled her to continue going to school for another two years, after which she joined his household.

Aminu's explanation of his venture into the polygamy practiced by his ancestors was simple. Though the custom had an economic purpose in rural areas by supplying labor for the fields, he was opposed to it when practiced by rich men as a means of acquiring property and ostentatiously displaying their wealth. This was degrading and oppressive to the women, and especially so when purdah was practiced. He would have none of this. He would marry more than one wife only if it meant that their living standards and educational level would be raised, and that they could learn to be independent and socially productive, almost in the same manner as a Westerner might calculate the number of children to have in his family. His marriage to Zahra, he felt, was consistent with his own emphasis on modernization and education. Yet one wonders how much of this was a rationalization and perhaps a desire to have his own "issue," (a possibility suggested by one of his close friends). Though there were five children in his household, they were all "given" to his household by other parents. When Zahra gave birth to her first child, a baby girl, in 1970, it did seem to give credence to this latter interpretation. However, as events turned out, Zahra never returned to his household after the birth. They were divorced and another wife was added in her stead.

Islamic custom has it that if a man has more than one wife, he must treat them all as equals. Aminu relates a humorous anecdote about an acquaintance of his whose third wife was educated and wanted a daily newspaper delivered to her door. Though the two senior wives were illiterate, they insisted upon equal treatment, so three separate copies of the newspaper had to be delivered. This seemed a silly solution to all concerned, until a modus vivendi was worked out whereby little envelopes containing the monetary equivalent of a daily paper were delivered to the two elder wives instead.

This egalitarian custom presented difficulties in Aminu's household as well. Since Shatu had relished her monogamous state, she did not exactly welcome her co-wife. She felt that her status was threatened and blamed close associates of Aminu for influencing him. But Aminu pointed out to her that education meant learning to get along with people. When he and associates had differences, he said, he continued to eat and drink with them and eventually won them over. It was part of her education to learn to like all women.

Aminu made it crystal clear to his current wives as well as their predecessors, that his public service would always take precedence over his private life, and that this was one of his conditions of marriage. They accepted the arrangement, with its by-products of trips abroad and relative freedom of action. If they found it unacceptable, they were free to leave, said Aminu. "Our nation is bigger than sex and family, and if they [the wives] are not satisfied with that, they must go elsewhere. . . . Of course, any grievances can be discussed. . . . If my absences are frequent and long, it has to do with my public affairs—Tradition has it that if a wife sees her husband talking with another woman, she would leave the house. However, Shatu has learned that I can do this and it means nothing."

He continued with his reflections, "I do get lonesome at times, but a lot of my energy is absorbed by my activity. I even get along without eating many times—maybe that's why I developed an ulcer . . ."[7]

One other major personal event of great moment to Aminu, crowded into these busy few months of 1967. On May 14, two weeks before secession was finalized in the East, Aminu's father died at the age of ninety-five. Yusufu had never really participated in his son's life, politically or otherwise, and for the last few years of his life he had done little more than sit quietly in a dark room at the entrance of his compound, almost as if he were waiting for the final moment. Aminu would brief him on his activities from time to time, and receive his blessings. For the last two decades, events had left Yusufu completely behind, but his rigid honesty and stubborn resistance to corrupt ways had always been a source of strength for Aminu. His legacy was all of five pounds, and his last request was that a prayer ground be maintained on his doorstep.

In the interim, the tensions between the regions in the country were growing. After the historic meeting at Aburi in January, the leaders of thought meetings were somewhat meaningless, for all negotiations were conducted by the military, and they were getting nowhere. In the East, "the Ibos would consent to discuss no constitutional solution that did not leave them with full control over their own security and economy."[8] By March, the Eastern Region took a giant step toward secession by decreeing that all revenue collected in the region on behalf of the federal government would be paid into the Eastern treasury. By May, federal authorities recognized that secession had been set in motion and would continue unless stopped by force. On May 25, when the federal government still had not acted on breaking the country into states, Tarka and Aminu and a few others asked to be relieved of their membership on the consultative committee. Two days later Hassan, representing vested regional interests opposed to the new states, asked for further delay, but Gowon rejected his request by telephone, saying that he would speak out on the states issue that very day—and he did.

In a history-making proclamation, Gowon announced on May 27 that henceforth Nigeria would consist of twelve separate states—long a dream of the minorities of both North and South. There was dancing in the streets, for the minority groups felt unchained. It was like a second liberation for all the masses. At the same time, however, Gowon declared a state of emergency throughout Nigeria.

Three days later, Ojukwu made his Unilateral Declaration of Independence, announcing that the Eastern Region had ceased to exist. In its stead was now the Republic of Biafra. The following day, federal troops crossed the border, a sea blockade was set up, and the civil war for the survival of Nigeria was on.

A country's grueling struggle to build a national existence has never made good copy for journalists, but the civil war with two and a half years of death, starvation, and destruction, created reams and reams of it. Nigeria splashed across the front and back pages of the newspapers and magazines of the world, with an explosive impact. Yet in retrospect, several years after the collapse of the rebellion, one wonders what people learned from this quantity of reading material. Does the world's citizenry know a bit more about the most populous of African nations—its people, its problems, its history? Within a year after the collapse of Ibo resistance, almost all but an infinitesimal group of the most interested observers are no closer to understanding the causes of the war than they were prior to this typographical eruption in black and white.

Within Nigeria, each side pleaded with the other to stop the bloodbath by granting them their goals—one to secede, the other to maintain the integrity of their nation. But outside Nigeria, the self-designated "Biafrans," through well-designed public relations, were able to arouse the sympathy of a multitude of would-be world humanitarians. Repetition of the emotionally charged phrases "genocide," "starving children," and "self-determination" had its effect. The world's mercy machine started rolling and, because of an inadequate understanding of the circumstances, was utilized to prolong the struggle. When it ended, Nigeria was left in much the same state as it would have been had the war not occurred.

But to say that the war, with its vast devastation and loss of an appalling number of lives, was totally unnecessary would be an oversimplification. More than that, it would ignore completely the role these catastrophic events played in Nigeria's revolutionary struggle to achieve a true national integrity and independence. The United States had its Civil War, Italy its Irridentist struggles, and other examples could be drawn from the world's history. Could these nations have done without their national revolutions? Smaller feudal groupings with divided loyalties had to be merged into a larger whole to forge a modern state.

The Ibos of the East had not been an oppressed people fighting for their freedom, despite the ethnic rivalries, riots, and killings which preceded the war. (Nor are they now, despite the many severe problems of reconstruction which follow civil strife on so large a scale.) If anything, they had a favored position in education, jobs, and status. While the struggle was in progress, it wasn't so obvious that whatever the claims or the justification of either side, the solution had to be found within a context of One Nigeria.

The political struggles in Nigeria had never produced a true ideological polarization, and the war did not change that. Only in the Northern Region had there been a continuing struggle involving ideologies—with the liberal party, NEPU, consistently challenging its conservative rival, the NPC—and even that changed after the first military coup.

Aminu had always tried to choose the side that would best serve his long-range goal of democracy for the masses. At first, he was in radical opposition to traditional rule; then he assumed a quiet but vigorous organizing role in unifying the North; now he stood in a position of leadership at the center, staunchly supporting the military establishment. Gowon, unlike Ironsi, had made it clear from the start that he would call civilians of all political hues, from all regions of the land, into public service to help run the government.

When the twelve-state format was announced, a military governor and a civilian representative from each state were appointed. The twelve civilian representatives, together with the chiefs of the military services and a few additional technicians co-opted for

The twelve states of Nigeria

specific purposes, were chosen to comprise a Federal Executive Council in Lagos—the equivalent of a ministerial council or cabinet, with a portfolio for each of the civilians. This cabinet would serve as the administrative arm of the government, with the Supreme Military Council sitting above them. Only three or four days after the proclamation of the new states, Aminu was notified that he was to be Kano State's representative. There had been no prior consultation, nor had Aminu any idea which portfolio was to be his. Major General Gowon (he achieved his new rank at the same time) said that, to avoid any leaks of information, "he slept with the list in his pocket." Only one or two appointees who lived in Lagos were consulted; the others, like Aminu, did not know which ministry was to be theirs until shortly before they were sworn in on June 12, 1967. Gowon evidently had followed the politics of his country closely from his military perch and knew whom he wanted to include in his government. With a few understandable exceptions, his civilian appointees were all *personae non grata* in the First Republic. (The leaders of the NPC in the North and the NCNC and NNDP in the South were either avoiding the limelight completely or quietly involved on a local level.) At first, the contacts between Aminu and Gowon were frequent, but as Aminu learned the ins and outs of his office, Commissioner of Communications, they met only to confer on pressing subjects.

Back home in Kano, the realignment of forces which had been taking place locally was formalized by Aminu's appointment. A group of Kano's leading citizens raised funds for a party in the cinema house in his honor. Several hundred invited guests showed up, including most of his former arch-opponents. The Sarkin Dawaki and Madaki, close to the pinnacle of traditional authority, and others from all sectors of Kano society, spoke in his behalf. A second party was organized, at which Ibrahim Musa Gashash, former Minister of Lands and Survey and regional president of the NPC, spoke freely—to the chagrin of his former followers and to the great pleasure of his former NEPU opponents. He said, in effect, "In the past, Aminu, you and I quietly disagreed and though we were victorious in the elections, we molested and harried you and your cohorts. Now that you are in the saddle, via the military, please don't do unto us as we did unto you!"

With most of the Kano leadership lining up behind Aminu, it was obvious that he would be very much in the picture when the Military Governor of Kano State, Audu Bako, appointed his state commissioners. Yet there was grumbling among his sympathizers for only one of his avowed disciples, Tanko Yakasai, was among those appointed. Aminu himself didn't seem put out by this. He subsequently explained the disparity in the proportion of NEPU people at the top of Kano State's government by pointing out that in addition to Tanko Yakasai, two or three others had been secretly associated with, or openly known as, NEPU sympathizers. There were also some former NPC members who were progressives; and in any case, we must ask who was available in Kano?

This new-found unity with a man who had earlier seemed a perpetually faultfinding traducer made it evident to the traditionalists that further changes would have to be made. Aminu's lifelong attempt to introduce local reforms in the North as rapidly as possible, had been consistently rejected by his opponents as explosive. Perhaps his ultimate goals were laudable, they said, but the speed and totality which he had demanded were too radical for them. The point at which these opponents lost control of the center might be considered the successful revolutionary change of class power in the North—from feudal to bourgeois.

Once the traditional leaders no longer dominated the federation or region, the speed of reform could be accelerated many fold. Thus when the intimidation and restraint imposed on the talakawa by the emirate structure was removed, they were quite ready to move at as rapid a pace as the powers-that-be chose to grant them. And the powers-that-were were ready to roll ahead.

True, some reforms had crept in gradually over the preceding years, but the essential focus of power had remained in the hands of the emir and his local authority. The elimination of the Emir's Court represented a cut-back of traditional power, but the emir was still handpicking the alkalis and thereby controlling the legal system of the North. He continued to appoint the councilors, district heads, and others, in this way controlling legislative and administrative powers and of course retaining exclusive executive control.

Aminu's role as a catalyst for this change was enhanced from his new perch as Kano State's representative to the Lagos government. Though he was well occupied with other matters of state, he followed the changes closely and looked upon each new local reform with great satisfaction. Those who broadened the political base and extended equal opportunity in each of the northern states—including the military and civil servants and at times even the reluctant local authorities—continue to regard Aminu as sort of patron saint of their cause.[9] This, to such an extent that his on-going concern with his home state has come in for criticism from some of his friends and allies when discussing his status as a national figure. "He is too much concerned with Kano affairs," was repeated by several political associates in one form or another, (such as Fred McEwen, Adisa, and Sule Katagum), though admittedly this criticism was levelled at him principally by allies in Southern Nigeria; native northerners generally see these reforms as Aminu does; as the jumping-off point for all subsequent forward movement, and a turning point in their national revolution.

To Aminu, the conversion from family-compact rule to a concept of public service, of *earning* the right to serve the people, represented class change. Even though the educated aristocrats might become the inheritors of the mantle of power in the new meritocracy, they could no longer rest on their birthright. They had to reorient their class relationship from the aristocracy to the bourgeoisie.

The movement toward reform of the traditional local government in each northern emirate had its hesitant beginnings as far back as the colonial period, for it had been in the interest of the British to introduce slow, controlled modernization. The policy had an inherent contradiction, however, since it was also in their interest to continue the existing hierarchical structure for efficiency of administration and control. When the Attah (Emir) of Okene insisted on a Western-style education for his children, the British Resident objected because he feared its liberating effect. But when the then Emir of Kano, Abdullahi Bayero, tried to break the traditional setup by introducing non-royal members into the Emir's Council (coincidentally eliminating any restraints put upon him by the power of the aristocratic families), he had the tacit support of the colonial administration. There were no elected councilors in Kano in 1959. After independence—by 1963, when Sanusi was deposed—there were some but only a minority (5 to 18). And by the end of 1965, all Local Authority councils had some elected members, and a few even had an elected majority.

Even the Hudson Commission, introduced by the British in 1956, recognized the need for modernizing the local political structure. It suggested a "provincial authority" with some power to spend money independent of the emir—in this way at least partially bypassing the Native Authority. Aminu was called upon to testify before the commission, but so were the emirs and their coterie of noblemen and kingmakers. The British were more impressed by the obvious opposition of the emirs than by the support of people like Aminu. So the recommendations of their own appointed commission members were never implemented.

Reform of the judicial system, running parallel to that of administration, had been one of Aminu's early concerns—dating back to his father's clash with the emir over his individualized interpretation of the law, and the subsequent denial of Yusufu's appointment as Chief Alkali. From the NEPU period of the 1950's and thereafter, Aminu's crusaders were in constant conflict with the law. Thousands of his supporters were arrested and charged with "verbal abuse of the emir." Even after regional authority was imposed upon the emir's Native Authority, the difference was hardly noticeable. The charges against Aminu and his supporters were changed to "verbal abuse of the Sardauna."

The core of their difficulties was the denial of any real due process. The alkalis were all appointed by, and beholden to, the emirs, and were subject to little or no restraint by either the British or their successors, the regional authorities. Legal counsel was denied, and open hearings or trial by jury were unheard of. To compound this situation, any appeal from the alkali's verdict had to be to the final native court of appeal, the Emir's Court, with the emir as final arbiter.

The inconclusive nature of the reforms introduced in 1959-1962 was summed up by Dr. John Paden when he said, "The consequences of such reform affected matters of legal structure, without entailing major substantive changes . . . [or] affecting the pattern of succession to judgeship."[10] Though Aminu advised Ado Bayero, upon his installation as emir of Kano, that he should expand

258

his council to bring in new men and retire the old, to divide the emirate into smaller units, and eliminate the Emir's Court, little was done to bring about these changes.

Not until Gowon's military regime did the Emir's Courts cease to exist, when the entire legal system in the North was incorporated into the state structure. In Kano, they were converted into Area Courts, with alkalis appointed by a judicial commission, consisting of civil servants and others who in turn were appointed by the Governor. A number of alkalis were " . . . retired, including Kano's Chief Alkali, in an attempt to upgrade standards."[11] The courtroom was opened up and counsel was permitted the defendant, who incidentally was no longer required to prostrate himself before the judge. Along with this drastic judicial change came a transfer of prison and police authority to the federal government, thus stripping the emir of any real enforcement powers. Unqualified personnel already within the apparatus would not be removed, but they would eventually be eliminated by attrition.

When Audu Bako, Military Governor of Kano State, introduced local government reform on November 11, 1968, he addressed himself to the State Executive Council and to the emirs, councilors, and members of the press, telling them that henceforth the emir's power would be decisively curtailed. Thereafter such power had to be exercised through artifice and subtle influence (not an insignificant one), no longer in overt form. The emir's complete control, through his executive function, his power of appointment and removal of the judiciary (alkalis), the legislators (councilors), his unchecked power to tax, and his total control of the police, had dwindled considerably. His own appointment had to be approved by the Military Governor; and his council, thereafter to be referred to as the "Emirate Council," would ultimately consist of himself as chairman, the traditional kingmakers, the District Officer, and other nominated members, plus elected members whose number would total to at least two-thirds of the council. On January 1, 1969, similar councils would start functioning in subdivisions of Kano State known as Administrative Areas, all with decision-making powers. When the Emir's Council was transformed to the Emirate Council, the post of secretary became vacant. The former secretary, one of three applicants, was turned down by the council, which chose another, who they thought was more qualified.

The Sarkin Dawaki, chairman of the kingmakers and once a powerful lord, testified indirectly to the effect of these changes when in one instance, he wrote to Aminu appealing for support and cooperation in insuring him the chairmanship of a particular committee, and another occasion when he chaired a public meeting to protest British sale of arms to South Africa. Though he might still administer his city district with an autocratic old world flourish, and perhaps ignore some of the new regulations in the process, it did not negate the fact that aristocratic old-style administrative arbitrariness would eventually be replaced by more modern methods, subject to constant scrutiny by the people's representatives in the first place and by the people themselves in the second place. In the long run, the emir and his courtiers could find a place in the new Nigeria only if they learned to conform and perform.

So far as Northern Nigeria was concerned, Aminu's victory was almost complete. Implementation of administrative fiat was still ahead, but the break had been made. Paradoxically, an elected government had done nothing; it was a military government that had effected Aminu's lifelong dream. The power would now be in the hands of the people—when the military stepped aside, that is.

But Aminu, now based in Lagos, found he had to transcend regional and local affairs that had occupied his time, effort and loyalties, over much of his political lifetime. He was involved with the deadly serious business of helping to "solve" a civil war. He and most of his fellow members of the Federal Executive Council never interpreted victory over the Biafrans to mean their total defeat. When an internecine struggle such as this would come to a conclusion, the victory could never be complete. Though a nation might be born in the process, there was always the afterbirth to deal with, before the infant could be sure of survival. "Out of our travails, out of a crisis of collective synthesis, a nation has been born."[12]

Neither vengeance nor vindication had ever motivated Aminu, even remotely. His years as a member of Parliament and as a representative to the United Nations had given him some preparation for a national role. But with those special tasks, there had always been an element of temporary escape from the battlefront, even though his efforts were useful and productive. Now the front had shifted to Lagos and the national scene, requiring that he think and act in those terms.

Previously, Aminu's relationships with southerners had been principally through his ties with the NCNC, as one of its vice-presidents. His past political bedfellows in the West remained close, but his role as a hero in the East, where the NCNC had its strongest base, had been sorely interrupted. Most of the Ibo leaders of the NCNC, from the Eastern Regional ministers on down, had been thrust aside by their fellow Ibos in the Ironsi government, only to be brought back from prison and from hiding by Lieutenant Colonel Ojukwu, leader of the rebellion. The fact that they were spared—though every bit as culpable and discredited as the northern political leaders put to death in the first coup—was a great source of friction between the regions.

In the sharp polarization that took place between January 1966 and May 1967, prior to the secession and civil war, Aminu's ties with the rank-and-file Ibos in the North and the East were, to all appearances, completely shattered. Because the Ibos in the North had thought of him and the party he led as allies, they were stunned by his and NEPU's inability to stem the polarization. Though it is reported that the refugees fled the North with his name on their lips, the best Aminu had been able to offer them was advice to leave quickly while going was still possible, and to shelter them en route wherever feasible. Their disappointment with him was great.

But as the realities of the civil war settled upon Nigeria, those Ibos who remained behind in Lagos and the rest of Nigeria (they numbered in the tens of thousands) could not forget their ties to him. Many an Ibo who had suffered some indignity, great or small, came to him for help. The official conciliatory attitude of the government permitted Aminu some leeway, so that he could move quietly behind the scenes to give what assistance was possible. One Kano woman was permitted to continue her job as caretaker at the Bayero College until she was reunited with her Ibo husband when he came out of the bush. Another, an Asaba Ibo, was released from jail through Aminu's intervention. A few nights afterward, Aminu was startled when a truck full of the Ibo's fellow villagers, representing ninety Asaba families, stopped to thank him for the release of their "brother" and for the risks he took. They left saying, "Men like you leave us with high hopes for the future of Nigeria." These appeals came in such numbers at one point that Aminu was concerned lest he be suspect among the less thoughtful and more impulsive soldiers, but he continued discreetly and quietly.

Stories like this are myriad. An Ibo woman, a former secretary at Dodan Barracks, after her release from custody, came to Aminu with private pleas to him from several Ibos remaining in detention. Again, when Aminu ran into two Ibo leaders in London, one of them embraced him, saying, "My leader! Why can't we stop this war nonsense?" And when he represented Nigeria during the attempts to find a peace formula at Kampala, he was greeted warmly by the Biafrans on the other side of the negotiation table—including Christopher Mojekwu (who had accompanied him to the Boy Scout Jamboree in his youth), and Chief Justice Sir Louis Mbanefo. (On the third day of the conference, however, when negotiations were reaching an impasse, their smiles changed to grimaces.)

These contacts with individual Ibos during the civil war years represented a carry over from the past. The tales of his mid-civil war efforts on their behalf spread rapidly by word of mouth, but they still represented primarily that select group in contact with him personally. Large numbers of Ibos who fled to the East before communications were sealed off undoubtedly retained some bitterness about Aminu's inability to do anything to stem the killings in the North. However, in the postwar reintegration process, Aminu's skill in human relations and his openhandedness during the rebellion have not gone unnoticed. Ibo civil servants and others of influence with the masses continue to look hopefully to Aminu to play a special role in the reintegration process.

Other than military action to end the rebellion, perhaps the Gowon government's most significant move was the creation of the twelve states and the civilian Federal Executive Council. This move, if it did not completely sweep away the thorniest obstacles to national unity, at least made it possible for them to move toward solutions in the foreseeable future. The gross inequality in the size and power of the regions was eliminated. Potential sources of dissension were disposed of by incorporating civilians from almost all known political beliefs into the government. The minorities that historically had been pushing for a degree of independence now had it, together with the reassuring protection of a national cover.

But the Ibo, to be properly integrated into a twelve state structure would have had to give up his formerly favored position in the middle and upper rungs of trained people in trade, industry, and government. Moreover, he would have had to sacrifice his hegemony over the minority groups within the Eastern Region, including the control of the oil-rich areas. This he would not accept, if instead, there was a possibility that he and his fellow Ibos could establish an independent state with its promise of additional top echelon jobs and status. So the Ibos fought on.

For the two and a half years of civil war, Aminu identified himself completely with the Federal Military Government. The senseless loss of life, with its terrible deprivation for the inhabitants of the East, seemed productive only of chaos and delayed national development. The Federal Government at first tried to convince the Ibos to renounce secession. When persuasion failed, they tried land and sea blockades. This tactic proved equally unsuccessful when the newly organized Biafran army overran the Mid-West Region, with the aid of Mid-Western Ibo defectors from the federal cause. The military government then realized that what they were trying to treat as a police action would have to be escalated to total war, with full mobilization. And for the conduct of the war, the cooperation of experienced and skilled civilians was necessary.

Although respected by the top military echelons, Aminu's great strength was with the people, and not particularly with the soldiery, but when the first decentralized purchases of arms proved cumbersome, and disorganized, Aminu found himself floating through Europe as chairman of the procurement committee engaged in arms purchases.

In general, however, Aminu's value to the government derived less from that of an administrator than from his international experience, his popularity with administrative personnel on all levels, and his keen understanding of mass response to governmental internal policy. Although distressed by the sinking international image of Federal Nigeria when threatened by the one-sided reaction of the world's humanitarian organizations and public media, he tended to shrug if off as someone else's department, with little he could do about it. If a division ever could have been made between the doves and hawks, it would have found him in the camp of the "step softly" group. Although he felt the war had to be prosecuted to the fullest, he tried to distinguish between the rebels actively engaged in military resistance and the large passive mass of Ibos who were not carrying guns. He felt the war was being fought against secession, not the Ibos, and kept looking ahead to the postwar period, when it would again become necessary to welcome this large slice of Nigeria back into the fold of national integration and unity. In light of this, starvation as a weapon of war never appealed to him, for many innocent, uncommitted Easterners, Ibo or otherwise, would cruelly suffer.

Aminu felt that patriotic organizations should and could play an important role in mobilizing public thought not only around winning the war, but also about winning the peace. He tried to convince the Military Government that support of such organizations as the Afro-Asian Solidarity Conference in Nigeria was essential to project Nigeria's cause externally and to offset the attempts of the Biafrans to establish themselves as an independent force in these and other international congresses.

The Military Government had banned all organized political activity, but application of such a decree could be flexible and Aminu from inside the government continued to push for liberal interpretations. Political activity was detrimental only if it meant jockeying for partisan advantage, not if it aimed toward harmony between people, or improving the war effort, or the country's international prestige and solidarity. If the government itself could not initiate this type of activity, organizations such as the Afro-Asian Solidarity Conference could be a logical funnel. He succeeded in convincing government leaders, at least to the extent that they tolerated the Conference activities and permitted its delegates to attend international conferences around the globe.

However, not all persons within this particular organization shared Aminu's views of its function—that of a unifying force for continuing radical activity toward federal victory and ultimate democratization of the country. Factional struggle carried over from pre-military days. Otegbeye led one group, Tanko Yakasai the other, with the degree of loyalty to the international socialist movement as the issue in dispute. Despite Aminu's attempts to mediate from his position above the ideological dispute, and his insistence that loyalty to the concept of One Nigeria was primary, Otegbeye's group withdrew at one point. Both factions remained on good terms with Aminu, frequently asking him to speak at symposia and meetings which each organized.

In June 1969, at an international conference in East Berlin, the Nigerian delegation was led by Yerima Bella, a long-time lieutenant and ally of Aminu, dating back to the NEPU days and at the time, the Commissioner of Community Development in the North-East State government. He and his fellow delegates created quite a stir by taking positions independent of the Eastern European bloc. Other delegations quickly learned that Nigeria's militant independence did not in any way permit its war-time arms purchases and its accompanying friendship with the Soviet Union to be interpreted as subservience. The Nigerians expected to criticize and be criticized on issues, not loyalties. At this same conference, a group of Eastern Nigerians who had requested recognition as an independent Biafran national delegation was rejected at the insistence of Yerima Balla and the official Nigerian delegation.

Aminu's role as referee between the two groups was once again invoked when he found that Otegbeye had been jailed upon his return to Nigeria. He had left the country unofficially, without the necessary travel documents, represented himself at the conference unofficially, and had returned unofficially, but found himself imprisoned officially. By his conduct, he most certainly had broken the existing laws of the land, but Aminu in arguing for his release, indicated that it was not in any way against the greater interests of the nation to release him. He felt strongly that a group such as this, allowing everyone to work together should be permitted, and could serve as an umbrella for radical activity that accepted a strong, independent One Nigeria as a basic premise, while coincidentally attempting to make this One Nigeria a better place to live in.

Great Britain's early rejection of Nigeria's request for military assistance and the immediate assumption by the Soviet Union of a role of military supplier, made more grist for Aminu's anti-imperialist mill. He felt that waging a war for national integrity, although an essential prerequisite for national progress, was not in itself an anti-imperialist move. Nor did he feel that a military victory won with or without Soviet arms would prevent close postwar ties to the West. Neither was the pro-Western foreign policy of Nigeria's first republic helpful. Thus, Aminu's unconventional interpretation of anti-imperialism rejected big power domination and welcomed Nigeria's newly acquired friendship with the Soviet Union without dropping its former Western allies, and tended to move the country closer to a true policy of nonalignment.

Evidently the world powers recognized new possibilities too, for the seemingly absurd and contradictory alignments which developed during the war could never be explained in a classical division of imperialist vs anti-imperialist. England, the Soviet Union, the overwhelming majority of African states and developing nations all supported the federal cause, with the United States attempting a tenuous fence-straddling. And the unlikely combination of the People's Republic of China, Union of South Africa, France, Portugal, and four Black African countries lent succor to the Biafran cause in one form or another. Simply, each country aligned itself according to what it interpreted as its own national interest and how it believed the forces would line up at the termination of the struggle. The discovery of great oil reserves in Nigeria during this time just accelerated the process.

The implications of all this led Aminu to conclude that he couldn't simply melt his efforts into the general goal of winning the war. He had to continue to exert such influence as he could toward making the defeat of a heart-rending attempt at secession a valid victory for his people. Thus he continued to encourage active discussions on university campuses, at meetings of consultative committees, and to support any action that would broaden public participation. Aminu's participation in the several attempts at peace negotiations was more or less routine. Personal contacts across the negotiating table were quite meaningless in the long run. The federal government seemed flexible enough and ready to negotiate almost any issue save that of One Nigeria, but the Biafrans would not yield an inch on this basic point, interpreting the Gowon government's insistence on it as a demand for full surrender. The concessions on relief arrangements were essentially made unilaterally by the federal government, which held the trump cards in this respect. They proposed many plans for supplying the Biafran civilians with food and medicines, but the Ojukuwu forces rejected any method that would not permit international arms deliveries to be filtered in along with the relief supplies. So regardless of the intensity of the international heat caused by the internal Nigerian friction, not until the fire was put out completely—through military defeat and the ultimate disappearance of "Biafra" as a cause and concept—could national reconstruction and rehabilitation begin.

In 1960, when Independence came, Nigeria was an emerging nation. In 1970, when peace came, Nigeria was an emerged nation —strong, centralized, with a popular and democratically oriented military government; industrially sound and potentially the most powerful nation on the African continent.

14.

WHEN

This tale of the growth of a man and a nation was conceived in time of crisis and civil strife, and completed during the period of reconstruction following the collapse of Biafran resistance. It would seem fitting enough to use this latter period as one of projection into posterity, of reexamination and reevaluation as to what role a man like Aminu can or might play in the "When" period of his nation's history. What is his own conception of his future role on the one hand, and in what form or fashion will circumstances permit him to function, on the other?

As originally conceived, this book was to be a straightforward biography of Aminu Kano. Yet it quickly became evident that his country's history was so inextricably interwoven with his own, that much attention had to be devoted to the detail of national development in order to find the essence of the man. If the story seems oriented toward Aminu, it was so intended. If in the doing, other national leaders seem slighted, it was not. Since Aminu is a product of Hausa-Fulani culture, events in the North have been described in detail, whereas events and personalities of southern Nigeria have been included only to the extent that Aminu was involved. Thus if any readers are moved to investigate further into the history of Nigeria to get other perspectives, it would be flattering indeed. If the reader has gained some insights into the quality of life of a man whose feet have remained rooted in the soil of his ancestors, whose body is of the stem of the present, and whose head is in the sky, hidden by clouds of the future; who matured during a time of computers and moon-walks, as well as emirs, herbalists, mud huts and camels, the book has been successful.

When the Sarkin Dawaki of Kano said of Aminu Kano that he never *became* a total political being, but was *born* into it, he was speaking for most of those who have learned to know the man well. Politics was in his pores, and poured out or just oozed depending upon the stimulus. His energy has been so consumed by the demands of his political existence that he has had little left for a private life. Though Aminu is obviously a friendly, affectionate person, his devotion to his politics and his countrymen has apparently shut out any really meaningful personal attachments, through what has been universally recognized as total political submersion. As he sees it, there just has not been time for them. His long absences from his home have separated him from both its pleasures and problems.

Because he is deeply moral (influenced undoubtedly by his early rigid religious training), he has loved his family, and has accordingly remained respectful to them. Since he also likes life and laughter, his years of single-minded concentration on improving the lot of his fellow countrymen must have created great inner turmoil. The temptations must have been great and the subsequent self-denial even greater, even though the days of fasting in his youth were meant to steel him for a life of relative austerity. If he has derived great satisfaction from his position in the nation, and from a sense of fulfilling his destiny, it did not lessen the extent of the personal strength involved. One can easily imagine that his frustration and dejection must have weighed heavily on him in 1965, when his whole political world was collapsing around him.

As we have noted previously, Aminu was married to a second wife, buried a close friend and had a committee meeting all in one day; reflective of the political blinders he wore. Perhaps this is true of statesmen or politicians anywhere in the world, but unlike many of these people, his subordination of private life and utter dedication to politics does not seem to be related even remotely to personal opportunism. Aminu has never greatly concerned himself with his own public posture or place in posterity. Rather he has been impelled by overwhelming need to be in a key position in order to accomplish his lifelong goals, whether in government or as leader in opposition. He has not been self-oriented, but consistently groupgoal oriented. Unlike most politicians of the Western world, Aminu never wanted to be a manipulator of the masses, to rise high to a position of prestige. He is more a man who early felt his mission in life was to bridge the gap from the isolation and darkness of feudalism into the blinding light of a world of modernism and technology; the new concept of civilization. In this struggle to shift the reins of power from the old to the new, he wants neither to antagonize nor to bow to anyone. His life has been filled with clashing ideas, bitter in nature, casting him as a symbol of resistance to the feudal hierarchy for the poverty ridden masses and young intelligentsia.

Yet he couldn't remain so indefinitely for those who looked to him for leadership in this struggle, for change and the very act of mobilizing for action tended to take him off the pedestal and subject his compromises—or lack thereof—to personal attacks. As NEPU, the vehicle chosen for this took shape, it picked up all the problems attendant upon political warfare; difficulties with finances, cadres, local tactical applications of general tenets, and alliances with the not-so-simon-pure and not-so-competent, the disaffected, and the aristocratic malcontents. Yet even making allowances for the caginess of political opponents and the adulation of his followers, the comments of everyone who knows Aminu are surprisingly free of rancor, vengefulness, or bitterness. He "attacks ideas or concepts, not people," friend and foe are quite ready to testify, and he carries no grudges: When a hand is proffered to Aminu, his hand is extended in ready response.

The traits in Aminu that are not so laudable (for there always are) a man such as he, always emotionally under control, seems able to hide. However, if he is capable of hiding these traits so well, that one is unaware of them, how meaningful are these negative qualities to his life style? If the only plaints about him are peripheral and at least in some instances, reflections of the commentator's disappointments or frustrations in regard to him, or if they are objections to his militancy, his speed or his impulsiveness, does this alter the projected image of a lifetime? Would his successfully hidden traits affect the essence of what the man has meant or could mean to millions of Nigerians, Africans and possibly ultimately to the world? They could, one supposes, but to date have not.

The abiding passive fatalism of the people of the North, Aminu links directly to lack of education. How else could the talakawa explain a high infant mortality rate save through the presence of jinns or by "God's will"? But when sanitary measures taken during the first weeks of a child's life visibly improve its chances for survival, what happens to jinns or God's will? When smallpox vaccinations were begun, the large mass of peasants regarded this health measure as though it in itself was a plague, and tried to avoid the vaccinations by bribing the sanitary inspectors. Today these same people, now more enlightened, clamor to be first in line. As a result, the World Health Organization predicted that Northern Nigeria would be almost completely free of smallpox in the early 1970's.

Aminu's new home is located in Kano's formerly desolate Dalla Hill area, where jinns abounded in great numbers during his youth. No one dared to live there then, but the jinns have disappeared now, and people of the North are jostling each other in their haste to secure land. They have learned, with Aminu's gentle urging, that even destiny can be influenced by one's actions. As their alienation ends and they awaken, he feels that a populist upsurge should ensue. His early crusade for enlightenment, starting with his intense concentration on proper sanitation for all, soon had the broad goal of education for all. With schooling comes economic and social development, and as they both arrive, superstition departs. Early recognition of the role that ignorance and fatalism in religion played in encouraging superstition and how these were manipulated by the power brokers of yesteryear, led Aminu into his early religious struggles to free society from such control.*

He accepted religion as deeply ingrained in his people, and carefully separated it from the traditions which were palmed off as religious observances by the rulers to perpetuate their rule. His father's parochial, rigid orthodoxy and the conflicts which arose from his application of it to the law, enabled Aminu the boy and young man to see through the hierarchy's attempt to use religion as an opiate. Instead, he regarded religion as the moral basis for a system of social justice. Allusions to Islamic doctrine were used consistently in order to reinforce principles of democracy and egalitarianism. NEPU's slogan, translated from the Hausa, was "To glorify God, association, and service to the community"—and any religious organizations sympathetic to these goals were encouraged.[1]

---

*H. G. Butler, Provincial Education Officer of Bauchi in the 1940's, characterized Aminu at the time as a "divine discontent."

Rather than shock the Northern Nigerian masses with unfamiliar values associated with modern institutions, Aminu and NEPU tried to cross the bridge in familiar forms— the same moral elements in tradition and religion. They tried to separate Fulani family-compact rule from the Islamic beliefs of the talakawa by resuscitating the Habe pre-Fulani history of the region. They pointed to Usman Dan Fodio, his son Bello, and his brother Abdullahi as great Moslem democrats whose tenets were subsequently distorted by their successors. At the same time, "Aminu Kano, who enjoyed a reputation for being devout, came close to fitting that relatively rare breed of active Moslems who believe the Islamic ideal to be a secular state."[2] In order to build a "bridge from then to when" and bring the old world up to date, in order to expand and unite his people into a One Nigeria, Aminu knew that ignorance and illiteracy had to be eliminated from each religious group, each village, each region.

His concept of strong leadership did not in any way seem to him to contradict this dedication to the freeing and secularization of society. The Sardauna's strength of leadership had never really distressed him, since the goals he had sought were what Aminu fought, not the man. Sardauna's personality and prestige and the fear he instilled in others were enlisted in the cause of traditional authority, introducing change only to the degree necessary to maintain it. The democratic forces needed strength of leadership and initiative, too, and Aminu hoped to provide these. He overcame any opposition within his party by the power of his ideas and his prestige in the organization. Duress, he believed, was not the only effective form of strength.

His recognition of the need for a strong leadership with mass popular support logically led him into socialist terrain. While in England, he had found some meaning in the orthodox Marxist-Leninist approach, but he realized that any attempt to transplant its dogma to the raw, unprepared soil of Nigeria would fail. He stuck to and continues to advocate socialism, but within the African, and more specifically Nigerian, framework, it assumes very special dimensions. According to C. S. Whitaker, "Maximum popular participation in government, providing the widest possible access to social roles and rewards, . . . rather than . . . the more doctrinaire meaning of public ownership of the means of production, is what the party [NEPU] had in mind when it proclaimed a belief in socialism." And Aminu himself suggested "a socialist commonwealth . . . in which there will be equal opportunities . . . [which will] do away with vested interests."[3]

The label "socialist" never frightened him. He actually sought out organizations with professed socialist goals, and in many cases tried to breathe life into them. On May 20, 1963, he wrote to an organization called the Socialist Youth of Nigeria, accepting the post of chief patron with pleasure. The stated aims of the organizition were to espouse socialism as the only path for Africa; to work for the unity of all African tribes; and to promote Pan-Africanism in an independent Africa. Aminu encouraged the budding new group, suggesting ways and means for it to function, for he continually looked to stimulate any organization that could work toward any of his national goals.

Socialism was, and is to him today, essentially a means for extending education and for eliminating privilege, since opportunity has to be made equally available to all, regardless of influence or family background. Sophisticated systems of dogma do not greatly interest Aminu the pragmatist. Big industries, such as textile manufacturing, oil, and utilities, that involve large investments, he perceives as requiring at the very minimum, joint government and private ownership, with government retaining control. Selective, rapid, and planned development, such as setting up a wool industry in sheep-breeding country, would take place when privilege is eliminated. Communication and education should be spread to rural as well as urban areas. Broad-based, horizontal private investment of internal capital—e.g., compulsory savings—should be used as much as possible in centralized planning for fixed economic goals. He knows and fears the possible effect of the common economic paradox of great foreign aid and investment leading to a country's even greater impoverishment. "The only help is self-help; . . . otherwise the country must mortgage its resources to foreigners."[4] Similarly, he feels that spreading political control to women, farmers, youth and trade unionists, including representation at the cabinet level, can give government the same broad base that compulsory savings and small individual investments give to economic planning.

With this relatively uncomplicated approach to government, remaining true to his early goal has been the key to Aminu's political orientation, not the tactics of the moment. The idealistic zeal of the early NEPU years he knew could not withstand the battering of one electoral defeat after another. The non-violent resistance of the early '50's gave way to "selective resistance to violence," and was followed by a more subdued role during Aminu's parliamentary period in 1949-1954 while part of a national coalition government. Alliances, coalitions, direct head-on collisions, local grievances— all had their place in an overall strategy, with a particular tactic attempted when it seemed to have a chance for success. Charges of radicalism or conservatism were raised as events developed. After the electoral losses and crisis of 1965, NEPU sold most of the party vehicles, dismissed their organizers and retrenched to a skeleton crew. Tactics had changed, but the thread that tied the democrats, the populists together remained their strategic goal, their revolution.

How does Aminu define the core of this revolution? A socialist commonwealth—equal opportunity—do away with vested interests—all non-specific, no blueprint. But Aminu, idealist, pragmatist, or politician sticks to his guns. Power to the people, democracy, populism, yes—and most important of all: eliminate the traditional family compact rule. If democratization of local government succeeds in breaking the emirs' power; if men of good will who are not self-seeking, take over for, with, and of the people, a revolution will have taken place. And if the base of the revolution is broad and popular, the leadership will be kept hewing to the straight and narrow. The ratio of public to private ownership in such a system would no longer be considered a decisive factor.

Has Aminu changed from radical to moderate and, if so, when and why? This question becomes meaningless when considered in the light of these ultimate goals. His political stance, his tactics have shifted with the demands of the times, during his and his country's maturing process. "I am more interested in the purpose of government than its mechanics—though the means should at least be good enough to lead to the ends desired," he said to a group of students at the University of Ife in 1968. His pragmatic tactical flexibility was summed up thusly: "The system doesn't have to be pure, but it does have to work." Again: "To approach the people one must use identifiable means, couched in words and images that they understand—analysis, simplicity, approachability, that which appeals to them directly. If their local needs can be related to the regional and national needs, ideology will result."[5]

Aminu believes with some observers that the power of the emirs was decisively broken when the twelve-state structure was introduced into Nigeria. "The political decline of the traditional northern leaders began with the January 1966 coup. . . . Since then, reforms . . . have sealed [their] fate. . . . The emirs have been reduced from a ruling ogliarchy to a prestigious traditional elite with limited constitutional powers," says Pauline Baker, political scientist.[6] The new bourgeoisie is heavily laden with descendants and relatives of the traditional authorities who maintain some power in this way, but it must be in a new form. The emirs who go along may survive, but in the limited fashion of a constitutional monarch or an Indian maharajah. Gowon and company drew Aminu, Enahoro, Tarka and Awolowo into government at the center, and exerted the entire government's influence on the military governors of each state. This combination of forces cut into the local power base of the emirs and chiefs by decentralizing and broadening the base of local government by eliminating the Emirs' Councils, transferring police power and the judiciary to the federal government.

One conceives of a revolution as either sudden, or total, or both. Unlike the British, who attempted to build a modern society by fusing it onto the old autocratic emirates, leaving the power structure intact, Aminu remains dedicated to the totality of his revolution. As he originally conceived this, power would be wrested from the ruling class, the masu-sarauta, and placed in the hands of the people. But complete removal of traditional forms no longer seems so crucial to him . . . and by the same token, neither does the speed of the time-table.

Kano Under the Hammer of Local Autocracy was the title of Aminu's first real attempt at political writing. Perhaps it is that the fervor of the emancipator has dwindled somewhat as his friend Sule Katagum suggested at one point, but Aminu is now convinced that the hammer has been taken away, lifting his country to a new and higher stage of struggle. Whether this transition of power has already passed the point of no return remains to be seen, but Aminu is evidently convinced that it has. His inclination at this time is to continue to encourage local democratic forms, while retaining control at the center, and for the moment, the current military government seems to him to be a proper vehicle to achieve this.

Projections regarding the future of Nigeria now revolve around plans for a constitution and the form which political organization will take when the military relinquishes power. In 1970, after the conclusion of the civil war, Supreme Commander Yakubu Gowon announced that a six-year transitional period would be needed before the country could return to civilian government. His proposed nine-point program, to be effected within that period was as follows:

1. Reorganization of the armed forces.

2. Rebuilding and rehabilitation of war-damaged structures and institutions, and the successful completion of the second four year Economic Plan.

3. Elimination of corruption from public life.

4. Settlement of the question of how many states Nigeria should ultimately comprise.

5. Formulation of an acceptable constitution.

6. Development of a revenue allocation formula between the states and the federal government.

7. Conducting a census of the population.

8. Organization of political parties.

9. Conducting elections and setting up a civilian government.

Because Aminu is a member of the Federal Executive Committee, and at the same time one of the prime contenders for top political office when civilian rule ultimately returns, some inner conflict about these nine points might be expected. As a representative of government, he must promulgate its program. At the same time there is a need to project his own image of Nigeria's future, separate and apart from that of the government. Coalition and cooperation with those who are not in complete agreement with his ideas have been as integral a part of his political existence as his independence of spirit. To Aminu the span of time necessary to implement this highly desirable nine-point program is not nearly so important as how these years will be utilized. Ghana's military administration was able to turn the government back to the civilians within a two-year period, but it was returned to the military not too long afterward.

Nigeria's civil war and its continuing ethnic and regional rivalry seem to preclude such a rapid changeover. A longer period of transition would be needed to permit local authorities to build up the mechanism for the change of power. Nevertheless, Aminu believes that if time went by and no significant dent was made during that period, the nation would suffer a severe loss. He therefore feels it incumbent upon himself to speak up in every way possible: in private discussions with leaders, magazine interviews, lectures, pamphlets, speaking engagements, and so on, in order to squeeze out as much progress as possible toward the achieving of the nine points as completely and as quickly as possible.

Long a proponent of equal opportunity for minority groups and for a breakdown of the larger regions into smaller units, Aminu is a strong supporter of the multi-state structure. However, he vehemently opposes any ethnic basis for this structure. Such institutionalizing of tribal differences and the disparity in size between tribes would raise the same danger of one group dominating the others—which proved to be the downfall of the first Federal Republic. As he said in December 1968, "What we have now is a judicious result of weighing factors of viability, ethnic similarity, historical connection, compactness, and administrative convenience."[7] Whether or not to adjust the number of states in the future is something he feels the individual groups within each state will work out. If disputes arise in this regard, he would probably tend to be on the side of more rather than fewer subdivisions, for he continues to feel that the base of government should be as broad as possible.

For an analysis of Aminu's attitude toward Nigeria's future political organization, one would have to review what remains of the core of his earlier concepts of party organization. During preparations for the constitutional conference of 1956, he made it clear that he was concerned about the interparty strife in other new African nations, and urged that Nigerian national unity be maintained at all costs during that critical period.[8] Over the years he was clearly disturbed by the disintegration of the ideological base for party organization, recognizing that the prevailing regionalization and ethnic orientation was tearing the country into shreds. When Aminu addressed the House of Parliament in 1964, he said: "I do not agree that the pattern of democracy in Western society is an ideal pattern. . . . The question of one-party, two-party, or even a multi-party system of government is not necessarily a guarantee of the essence of democracy. There is more in the temper of society, the ease and smoothness of transition and change, the tolerance of difference, etc.; these are the ingredients which evolve a democracy in a given country."⁹

To avoid a repetition of the bitter strife of those years, Aminu seriously considers some form of one-party democracy, but he hastens to add that this should not be imposed. Guidelines could be worked out requiring one or more parties to be national in scope, banning all regional or tribal parties. A single national program should be accepted by all, and the party or parties would be measured against this program. Within each party leadership, allowance could still be made for differences in personality, and in speed and energy of action. The single-party government of Tanzania has greatly interested Aminu, causing him to visit his friend Julius Nyerere, its president, several times before the falling out between their two countries over the Biafra conflict. At the time, Tanzania's one-party system seemed to eliminate some of the abuses of multi-party government (while coincidentally introducing new ones), but not until military government took over in Nigeria did he consider that system as a real possibility for his own country.

During the Ironsi regime, Ibrahim Imam presented a paper to the Kaduna Discussion Group wherein he presented the case for one-party government. Since the people, he said, were not prepared for multi-party democracy, they would do better with one party organized on a democratic basis. Anyone who wished should be able to join, but it should have a system akin to democratic centralism as the prevailing principle (pyramiding of committees from the lowest village level to the highest national level, with each committee empowered to act for that below, between congresses).

If such a system could be worked out, Aminu would probably support it now, as he did then. Since he has never been a stickler for form, however, he will go along with any acceptable system so long as it leaves room for national development. He feels that if such a national party could be formed, it should be first by agreement among the top leaders, then broadened to include everyone—in this

way guaranteeing its national character. Even if political organization were not restricted to this one party, such an approach would
at least assure it a relatively dominant position. The way would not
be smooth if this procedure were followed he surmises, for strong
differences exist among the most influential leaders. Some of them
have in fact never even professed a belief in socialism in any form.
Notwithstanding, this still should not present an insurmountable
obstacle, since national goals would be the unifying force. "Isms"
could be avoided by outlining the desired ideals without placing
them in categories. After this was done, the issue of how many parties
could be settled.

The leaders of the country in projecting possible forms for
future government have also considered the feasibility of a presidential system. Aminu, after weighing all factors though remaining
open, tends to reject it. He feels that tribalism and local loyalties
will probably linger for a long time and that it will be difficult for
one man to get the backing of the entire country. Rather, the executive head should be chosen by a parliament, He in turn should
choose his own ministers of government, via alliances, with greater
attention paid to gaining broad representation from all sectors, geographic as well as social, rather than to selecting individuals with
whom he would be most comfortable—United States style. Incidentally related concerns of Aminu are the greater concentration
of power in the hands of an individual rather than a party, that is
implied in a presidential system, and his increased vulnerability to
possible assassination—or dictatorship. He feels that a successfully
organized national party would not necessarily affect the framework
of the federal government. Each elected member of a legislative body
would still represent a local constituency, and function accordingly,
whether in a bicameral presidential system or a variation of the
parliamentary form. However, the national orientation and goals of
a countrywide party would tend to unite the people rather than
split them, as did the regionally oriented parties of the past.

Although Aminu's relationships with Ibos, both in the prewar
period and during the civil conflict, have already been discussed,
when the questions of one-party government and national orientation and goals are raised, a few words should be said about Ibo
reintegration. "A reconciliation of the mind," Aminu has said, "must
come first, eliminating any feeling of alienation, of being left out of

the national planning, whether Ibo or any other ethnic group is involved.[10] He has endeavored to foster such reconciliation through self-help, as for example when during the early reconstruction period he helped a group of young Ibo students in the East Central State, to regain their pick-up truck from the Rehabilitation Commission in order to resume the community service they had begun. Believing that an individual's fate is determined by himself, rather than vice versa, Aminu encourages Ibos to move actively on their own behalf and that of the nation. Growing segments of Ibo youth, women, and organizations engaged in self-help are looking for people in national government to whom they can turn for fair and considerate treatment. The extent of his past and present associations with Ibos raises the possibility that Aminu will play a special role in the postwar reintegration process. Historically there has been a well of good will among Ibos toward Aminu and the disbanded NEPU he once led, and he proposes to encourage this spirit as much as possible. He chooses to think that any Ibo hostility toward him in the past was based on the ethnic antagonisms which started in 1966 and culminated in the civil war, and that will be buried with it in the long run.

It is his considered judgment that, although ethnic rivalries will linger for some time, they are on the wane. This process can be hastened, he believes, first by permitting free movement of all people into all parts of the country and by making schools and other institutions, regardless of their location, available to all groups. The past custom of sabon garis, which isolated people not indigenous to an area, and of separate Ibo, Yoruba, and Hausa schools, should be eliminated—as has been done in the Kano Community Commercial School, which Aminu sponsors. Second, by shifting the forces of power from the local to the federal government, inequities can be corrected much more readily. Roads, schools, and public works, if supported financially by the federal government, can be allocated fairly. State governments will have to become less parochial and sacrifice some sovereignty to the national interest. Third, the imbalance in the level of education between north and south should be corrected; at the same time, efforts should be continued to raise the general level throughout the country.

Aminu ties Ibo reintegration into the idea of national parties and goals to achieve ethnic unity. He feels that Ibos are being welcomed back to the north (where their skills are still in need) in greater and greater numbers. The question is not primarily jobs. The fact that, in the past, one-half to three-fourths of the Ibos have been involved in private business, in one capacity or another, makes it relatively simple to reabsorb them. Although their home base continues to be the East Central State, the Ibo of the future could be as much a northerner as a Nupe, Hausa, Fulani, Kanuri, or Tiv. If the educational level of the northerner is raised sufficiently, all can compete on equal terms, be they Yoruba, Ibo, Calibari, or Hausa. Aminu of course does not perceive this as a smooth process without serious problems (witness the reception given the Ibos in the early postwar months in Port Harcourt and other areas of the Rivers and South East states). If this new nation-wide value system is permitted to grow, such inequities as the existence of 214 secondary schools in the Western State (population, 12 million), and four in Kano State (population, 6,000,000) can and will be corrected.*

As for foreign policy, Aminu feels that nonalignment is eminently correct for Nigeria, but considers the first Federal Rebublic's interpretation of this stance as close to scandalous. While serving as United Nations delegate, he felt that its support of U.S.-led opposition to admitting the People's Republic of China to the U.N., its timid and inaudible views on the Vietnam and Rhodesia questions, and its lack of diplomatic and commercial links to countries with centrally planned economies were hardly nonalignment. A forthright, courageous policy of nonalignment, in solidarity with other African and Asian countries, even to the extent of a joint African command, could yield Nigeria a national prestige commensurate with its size, strength, and potential for dignified leadership of the Third World.[11]

It is surprising that Aminu's lack of concern for his personal welfare can be so all-pervasive. The twin curses of bribery and corruption have permeated the inner fiber of the nation; yet he has been able to wander in and out of nepotistic and corrupt circumstances without seeming to become either contaminated or greatly disturbed.

---

*These figures were quoted in 1969-1970. Undoubtedly there have been changes since.

His attitudes toward family, and nepotism where it exists, he explains in this way: "I do what is expected, but make it clear to my family what my limits are. I am more concerned with the under-privileged in the family—the children, the elderly." (Recall his father's early advice to go out of his way to help those least able to help themselves.) "I found Sufi's sister [a distant relative] a job in a textile factory, but when it comes to Mustafa's son [Aminu's nephew], it's different, because Mustafa is in a position to help his own.

"I sent several people to Mecca, but not necessarily from the family. Rakaiya, in Jos, was one of the first to suffer for NEPU. She sold food in the market, but no one would buy; her NPC sons made her an outcast. There was a need to build her prestige, so the party promised to send her to Mecca. After the coup and the disappearance of the party, *I* had to fulfill this responsibility. Then there was my old aunt, whom many thought of as my mother. Her grandfather called her 'Hajia' from birth, and I had to fulfill his prophecy [a woman is referred to as Hajia if she has completed a trip to Mecca]." Although many Hausa-Fulani households have very close family interdependency and loyalties, Aminu feels that his community is the nation.

He remains aware of his family responsibilities, but tries not to permit them to interfere with his political goals. It is not "My family (or friends), right or wrong," but it is to worship at the altar of national unity and improvement, whether friend or family, acquaintance or stranger. Nepotism may have served as a sort of built-in social security system, but when one probes deeper, one finds that intratribal loyalties have bred intertribal rivalries and this became the political division rather than class. Thus national interest became secondary. The other side of that coin has been corruption, pure and simple. One is always safer taking bribes from friends and relatives than from strangers.

Family loyalty cannot and should not permeate levels of government, Aminu strongly feels, nor should it be confused with corruption. Appeals to tribal loyalty for support should be an offense. Merit, morality, responsibility, and seniority must be the only bases for advancement.

One would suspect that the proponent of such a social philosophy might tend to be friendless and lonely, but with Aminu the reverse seems to hold true. Try to visualize, on a Sunday morning, dozens of men seated in a relaxed fashion, against the wall outside Aminu's home. Or picture his living room filled with silent or chattering young and old men (and an occasional woman, particularly when he is at home in Lagos). No he is not alone. Some certainly come with official entreaties or on business, but others come with none. Many of them just come to listen or to participate in the conversation centering around this little brown-as-brown-can-be (not black) man—casual, informal, yet always alert. Whether he relaxes slumped in the middle of the sofa in the crowded sitting room, picking absent-mindedly at one part of his anatomy or another; whether he sits apart in his library or dining room, in Kano or Lagos, sorting out the questions and problems of those present, in groups of no more than four—he is not alone. As he speaks rapidly, at times approaching the point of stutter, his palms and long graceful fingers open and close, and his head nods for emphasis. He feels at one with those engaged in discussion around him, and they seem to feel the same with him. He reserves his hours of solitude, reading, planning and self-examination, for the wee hours of the morning, after all his visitors have left. He sits in his library, surrounded by an extensive collection of Fabian Society literature, books on Communism (Chinese, Russian, British, and Marxist varieties), Islamic and other religious works, (including even a bulletin of the Muslim and Druze Division of Israel's Ministry of Religious Affairs), books on the Nazi conception of the law, and American political commentary—literally thousands of volumes. Or he works during the early morning hours, after he has awakened and before he leaves for his office. Normally, four or five hours a night are enough to sustain him.

When Joseph Tarka, Commissioner of Transportation, said "Aminuism is beginning to triumph," he most assuredly was not implying the beginning of a cult of personality. (If anything, Tarka seems ready to take on a greater share of the national leadership himself.) Rather he was trying sincerely to convey his feeling that the sum total of Aminu's life was beginning to take shape now. No longer were his ideas supported by an isolated, dedicated opposition but were now a dominant force in Nigeria. Tarka, and others interviewed, almost unanimously associate this "triumph" with a universal acceptance of Aminu's long-held national goals, not with any demagogic misrepresentations, or any undercutting of these goals for opportunistic gain.

Western State Commissioner of Information Adisa[12] has listed Aminu's most characteristic attributes as unflagging nationalism, lack of personal ambition, a forthright and honest humility to those of high or low station, and courage. Federal Commissioner of Information Anthony Enahoro said of Aminu: "He was a radical. If he didn't join the NPC, he must have been strongly persuaded [in the other direction], since it was so easy to cross the carpet and benefit personally." And, "I describe myself as centrist, [but] he is decidedly left of center and one of the more progressive-minded."[13] And Umaru Dikko, Commissioner of Finance in North Central State, characterized Aminu Kano in this way: "He cares about suffering. . . . He accepts his situation and functions, whether leader or no, for ideas are most important to him."[14] From three completely different positions three different ways of saying the same thing.

Aminu remains a man devoted to ideas and people as he sees them, mature enough to approach national problems soberly, intelligent enough to address himself in understandable and popular form to the common man or to the educated activist elite, and courageous enough to face up to these problems, where others may hesitate.

"We would still be far from learning anything from . . . crises, unless the ruling class, in working out the constitution, is prepared to surrender power to or share it with the people, if that class does not want to lose all it has and plunge the nation into disaster," said B. O. Adebisi, lecturer at the University of Ibadan.[15] Aminu's approach to these above-mentioned crises would seem to be just that. "Anyone who wants to be a leader must be the servant, not the boss, of those he wants to serve," Aminu responded to an interviewer in August, 1970.[16]

As Nigeria responds to the inexorable pressure upon it for change to modernity, whether evolutionary or revolutionary in form, Aminu will predictably continue his historic role of catalyst— cajoling, guiding, helping to push or pull the nation into its new suit of clothes, waking the people to their newly emerging responsibilities as well as their independent rights, and, with enlightenment as a base, to try to help eliminate alienation and social immobility born of ignorance; and to help his countrymen emerge with thoughts that sing free of past chains.

He has had a way of making his mark felt from outside the government as an individual (up to the early 1950's) as a leader in pure opposition (1951-1959)—as a leader of a party in coalition at the center, (1959-1964), as an individual again during a regime devoid of politics (Ironsi)—and as a leader within the highest civilian policy making body of military government (Gowon).

Inside or outside of government, military or civilian, he has found a niche for himself, and undoubtedly will continue to do so, regardless of the duration of the transitional regime. "The disrupters waiting in the wings, [ready to step in] if the forces of national unity don't unite, . . ."[17] will continue to have Aminu Kano to deal with.

NOTES

Much of the material in this book was derived from extensive on-the-scene personal interviews. The notes and recorded tapes of these interviews are all in the personal files of the author.

CHAPTER I

1. Louis Fischer, *Gandhi* (New York: New American Library, 1954), p. 18 (freely extracted).

CHAPTER II

1. Michael Crowder, *The Story of Nigeria* (London: Faber & Faber, 1962), pp. 43-45.
2. H. R. Palmer, "The Kano Chronicle," *Journal of The Royal Anthropological Institute,* 38 (1908), pp. 58-98.
3. Aminu Kano, personal interview with author, Lagos, June 27, 28, 1969.

CHAPTER IV

1. Sir Ahmadu Bello, *My Life* (London: Cambridge University Press, 1962), p. 31.
2. Bello Dandago, Sarkin Dawaki, personal interview, Kano, August, 1969.
3. Abdu Mani, personal interview, Kaduna, August, 1969.
4. C. S. Whitaker, Jr., "Three Perspectives on Hierarchy," *Journal of Commonwealth Political Studies,* March, 1965.
5. Aminu Kano, *Kano Under the Hammer of Native Autocracy* (Kano: July, 1941). Handwritten copy of unpublished manuscript in author's file.

CHAPTER V

1. Aminu Kano, "My Resignation," *Kano Daily Comet,* November 11, 1950.
2. Aminu Kano, *Kano Under the Hammer—*, op. cit.
3. Sani Gezawa, personal interview, July, 1969.

4. Aminu Kano, "Bauchi Discussion Circle Debate on Indirect Rule," 1944. Personal notebooks, handwritten copy in author's file.
5. Sa'adu Zungur. Personal notebooks, received from Aminu Kano.

CHAPTER VI
1. James Coleman, *Nigeria, Background To Nationalism* (Berkeley & Los Angeles: University of California Press, 1965), p. 356.

CHAPTER VII
1. Aminu Kano, personal diaries, December, 1948.
2. Ibid., August, 1948.
3. *West Africa Magazine,* August 5, 1967.

CHAPTER VIII
1. A. J. Spicer, London, September, 1969; Aminu Kano, Lagos, June, 1969. Personal interviews.
2. C. S. Whitaker, *The Politics of Tradition* (Princeton: Princeton University Press, 1970), p. 270.
3. Richard Sklar, *Nigerian Political Parties* (Princeton: Princeton University Press, 1963), p. 94.
4. Ibid., p. 94; Aminu Kano, personal interview, Lagos, June,1969.
5. Abubakar Imam, personal interview, Lagos, August, 1969.
6. Maitama Sule, personal interview, Kano, July, 1969.
7. Aminu Kano, copy of letter in author's file.
8. C. S. Whitaker, "Three Perspectives on Hierarchy," offprint, p. 4.
9. James Coleman, op. cit., p. 39.
10. A. J. Spicer, personal interview, London, September, 1969.

CHAPTER IX
1. Capt. Hugh Clapperton, quoted in K. J. Bryant, *Kano, Gateway to Northern Nigeria* (Zaria: Gaskiya Corporation), p. 4.
2. Heinrich Barth, Ibid., p. 5.
3. Dr. John Paden, "Aspects of Emirship in Kano." Paper presented to Conference on West African Chiefs, University of Ife, Nigeria, December 17-21, 1968.
4. M. G. Smith, *Government in Zabbau.* (London: Oxford University Press, 1960), p. 260.

5. C. S. Whitaker, *Politics of Tradition,* op. cit., p. 461.
6. Ibid., p. 354; Aminu Kano, personal interview, June, 1969.
7. Aminu Kano, personal interview, Lagos, June, 1969.
8. Inuwa Wada, personal interview, Lagos, August, 1969.
9. Louis Fischer, op. cit., p. 36.
10. Aminu Kano, personal interview, Kano, August, 1969.
11. Uba Adamu, personal interview, Dambatta, July, 1969.
12. NEPU song, quoted in C. S. Whitaker, *Politics of Tradition,* p. 407.
13. Maitama Sule, personal interview, Kano, July, 1969.
14. Dr. R. A. B. Dikko; Aminu Kano, personal interviews, Lagos, August, 1969.
15. *Nigerian Citizen,* October 2, 1952, Sadauna of Sokoto, quoted by Billy J. Dudley in *Parties and Politics in Northern Nigeria* (London: Cass, 1968), p. 83.
16. See Billy J. Dudley, *Parties and Politics in Northern Nigeria,* pp. 185-190.
17. C. S. Whitaker, *Politics of Tradition,* p. 392; Aminu Kano, personal interview, August, 1969.
18. "Report on Kano Disturbances," Appendix B (Kaduna, 1953), quoted by B. J. Dudley, op. cit., p. 25, note #83.
19. Ibid., May 16-19, 1953, quoted by James Coleman, op. cit., p. 400.
20. Joseph Tarka, personal interview, Lagos, August, 1969.
21. Anthony Enahoro, personal interview, Lagos, August, 1969.
22. C. S. Whitaker, "Three Perspectives on Hierarchy."
23. C. S. Whitaker, *Politics of Tradition,* p. 351.
24. *Nigerian Citizen,* December 19, 1959, quoted in C. S. Whitaker, *Politics of Tradition,* p. 350.
25. C. S. Whitaker, "Three Perspectives on Hierarchy," Offprint, p. 8.
26. Sule Katagum, personal interview, Lagos, July, 1969.
27. C. S. Whitaker, "Three Perspectives on Hierarchy," Offprint, p. 17.
28. Maitama Sule, personal interview, Kano, July, 1969.
29. Billy J. Dudley, op. cit., p. 178. The assumption is made that these figures are for literacy in English. The author indicates that approximately 5% more are literate in Arabic.

30. Aminu Kano, *Notes From The Jailhouse.* Copy in author's file.
31. Richard Sklar, op. cit., p. 419, note #100.

CHAPTER X

 1. Aminu Kano, "Parliamentary Speeches," (Kano: Olusei Press Ltd.), August 19, 1960, p. 67; April 19, 1960, p. 75-76; August 13, 1960, p. 70; April 2, 1964, p. 94; April 14, 1960, p. 77.
 2. C. S. Whitaker, *Politics of Tradition,* p. 408; Aminu Kano, personal interview, August, 1969.
 3. NEPU National Headquarters Press Release, September 20, 1962.
 4. Aminu Kano, "Parliamentary Speeches," op. cit., April 13, 1960, p. 81.
 5. Aminu Kano, "Notes on Democratic Alternatives in Africa"; also "Parliamentary Speeches," April 1, 1964, p. 25.
 6. Aminu Kano, "Parliamentary Speeches," April, 1969, p. 89.
 7. NEPU Manifesto, Kano, 1950.
 8. C. S. Whitaker, *Politics of Tradition,* p. 411.
 9. Ibid., p. 411.
10. Billy J. Dudley, op. cit., p. 109, including note #47.
11. Ibid., p. 194, note #60.
12. C. S. Whitaker, *Politics of Tradition,* p. 280.
13. Aminu Kano, personal interview, London, September, 1969.
14. Dr. John Paden, "Influence of Religious Elites on Political Cultures in Kano" (Kano: Unpublished Doctoral Thesis), pp. 502, 3.
15. Aminu Kano, personal interview, Lagos, August, 1969.
16. Dr. John Paden, "Influence of Religious Elites . . . ," p. 509.
17. Ibid., Part II, "Brotherhood Patterns of Integration."
18. C. S. Whitaker, *Politics of Tradition,* p. 397.
19. Copy of this letter is in author's file.
20. Dr. John Paden, "Influence of Religious Elites . . . ," p. 62.
21. Billy J. Dudley, op. cit., p. 185.
22. R. Harris, "Nigeria; Crisis & Compromise," in *Africa Report,* March, 1965, p. 28.
23. Fred McEwen, personal interview, Lagos, August, 1969.

CHAPTER XI
1. Aminu Kano, personal diaries, April 14, 1965.
2. Letter from Minister of Trade to Aminu Kano, August, 1969.
3. Aminu Kano, personal interview, Lagos, August, 1969.

CHAPTER XII
1. Margaret Eipper, master's thesis (unpublished), Spring, 1969.
2. *New Nigerian,* January 19, 1966.
3. Martin Dent, "The Military and Politics: A Study of the Relations Between the Army and the Political Process in Nigeria," collection of papers edited by K. Kirkwood in *Africa Affairs* #3, p. 130.
4. Billy J. Dudley, op. cit., Preface, p. X.
5. Nuhu Bamali, personal interview, Kaduna, July, 1969.
6. Ibrahim Imam, "Peter Pan's Fib on the North and the Coup; A Cultural Analysis." Unpublished paper.
7. Aliyu Gwarzo, personal interview, Kano, July 15, 1969.
8. Sani Zangon Daura, personal interview, Kaduna, July, 1969.
9. Naibi Wali, personal interview, August, 1969.
10. Alpha Wali, personal interview, August, 1969.
11. Nigerian Military Government; First Hundred Days, & the Terms of Reference to the Committee for Constitutional Review.
12. *New Nigerian,* June 11, 1966.
13. Fred McEwen, personal interview, August, 1970.
14. Government Statement on Current Nigerian Situation, 1966, p. 4.
15. Martin Dent, op. cit., p. 129.
16. Ibid., p. 135.

CHAPTER XIII
1. Ali Abdallah, personal interview, Kano, July, 1969.
2. Martin Dent, op. cit., p. 136; Aminu Kano, personal interview, Kano, July, 1969.
3. See Plekhanov, *The Role of the Individual in Society.*
4. Martin Dent, op. cit., p. 115.
5. Ibid., p. 139.

6. Umaru Dikko, personal interview, Kaduna, August, 1969.
7. Aminu Kano, personal interview, July, 1969.
8. Father James O'Connell, *Africa Report,* February, 1968, p. 10.
9. Alpha Wali, personal interview, Kano, July, 1969.
10. Dr. John Paden, "Aspects of Emirship in Kano," op. cit., December 17, 1968.
11. *West Africa Magazine,* April 6, 1968, p. 392.
12. Ukpabi Asika, "Reflections on Political Evolution of One Nigeria," pamphlet, March 14, 1969.

CHAPTER XIV
1. C. S. Whitaker, *Politics of Tradition,* pp. 394, 395.
2. Ibid., p. 405.
3. Ibid., p. 406.
4. Aminu Kano, "Politics and Administration in Post-War Nigeria," University of Ife address (mimeographed copy in author's file), December 10, 1968, p. 7.
5. Aminu Kano, personal interview, Lagos, August, 1969.
6. Dr. Pauline Baker, "The Politics of Nigerian Military Rule," *Africa Report,* February, 1971, p. 21.
7. Aminu Kano, University of Ife address, op. cit., p. 7.
8. Richard Sklar, *Nigerian Political Parties,* p. 373, note 103.
9. Aminu Kano, Parliamentary Speeches, op. cit., April 1, 1964, p. 84-5.
10. Aminu Kano, Drum Interview, August, 1970.
11. Aminu Kano, University of Ife address, op. cit., pp. 5-6.
12. E. Adeoye Adisa, personal interview, Kaduna, August 19, 1969.
13. Anthony Enahoro, personal interview, August 18, 1969.
14. Umaru Dikko, personal interview, Kaduna, July, 1969.
15. B. O. Adebisi, *Nigerian Opinion,* January-February, 1970, p. 11.
16. Aminu Kano, *Drum* Interview, August, 1970.
17. Dr. Pauline Baker, op. cit., February, 1971, p. 21.

INDEX